Women's Choices

Women's Choices

Philosophical problems facing feminism

Mary Midgley and Judith Hughes

St. Martin's Press New York

ISBN 0-312-88791-4

Library of Congress Cataloging in Publication Data

Midgley, Mary 1919–
    Women's Choices.

    includes Index.
    1. Feminism—Philosophy.   2. Choice—(Psychology)
I. Hughes, Judith. II. Title.
HQ 1206.M49 1983   305.4'2   83-16049
ISBN 0-312-88791-4

For Geoff and Ted with love

Contents

Acknowledgments

Simone de Beauvoir has said that, until she began to work on her book on women, she did not think there was much in the subject. How deeply she found herself mistaken appears from her more than seven hundred pages. Anyone else who starts on it is likely to have the same kind of experience, and moreover to find that they owe her a great deal. We want to acknowledge this debt, and also another, no less deep, to Elizabeth Wolgast, who, in the enormous, sinister and chaotic landscape which Simone de Beauvoir revealed, shows some firm ground on which we have tried to follow her. Both from her book and from discussion with her we have learnt a great deal which has helped us to avoid thinking that this is a wholly impossible enterprise.

An amazing number of other people have helped us with this book too. Indeed it is remarkable that we have any friends left.

Iris Penny, with great kindness, gave us the run of her bookshop, The Bookhouse, and the benefit of the experience she has gained there. Lord and Lady Kennet and Michael and Myra Bavidge read the original manuscript and made us think more deeply about many important topics. Jean Crocker and Jane Heal provided us with diverse and stimulating views about language, and Ted Hughes was always ready to use his remarkable ability to discover apt examples from a wide range of disciplines. From Martin Midgley we learnt how it is possible for young men to understand and try to co-operate with the new assertiveness of women. The typing of this manuscript was done with customary cheerfulness, speed and accuracy by Moira Dearden and we are very grateful to her.

Among the others who have given us valuable advice and

suggestions, we would especially like to thank Professor D.W. Elliott, Shirley Williams, Mary Warnock, Leslie Abdela, Angie Tinkler, Heather Scott, Dorothea Kerslake, Katherine Waddington, Mary Shepherd, Ann Charlton, Willie Charlton, Jane Feinmann, Sylvia Feinmann, Steven Smith, Alan Craft, Geoffrey, David and Thomas Midgley and Lorna Rusbridge. Thanks, too, to Joanna, Daniel and Edward Hughes for their co-operation.

Part One:
Introduction

1 The need for new maps

We cannot rely on existing ideologies as they are all products of a male supremacist culture.

(Redstockings' Manifesto, New York 1969)

1. Seeing the problems

Feminism is not just an eccentricity. Nor is it it the only cause which will save the world. It is an element which we all need for our thinking on a great range of important matters – social, political, psychological and moral – and whose absence has always weakened that thinking. The surge of excitement over the women's movement in the last fifteen years has been very confusing. It is not surprising that many people have simply refused altogether to think about its meaning. But that surge is subsiding now into more intelligible shapes. The job is becoming both easier and more urgent. The spate of feminist books is beginning to take a different and more constructive form. At first in the late 1960s and early 1970s they were predominantly rather general books about women's miserable lot. Later, this main stream divided to deal with more specific injustices – fields such as law, language and education. More recently, however, it has become clear that these need a context. To supply it, we are now getting more thoughtful critiques and histories of feminism itself, and of feminist attitudes. Writers are becoming more conscious of their own problems of method. They are beginning to stand further back; they want to weigh and judge the various parts of the initial campaign. The splits and clashes between these parts have in fact made this more careful approach necessary. It has become clear that, in spite of strong efforts to form a single movement, women – like any other group – have not one aim but many, which can conflict. They need priority systems. And they are not all going to agree upon the same one.

3

This is no tragedy, but it is a real problem which must be faced. Disagreements need to be understood. Any group which tries instead to conceal them behind a spurious façade of unity is bound to be fatally confused, and to waste its efforts. There is a difficulty about the whole idea of a 'women's movement'. There is not a single 'poor people's movement'. Is the women's movement more of an organic whole? If so, how? This question calls for a lot of thinking, and in the last few years it has started to get it.

This book is a part of that new, more reflective enterprise. It is an attempt to locate the various strands of feminist thinking, and to show the conceptual problems of combining them – problems that cannot be avoided, however little interest we may generally have in philosophy. In their traditional forms some central feminist ideas clash, as it turns out, both with each other and with other ideas equally essential to our thinking. We need, then, to alter the traditional forms. But to do this will involve breaking the isolation in which women's problems are often considered, and altering a much wider background of thought as well.

One part of that background which specially needs attention is that cluster of political concepts which roughly constitutes 'leftness'. The present-day women's movement developed out of, and drew its ideas from, the crop of revolutionary movements active in the 1960s; by chance, but significantly, it was the last of these to arise, except for Animal Liberation. It therefore took over unchanged the language of its predecessors, a language which for its purposes turned out to have rather grave drawbacks. Leftness itself is of course much older than this, dating from the French Revolutionary Assembly, where it signified a devotion to liberty, equality and fraternity. Reading 'sisterhood' for 'fraternity', these have been the guiding ideas of today's women's movement. Of course they are magnificent ideals; and at a glance they look simple. But in fact they are all deeply ambiguous, and confusion over their meaning is a strong source of the conflicts mentioned above. Moreover, they can clash with each other. There is a notorious general difficulty about reconciling equality with liberty. In general politics, unbridled commercial freedom can lead to economic injustice, and totalitarian structures designed to ensure equality can turn out to wreck personal freedom. Indeed, these two principles collide so often that in contemporary Western political thought they are widely seen as incompatible. Marxist thought developed the commitment to equality (and fraternity), while nineteenth-century liberalism concentrated on liberty and individualism. More recently the concept of liberty, particularly individual liberty, has become associated at least as closely with those political sentiments which lie to the right of centre as with those to the left, if not more so. Union pickets do not commend those who cross their lines for exercising their freedom.

Nowhere is the bitterness of this conflict seen more clearly than within the women's movement itself, which is now generally agreed to have divided into two distinct streams. Socialist feminism, aiming primarily at equality and working towards it through normal political channels, sees itself as being diametrically opposed to radical feminism, which aims above all at liberty from male domination, and has now come to see its best hope of this in some kind of separatism. (Both streams, rather confusingly, tend to use Marxist language, but with somewhat different meanings, a problem which we must discuss.) The anger with which Betty Friedan's book *The Second Stage* has been received in America by some radical feminists is a graphic illustration of the perceived competitiveness of the two ideals. To the radicals, that book is a sell-out. They bitterly resent it because they see disagreement not just as a genuine difference of opinion but as a betrayal. They want a unanimous movement, and it follows that she who is not with us is against us. For people who are trying to redesign something as vast and complex as the relations between the sexes it would certainly seem more natural to expect some disagreement, and to allow for quite a long period of rethinking before any truth emerged which was clear enough to be worth fighting each other for. And if women, as women, can be expected to have any distinctive kind of approach, we might suppose that they would be less contentious, less intellectually arrogant and sweeping, more sensitive to the complexities of the case than men. But unfortunately the simple, sweeping, warlike style of thought, which prefers to locate an enemy at once and present choices as stark dilemmas, is traditional in the French-Revolutionary approach. And this was the style current in revolutionary circles in the 1960s. To adopt it is very easily seen as a test of loyalty. Once adopted, therefore, it is extremely hard to unseat. Extremism itself then appears as a virtue, independent of both its usefulness and its suitability to the topic – and this is what seems to have happened to the women's movement.

The general problem of over-simple, unrealistic dilemmas will be central to this book. But besides this, French-Revolutionary thinking produces, by its special view of equality and liberty, another, more specific kind of trouble, namely social atomism.[1] It deals in people as standard, quasi-mathematical units. It sees individuals as a species of billiard balls, each rolling separately onto the communal table, essentially isolated from each other, each inevitably pursuing its own single interest, and related only contingently by an optional contract. The idea of natural emotional bonding suggested by 'fraternity' has never been developed, and until lately even the crude fact that it was sex-linked was not noticed. Moreover, the idea of liberty has been developed in a way that tends to make all such natural bonding look like an odious imprisonment. Of course, for certain political purposes – when illicit bonds have to be broken – this destructive approach can be very useful, even vital. And French-Revolutionary thinking was formed mainly as a solvent to get rid of such bonds.

When people turn to more positive, constructive work, however, more is needed. If we ask what kind of life, and particularly what kind of personal life, the free society should aim at, these two formal and negative ideas are of little help and can be a serious burden. In discrediting the artificial bondings of a class-ridden society, they obscure also the natural bondings between people who are not only individuals but social creatures as well. We throw out this baby with the bath water at our peril. Yet the ideals of equality and liberty still remain two of the central tools of feminist thinking, while the third – sisterhood – does nothing to resolve their conflicts, but instead introduces a whole new set of problems of its own which have so far scarcely been noticed. We need to rethink all these concepts and to ask what *other* ideals, besides these three, a humane life needs.

2. Practical problems; work leaves the home

This rethinking is urgent because of a drastic, concrete change in the world. All of us, not only women, are being forced to change the way in which we relate our work to our homes. In the last two centuries work has largely moved away from people's homes into specialized workplaces such as factories and offices. These have usually been designed by men for men. They have tended to admit women, if at all, only in subordinate and non-controlling positions. This had the unintended effect of leaving large numbers of women in a situation which is often thought of as traditional, but which in fact was quite new – confined to a home where nothing much went on that seemed to have any serious significance. Large areas of traditional women's work simply evaporated. All the more prestigious and impressive parts of teaching, nursing, medicine, social service and the like were professionalized and packed off into institutions. Spinning, weaving, brewing and much other small domestic manufacture went into factories. (Mrs Beeton probably shows us the last gasp of partial domestic autonomy before this process took effect.) At the same time the increasing mobility of labour tended to break up neighbourhoods, steadily weakening the friendly networks through which some of these functions still did get shared. It is not surprising that the women left at home began to be troubled by a sense of isolation and futility.

This uneasiness could not be dispelled by the romantic attempts of Victorians such as Ruskin to idealize women's secluded status as something spiritual and exalted, and so to keep it out of the mainstream of life. That vision failed to convince, because it was out of tune with the real values of the age, which were active and practical. In a culture such as Buddhist Tibet, or even medieval Europe, where contemplation is believed to have a vital function, people can reasonably be expected to embrace a secluded, monastic life. But industrial countries in the nineteenth century did not have that belief. Both in a good sense and in a bad one, they were utilitarian. The good sense called for vigorous, enterprising action to right terrible social ills. The bad sense meant that aims were limited to certain crude and measurable benefits, notably money. By both these standards the narrow, inward-turning life prescribed for women rated low and looked futile. Women therefore refused to stay content with it, and tried to follow the work out into its new locations. But they found that here, apart from menial grades and certain special enclaves like nursing, they were largely excluded.

3. Why equality does not always help

Of course, there has been a great deal of progress towards changing this situation. But it never gets beyond a certain point, and essentially this is still the problem for women's work today. In meeting it, feminists have relied largely on the notion of equality. They had demanded that women should be treated as men are, but we need to ask whether men ought to be treated like this in the first place. Is it a good thing, for instance, to have hardly any time to see one's children? Or to have one's value measured by one's wage packet? Or to overwork so that one dies of thrombosis at fifty? Unless these are good things, it is not obvious why women should demand an equal share of them.

The notion that what women need is simply to be treated like men is the one expressed by the charge of *sexism*, which combines the idea of their being oppressed with that of their being treated differently from men, as if these were one and the same offence. On the model of 'racism', this charge assumes that sex differences are mostly imaginary and have been invented by men in order to show women as inferior. We shall avoid using the word 'sexism' in this book altogether because we think this assumption most misleading. Many of the sex differences seem to be real, and difference does not involve inferiority. The point is discussed in Chapter 6.

Are the drawbacks that have just been mentioned regarding men's work, however, perhaps inevitable? Are they just the price of doing 'real work', rather than the flimsy substitute work in which unpaid women at home are currently indulging? If this work seems unreal, there is surely something wrong with the way we are thinking about work and relating it to money and esteem. The work done by women at home, especially in caring for children or the old, is as real as work can be.[2] Is there something servile or ignoble about it? It is really a very odd form of snobbery which believes so. Russian women, provided with crèches and economically compelled to go out to work full-time, bitterly resent being deprived of the chance to make a home for their families.[3] Yet much Western feminism still seems to make their situation its goal.

It is easy to see how all this comes about. For quite understandable reasons Labour movements have centred their efforts on raising wages, and have had no particular interest in providing for a flexible distribution of time. In particular they have tended to frown on part-time work, and especially on the part-time work of women, as a dilution of labour. The tendency of women to bargain money for time exasperates them. For most women, however, during a crucial part of their lives control over the distribution of time is a first priority. Over time, their needs are quite different from those that have been viewed as central for men. And where needs are different, the notion of an equal right to the same treatment is no more use than a hole in the head.

To a tidy-minded planner, then, things might look like this. The process of institutionalizing work – of corralling it all neatly into certified and inspected workplaces – spread smoothly across the populace until it reached those awkward customers, women. At this point the machinery mysteriously snarled up, and things began to go wrong. Or – to look at it another way – the process of equalizing all citizens, of standardizing their pay, status, career structure and property rights, spread smoothly until the same point was reached, when it suddenly ran into inexplicable difficulties.

For conventional, lazy-minded thought, this strange event has no puzzles. It simply concludes that Ruskin was right. Women are above or below consideration. In any case they are impossible, and must just be left out of the system. French-Revolutionary rationalist thought, by contrast, grits its teeth and determines that whatever the difficulties and however little everybody likes it, women are going to be integrated into it on the same terms as men. If they resist, they will be denounced as 'unreconstructed'. But at this point it seems reasonable to suggest that we had better call a plague on both their houses, and see to it that instead something is done about the system. In any case, current un-employment problems indicate this strongly. Even for men it is no longer plausible that work should be made up into the largest possible bundles for the smallest possible number. The division of workers into an élite possessing real, full-time jobs and a shadowy mob of neglected diluters is no way to pursue the traditional ideal of equality, let alone real justice. Yet those who promote it undoubtedly do not notice this defect. This is because their eyes are firmly fixed on one aspect of equality – the equality that they would like to bring about between their own pay-bracket and another, selected, one which is slightly higher. Without a background of other ideals to supplement it, the notion of equality can do nothing to correct this bias.

This criticism of feminist reliance on traditional left-wing concepts does not, of course, mean that we should rely on right-wing ones instead. Neither political extremity has been designed to fit the case of women. In this changing age both are obscure even on their own ground, and both have, moreover, the same drawback of seeming to demand extremeness simply in itself as a pledge of sincerity. The mere fact of political opposition has a tendency to breed false antitheses. Will you have equality or liberty? Peace or justice? Employment or leisure?

Feeling or reason? Bath or breakfast? Children or a career? Is society formed by the social contract or by natural feeling? Are women just like men or quite different? If you try to say 'both' you are accused of wanting to eat your cake and have it, and it is added that she who is not with us is against us ... What in fact is usually needed, especially in a rapidly changing world, is fresh thinking, to devise specific new ways of reconciling claims and half-truths which conflict, often because of changed circumstances. Theorists, trained in controversy rather than in practical or conceptual plumbing, tend instead merely to heat up the argument. They easily become so obsessed with its existing forms that they find it very hard to stand back and see what has gone wrong with the premises of both sides. Controversies ossify thought, and prevent it from developing in the way needed to accommodate new insights. They freeze it in a posture hostile to change.

4. Antiques in the feminist tool kit

This tendency is a peculiarly unlucky one for new movements, which have to start life by using the intellectual tools available in their day. In the 1960s, the women's movement was in this sense new. (There had of course been feminists before, but never such a general surge of support for them, nor such a widespread attempt to develop their ideas and apply them in practice.) Reaching quite naturally for the conceptual tools available, the pioneers found them in three prevalent ideologies of the time – Marxism, Nietzschean individualism (channelled through Sartre and Simone de Beauvoir) and Skinnerian behaviourism. Marxism supplied the idea of an oppressed class, which must unite to seek revolution rather than attempting reform and compromise with its oppressors. Individualism countered traditional self-sacrificing female submission by pointing out the possibility of fruitful egoism – of resisting the claims of others to concentrate on one's own self-fulfilment. And behaviourism made change seem easy by ruling that the present position of women was only a chance product of conditioning, with no roots in human nature.

As ways of correcting former biases all these ideas had a real use. But their price was heavy. In the first place, these three ideologies are radically different, they do not fit together. Attempts to use any one of them fully tend to make continual trouble with the rest. Beyond this, too, each has its own very serious drawbacks. Marxist models of class warfare do indeed have some useful analogies with clashes of economic interest between the sexes, but in many other ways they fit the case of women very oddly (we shall discuss this problem in Chapter 4). A constant battery of sarcasm and paradox is needed to keep the comparisons looking at all plausible, on top of the difficulties which afflict Marxism in its own political sphere. As for individualism, it is indeed a splendid solvent for bad and unconsidered personal predicaments; it makes people start to think about the mess they are in. But once the thinking has started, individualism often does not help them much further. It is too undiscriminating. It tends to dissolve not just bad bonds, but all bonds – including of course the political ones needed for Marxism. And since most fulfilling human occupations are not solitary, it may leave its determined votaries with nothing much to do. As for behaviourism, it too is a potent destructive solution, handy for getting rid of false and pernicious beliefs about natural causes (that is why huge bottles of it were for so long kept on the shelves of enlightened social scientists). Yet its positive doctrine – the view that behaviour can have no cause except more behaviour – is highly incoherent and implausible. This makes it a serious obstacle to feminists who are trying to understand important phenomena which seem to have natural as well as social causes, such as sexual and maternal feelings. In other contexts, people are now beginning to notice that this view about social causes is not a clear one, nor does it actually work as a remedy for fatalism, which is supposed to be its main function. Social causes can be just as alarming as any other kind. The bottles should be put away, and problems of causation reconsidered in a less dog-

matic, more empirical fashion. These and other difficulties naturally need much fuller discussion. The present remarks are merely
signposts to indicate trouble-spots which we shall visit properly
later.

However what is surely much less doubtful is the effect on a
new movement of relying so heavily on old material. It has been
important to the women's movement to proclaim its newness,
to point out how thoroughly previous culture has been distorted
by being left in the hands of men. It would seem natural, then,
to expect that existing schemes would be used with caution,
reluctance and constant criticism, that careful selection and re-
moulding would quickly produce very different concepts and a
different style of reasoning. This has not happened. The most
outstanding case, of course, is that of Marxism, already one of
the most jargon-ridden and orthodoxy-obsessed of existing
faiths. Much feminist literature is sunk in the kind of unreadable
Victorian Germanic language through which only the acclimatized faithful can keep awake. Behaviourism, for its part, carries
only the less elaborate language of the classroom. But that is far
more noxious than is commonly realized. Unfortunately, it is
possible for academic psychologists to become accustomed to
saying things in their professional work which they would not
dream of saying or believing in their everyday lives, and technical
terms can sometimes make this process very easy. Surely, on any
general, non-technical subject special terminology ought always
to be suspect. If what is being said cannot be translated into
everyday speech, there is very often something wrong with it. It
may be valid and harmless in the sphere where it was first
invented, but may still blind its users fatally elsewhere because
it allows no space for vitally relevant factors. Common speech
may look less impressive, but it always allows that space.

Without this precaution it is scarcely possible to keep watch
on the mistakes built into a theory. Feminists need to be aware
of this danger, which is a much wider one than can be dealt with
in this book. Even if all the detailed criticisms we make here are
misguided and can be ignored, it would surely be as well to be in
a position to make *some* criticisms of the ideas one uses. But if

the theory's terminology is taken up as a package deal, this is extremely hard.

With individualism the problem is rather different. There is much less jargon here. Nietzsche avoided it, and indeed wrote beautifully. The defect of his style is not jargon but rhetoric, paradox and special pleading. Existentialism did add a jargon of its own, but that now seems largely forgotten. We read Sartre and de Beauvoir mainly in their popular works: their views, far from belonging to the classroom, are familiar and form part of the ethos of the day. The trouble about them lies in their actual mistakes, especially their one-sidedness. There is, however, also a formal peculiarity about these individualist views – namely the incongruity of their being a popular, widely accepted orthodoxy to the extent that they now are, when their central theme is resistance to orthodoxy. Corporate individualism is a strange thing. A convert who takes up Nietzschean immoralism today is not making a bold, solitary exploration but is getting on a well filled bus which has been been passing his door for the best part of a century. Nietzsche himself foresaw this absurd possibility, and cheerfully denounced those who would suppose it possible to be his disciples.[4] He saw his destructive work as simply the first step towards something far more splendid and quite unknown, but he is now respectfully treated as a master, a terminus.

5. Individualism and misogyny

Another point about Nietzsche that makes his influence on modern feminist thought surprising is his attitude to women. ('Man should be trained for war and woman for the recreation of the warrior; all else is folly.')[5] He got the nub of this from Schopenhauer,[6] who is the source of most genuine modern misogyny (as opposed to the vintage, early Christian variety), and added his own developments. He certainly passed it on to the existentialists, who built it into the modern notion of personal liberty as essentially a freedom from emotional ties, an armour against intimacy. In origin this means above all a protection for men from emotional claims, especially from the claims of women. Here, too, many feminists have responded by demanding that women should have an equal right to this same privilege of emotional isolation. But is that what they really want? How many of them? And for how long? It is after all just one ideal, one option. Freedom ought surely to mean a wide range of options, and as clear a view as possible of what each of them means, not the acceptance of a single one that is powerfully presented as unavoidable.

Schopenhauer's misogyny seems to have been the product of a savage private despair about personal relations, in particular the resentment he felt towards his lively and popular mother, who did not seem to care for him enough. It was a central vice of his thought – and of that of his followers – to project his own emotional conditions without hesitation onto the cosmos. Such theorists often convey aspects of the truth very well; but if their limitations are not seen through, if they are accepted at their own valuation, as universal sages, their effect is appallingly reductive. This seems by now to have been pretty well understood in the case of Freud, who also drew a great deal from Schopenhauer, including his very similar misogyny. Freud has had a bad press for this from feminists, and on the whole with good reason. In fact of all the major modern prophets, he is the one whom they have attacked most sharply. It is not clear why Nietzschean thought should be so much more respectfully treated.

All these ideologies have their uses, of course. And it is natural enough that the rising feminist movement should have wanted to indicate its connexion with them, to show its academic credentials by invoking them, and also to get out of them what political mileage it could without being drawn out of its way. They are good servants but bad masters. Unchallenged, they tend always to narrow the range of choices available to thought. But wider thought is an essential tool in widening the range of practical choices, and that widening is what we need. As Virginia Woolf put it,

It would be a thousand pities if women wrote like men, or lived like men, or looked like men, for if two sexes are quite inadequate, considering the vastness and variety of the world, how should we manage with one only? Ought not education to bring out and fortify the differences rather than the similarities? For we have too much likeness as it is, and if an explorer should come back and bring word of other sexes looking through the branches of other trees at other skies, nothing would be of greater service to humanity; and we should have the immense pleasure into the bargain of watching Professor X rush for his measuring-rods to prove himself 'superior'.[7]

The trouble with Professor X is that he is stuck like a fly in the drying jam of his own preconceptions, which were largely framed with a nervous eye to his own fears. We do not want to echo him and produce his female counterpart. We need to try, so far as possible, to look at the problem from the standpoint of some newly discovered third sex, looking down with a startled eye from its tree at the extraordinary arbitrariness of many human customs.

6. Partiality and politics

Can that kind of impartial perception, however, be our aim? It runs contrary to the current feminist idea that women ought to consider exclusively the interests of women, and moreover that men cannot possibly understand what those interests are, so that it is not possible for a man to be a feminist. Women, correspondingly, are supposed not to be called on – nor, presumably, even able – to take any account of the interests of men. They should therefore say, with the New York Radical Women, 'We take the women's side in everything. We ask not whether something is "reformist" "radical" "revolutionary" or "moral". We ask, is it good for women or bad for women?'[8] Taken literally, this would mean that they do not care how badly somebody is treated provided that person is not a woman – it might, presumably, be a child – and are not even interested in any other questions about policy except 'does this benefit our group?'. Is this remarkable narrowing really possible? No doubt a lot of it is simply rhetoric. Anyone trying to make practical changes is in fact forced to weigh the various interests involved. And most people who do this do it in a far more normal way, working together with anyone who will help them. They fit their feminism into a background of general concern for the human race. In general people of goodwill tend to assume that, at a deep level, the interests of different human groups converge, so that help given to one is not finally torn from another, but will tend to enrich everybody in the end. They work primarily as people, not as partisans. When two groups live together, as men and women do, this idea obviously makes a lot of sense, and we shall see reason to take it very seriously. The rhetoric, however, remains and cannot just be ignored. It supplies arguments, even where it is not fully accepted. And of course it does contain parts of the truth.

What does the proposal of total partiality amount to? An obvious analogy is the position of an advocate as opposed to a judge. Counsel for one side has been heard. He has, in fact, been speaking for a fair number of centuries. Counsel for the other side, when finally given the floor, can reasonably point out that the case must not go straight to judgment. The arguments so far presented must be answered, and this will need a one-sided approach, to balance the bias in what has gone before. But this can scarcely mean that this speaker must imitate all the faults of the first one. Extravagant bias is a weakness, even in an advocate. Arguments which pay no attention to the case against them are shallow; they will not convince.

This raises the question, whom are we trying to convince? Who are the judge and jury? We cannot be preaching only to the converted. Certainly judging – deciding on the conflict of interests – is rightly delayed till both sides have been heard, but it cannot be put off for ever. Those who attempt it must try to be impartial. Who are they? From one angle, they must be the general public, the people whose help is needed if things are to be changed. This has to include both men and those women who, however keen they may be on their own interest, still mind about other people's as well, and also those who do not currently accept the feminist picture of what those interests demand. (There will figure here a multitude, constantly renewed, of young girls who dismiss the whole topic because they do not expect to suffer from discrimination themselves. If feminism is presented solely as self-interest, it is hard for any argument to reach them.) From another angle, however, the jury is within; it is each one of us. Unbalanced partiality cannot be a good way to form one's own opinions, because it is deliberately ill-informed. People who refuse to know the case against them cripple their own judgment. This misfortune was oddly exemplified by some girl students who lately signed up for a university course on sociobiology in order to understand their enemies, and then refused to read any sociobiological texts on the ground that they were probably sexist and had certainly been written by men. This way debates do not get far, even in law courts. That reaction, in fact, almost suggests a religious rather than a political scruple, yet there is not supposed to be any religious element in feminism. Or is there?

7. Seeing the light

Mention of a connexion with religion tends to shock feminists. It is an ideology that the movement has hardly used at all. Yet someone beginning to read the literature can scarcely help being struck by the analogies. So many women, describing the revelation that came when they discovered the movement, write in a way reminiscent of religious conversion. 'It was like a Christian conversion, suddenly we found these friendships', writes Catherine Hall.[9] After despair they saw the light. Life, which had before been utterly meaningless, suddenly gained a meaning. Everything was transformed. They stepped from desolation into a joyous fellowship, and the world would never be the same again. Now what they find is of course not a god, but fellowship with those who share their condition. One thing which this shows is the depth of their previous isolation, which we must discuss in a moment. The change might look, then, merely like the relief of a personal need, like recovery from sickness. But it is more than that, because the new-found group is seen as one to be not only welcomed but served. That outgoing identification with others and self-giving for a cause which are characteristically religious lead past the immediate enjoyment of society to the forwarding of a group ideal. (Political conversion only works like this when it has a religious element.) It does seem that one thing which is happening is relief from the blinkered narrowness of modern life, from the depressing idea that one should live only for onself and (at most) one's children, who are considered as one's extensions and representatives. People, especially in the churches, who have exalted 'the family' as a sufficient social ideal seem to have overlooked this dreadful narrowness. But why, when the human spirit breaks out of such a prison, does it join this special group, defined by gender, rather than others?

To understand this we need to comprehend the nature of the previous despair and isolation; and it will startle many by-standers that these could be so deep. Older women, in particular, may be puzzled to see how at this age anyone could suddenly need to discover the fellowship and support of other women, something which seems as much a condition of normal life as the air we breathe. How have they been living? We need to grasp how deeply the conditions of modern life - the frequent moves, the inhospitable towns, the impersonal crowds, the lethal roads - isolate young housewives from each other, and how little their early life at work, when there were no children, prepares them for a life in which there will be children and nobody else. Their earlier friends are likely still to be in that different world, or a different town. There is no village green, no neutral space where they can make friends while the children play. The children themselves are often confined in a way that is unnatural to them, and take it out on their mothers. And because the women come from a world where all this was not mentioned, they are not prepared for it, and know no one with whom they can discuss their difficulties. To understand their step out of darkness we need to grasp their earlier sudden collapse into it, when they gave up work to start a family. What they need is sympathy, understanding and constructive help with these particular problems. This they get only from fellow-sufferers. It is not surprising if the resulting bond is powerful, nor if the movement based on it shows both the peculiar strength and the peculiar faults of a religion.

The most obvious bad result is an intolerance, a deliberate embattlement, not only towards men but also towards dissenting women, which leave little room for attempts to convince them. There has been a noticeable reaction against this violence lately, and some readers may think that here we ought simply to ignore it. But the early manifestos are still selling fast, and so are new ones which echo them. Wild though they are they have real merits, and the ideas they express are still alive. If their message is to be worked through, their arguments must surely be taken seriously and answered. In any case, extreme positions are often useful compass-bearings to map the more realistic and moderate ones: it is a mistake to ignore them.

The stereotyped hostile reaction to a stereotyped caricature commonly invoked by the term 'women's lib' is becoming a serious nuisance. We need to break out of conditioned reflexes on both sides. Anyone who reads this book will probably be tempted by a great many of them, and also by a more subtle form of non-thought, mislabelled 'moderation'. This will suggest that what we need is to believe roughly half of what we hear – it does not much matter which half – and to do roughly a quarter of what any extremist is demanding. While this is less dangerous than many forms of non-thought, it really must not be mistaken for new thinking. What is needed is a shift of standpoint, after which different things will look extreme and different people will be called extremists. Measures which now look radical will look only sensible (and in fact some of our proposals may be of this kind). The question is not how far you go, but in what direction; and this brings us back to the more general issue – what kind of a cause, what kind of a movement, is feminism?

8. What is feminism?

This question is less simple than it seems. Janet Radcliffe Richards discusses it well in the opening section of her book *The Sceptical Feminist*. She suggests that the most useful sense for the word 'feminism' is to mark the simple conviction that 'women suffer systematic injustice because of their sex'. As she knows, many feminists will not think this half enough, because they do not rank anyone as a real feminist who does not also share in a distinctive belief-system and way of life. Genuine feminists, as she says, are currently

> ... at the very least, supposed to have committed themselves to such things as consciousness-raising groups and non-hierarchical organization, to the forswearing of femininity of appearance and demeanour, and to belief in the oppressiveness of families, the inherent equality of the sexes (or the superiority of the female) and the enslavement of women as the root of all oppression.[10]

As she points out, however, it is awkward to impose these restrictions while feminism is also widely seen – and indeed sees itself – as '*the* movement which represents the interests of women'. She concludes:

> Since there is no doubt that feminism is commonly thought of as having a monopoly on the representation of women's interests, and since all feminists, however firm their ideological commitments, must want as many people as possible to be willing to listen to arguments about the position of women rather than reacting with hostility whenever the subject of feminism comes up, it is in the interests of everyone who cares about justice to have as many people as possible thinking of themselves as feminists.[11]

Heresy-hunting, in fact, is here a sign of bad faith, of not caring enough about justice. Nobody who really wants a new course of action to be taken can afford to disown supporters who also genuinely want it, simply because in other ways they have a different standpoint.

The problem is a familiar one; it is common to many causes. Where something is resoundingly wrong – like torture or wife-beating – it is usually wrong for a great number of reasons. Its opponents can therefore be a very varied set of people, acting on varying principles. Once a particular abuse is remedied, they may not be able to work together so harmoniously over the next one. Most effective reform is in fact carried out by temporary coalitions of this kind rather than by single, unanimous groups. Yet the sense of lasting solidarity is also a very great support for reformers. They naturally want to form parties. How are these needs to be reconciled? To leave the party name rather wide, as Dr Richards suggests, and to pin it to issues that can unite a wide variety of people is a good way to win supporters. To insist on narrowing it to something more sectional, and not yet widely understood, is a sure way to lose them. In particular it seems strange to pin it to a style of life rather than to actual policies. Most *political* movements do not do this. Is there any overriding reason why women have to?

Styles of life disqualify people from membership of a particular reforming group when they show that they cannot sincerely accept its policies. A slave-owner cannot join the anti-slavery society unless he can show almost unimaginably good reasons for not having freed his slaves. Similarly, someone who is currently treating women unfairly cannot be a sincere feminist. How much further can we go? On the Marxist model it is often suggested that no man can be a feminist, just as nobody outside the working class can be accepted as a genuine fighter for that class. This is an idea with much point, but also with drawbacks, since it disqualifies for instance Marx himself, along with Engels, Trotsky, Lenin and most of the revolutionary heroes. It is hard even to insist that a champion of the working class cannot be a capitalist, since that genuine hero Engels was one all his life and supported Marx on the profits of his factory. Judgments like this have to take account of the circumstances of the particular case, particularly of the alternatives available. Since men do not have the alternative of ceasing to be men, it is hard to approximate their case to that of the slave-owners. Are there any respectable parallels for this sort of incurable exclusion? The most obvious ones are not attractive; they all concern racist groups. The Nazis would not have accepted a black convert, however sincere his (doubtless confused) Nazi convictions might have been. The National Front would probably take the same line. In a way that at first looks similar, the Black Power Movement excluded whites. But that exclusion was not from a whole campaign or political ideal, only from a special kind of organized group formed to support it. This is quite a different matter, and the difference is important for feminists.

There is a real problem about direct co-operation between those who are accustomed to running things and those accustomed to being run, a problem whose dimensions the first group cannot easily assess. Dale Spender gives a melancholy but touching example of this when she describes a workshop convened to discuss the best way to combat sexism in education, containing five men and twenty-eight women. Using her invaluable tape recorder, she tells how the men talked for three-quarters of the time, and also determined the entire direction of the discussion. The instructive point here is the conflict between conscious intention and performance. This kind of experience (which is commonplace) shows that women's groups are not being silly in preferring to operate on their own. They need to develop their ideas in this way, and also to acquire the habit of expecting to be listened to. But, evidently, what they have to say at the end of this process ought to come back into the common treasury. It can no more be impossible for men to understand it than it is impossible for women to understand the entire writings of males. (Kate Millett's excellent criticisms of the writings of authors like Freud and Lawrence are a sufficient proof, if one were needed, that sex difference is no bar to understanding.) The jointly owned doctrine thus formed can reasonably be called feminism.

When it comes to excluding from that term *women* whose views and habits are not considered extreme enough, the problem is even graver. As soon as we get beyond our own English-speaking backyard, conformity is simply not available. The problems women face in different cultures differ hugely; and since their style of life is anyway different from ours, the changes they need are also usually different. Women from Third World countries are often astounded at the idea of attacking the family, for it is quite likely to be the only institution that affords them any protection. Women from Communist countries tend to see the family as an area of fulfilment denied to them by the state. Yet it is perfectly natural to speak of all these women, when they try to lead movements to improve the conditions of the women around them, as feminists. If we restricted that term to people signing up for certain current Western proposals, we should need another name to cover the wider sense. And, since familiar words can always reach a wider public, there are obvious reasons for pinning the word to its old general sense, covering everyone who works to redress injustices peculiar to women. That includes both these non-Western campaigners and also people like John Stuart Mill, Henry Sidgwick, Josephine Butler, Susan B. Anthony and Emily Davies, for whom the word was originally coined. Since many of the main arguments now used are Mill's, it would be specially odd to exclude him.

Within this wide range, other words will of course be used to define more sharply the various ideas which different people at different times see as crucial to 'true feminism' – that is, as the best background for that work of redress. Because these have already begun to multiply, the one word 'feminism' cannot discriminate among them. As in any growing movement, people are branching out in different directions, of which socialism and separatism are only two. Within a given branch heresy-hunting can be in order. Opinion-based groups do need a real unity. But it seems wild to expect agreement across the whole range. The 'women's movement' is defined by its public, by a group to be served, not by any doctrine. That public is bound to have many interests and ideals. In this it resembles the Labour Movement rather than Marxism, and even Marxism has now divided to accommodate – more or less by agreement – a rich crop of sects. We need, too, to get rid of the excessive abstraction that has always hampered Marxism, to stop talking as if 'women' were always a standard article facing a standard set of problems. They are not.

In particular, our use of what looks like a single English language obscures great differences between the USA and

Britain, both in the actual situation and in the accepted style of controversy. California, for instance, constitutes a splendid laboratory for social experiments and for the taking of doctrines to their logical extremes, whose results outsiders are entitled to use without feeling bound to repeat them all locally. And, more generally, the notion of separatism, which looks very puzzling on this side of the Atlantic, tends to seem more natural to Americans. The idea of a society containing many quite distinct groups, sometimes differing by their cultural origins, sometimes by deliberately segregating themselves for the sake of their views, has largely replaced the older one of general assimilation as a solution to the American problem of immigration and the clash of cultures. Many such small groups already exist and prosper. The idea of adding women to them as one more quasi-ethnic group – even as a 'minority' – [12] evidently seemed a natural one in the 1960s. Looked at in that way, the woman question appeared as just one more item in that vast piece of unfinished business, the fulfilment of the promises made in the American Constitution, and the attractions of treating it as much like the other items as possible were obvious.

The striking differences of this case were nothing like so visible as they are in the smaller and more homogeneous societies of Europe, where separate communities are a rarity and the prospect of forming a new one gets looked at on its merits. Australia, it seems, is different again, accounting for Dale Spender and Germaine Greer. And even within Britain there is a real difference between the various regions, and between them and the capital. Pressing needs and interests, which are determined by age and domestic situations as well as by geography and political traditions, produce enormous diversity within the women's movement. Circumstances determine whether a group is preoccupied with wide doctrinal issues or whether it devotes its energies to devising ways of finding out what is in the family wage-packet, or of coping when a drunken man comes home to smash the furniture.

9. Putting women's problems in their context

In general, urgent remedial issues centring on gross injustices tend to unite the movement. What divides it is dissension about the positive ideals which should prevail after the remedy; about the proper direction to Utopia. Here it is useless for every sect to regard itself as the leader, and others as merely sluggish in following its chosen direction. Some schemes are not alternatives at all, but quite distinct and compatible projects. Others are real alternatives, involving real disagreements. Then we cannot avoid saying with Cromwell – and with Janet Radcliffe Richards – 'I beseech ye my sisters, in the bowels of Christ, think it possible that ye may be mistaken'. Anyone who has seen a few intellectual fashions come and go knows that all these suggestions are in any case going to look different shortly. They need work. None of them contains the whole secret of salvation. And it is not, after all, only women who are oppressed.

We have to abandon the crude stance of a mere pressure group, blind to all aims except shouting for its own corner, and look at a much wider scene. But this is unavoidable anyway if we are to make sense of our present difficulties. What has gone wrong is not just that men are oppressing women. Nor – to look at it the other way – is it just that certain women have become deranged and are shouting for things they do not really need. It is that industrial civilization is getting out of gear, and the whole relation between private and public life – between our domestic and our official functions – is becoming distorted. A barrier is building up between them which is impoverishing life for everybody, not just for women. The reason why women are the ones to shout this is that their lives stretch right across the barrier and are the first to be pulled out of shape by the change. Their protests are therefore a red light, a warning of dangers which affect everybody. Perhaps, too, as well as being more directly affected by the distortion, they are more aware of it and rightly less willing to tolerate it. Jung, discussing the kind of systematic suppression of emotion that is aimed merely at keeping up appearances, wrote that this is 'an art in which men particularly excel, while women with very few exceptions, are by nature averse to doing such violence to their emotions'.[13] This seems right. Women do tend to notice, and to show, grave emotional evils which men prefer to conceal; this does everyone a service. But apart from this, at present their predicament actually is worse. If they once lose their foothold in the outside official world, they are very liable to get trapped in homes which contract and crush them. This trapping ought not to be looked at on its own, as an accidental, isolated injustice that can be dealt with by giving first aid to the worst cases. Homes ought not to be prisons at all.

To understand how they are tending to become so it is worth glancing at some of the current evidence – for instance, at a very thorough and impressive survey of the social origins of depression in women in big cities today carried out by George W. Brown and Tyrril Harris.[14] They interviewed 458 women in the central London district of Camberwell to find out what causes predisposed them to depression – a condition to which, as was already known, women were twice as liable as men. Of the Camberwell women 13.3 per cent proved to be clinically depressed, as compared with 5.8 per cent in a traditional rural area chosen for a comparative study (the island of North Uist). All these cases were grave enough to convince investigating psychiatrists that they needed psychiatric treatment, though many of them were undiagnosed and receiving no treatment at all, or merely tranquillizers. As the authors remark, 'No-one who has interviewed women in a general population survey can be anything but impressed by the determination of some to carry on with their lives as though little was wrong in spite of an intolerable burden of symptoms'.[15] We are not talking about hypochondria. Apart from those who reached this standard there were, as might be expected, a great many less extreme cases.

Careful investigation found four 'vulnerability factors' which sharply increased the likelihood of serious depression once there was a 'provoking agent' – a disaster or grave worry. These were: (1) the presence at home of three or more children under fourteen; (2) the lack of a confidant (preferably a sympathetic husband); (3) not going out to work, and (4) (an irreversible factor which will not really concern us) having lost one's mother at an early age. Women with children at home were twice as liable to depression as those without. And, among them, working-class women were nearly four times as liable to it as middle-class women – a difference which seemed largely due to the other 'vulnerability factors', not to their greater liability to disaster. Whether these figures are changing is not known, since this is the first survey of its kind, but it is clear that both sorts of causes are on the increase. Women's employment is collapsing in the inner cities, while 'provoking factors' concerned with housing, family finance and the security of husbands and children are rising.

To forget sympathy altogether for the moment, the social cost of this depression is high. Not to mention the prescription bill for such things as tranquillizers, depression in general, even when it falls short of the clinical stage, does not qualify people to look after children. Brown and Harris looked into just one aspect of this, the incidence of serious accidents to children, and found that among the cases and near-cases of depression it was twice as high as among other women in the sample, or the same women when not depressed. It looks likely, therefore, that some of the child neglect which is often attributed to mothers going out to work can also result from their not doing so. Why should the combination of children and no employment have this effect? Don't mothers love their children? No doubt they do, but there is at least one crucial respect in which children cannot possibly be substitutes for adult companions – namely, in supporting an adult's self-esteem. Essentially, depression seems to be a deep failure of self-confidence, an inability to hope or to believe any longer in one's own power and value. To reassure depressed people, other concerned adults are needed. But the care of small children can, without a real neighbourhood or an extended family, confine a woman to her home in such a way that she meets no other adults. If her husband does not help her there is nobody to do it. The result is that what should have been a passing crisis leads not only to chronic and sometimes incurable misery, but also to a social paralysis which is everybody's loss.

The move from a merely medical and psychoanalytic view of depression as a personal condition to the social enquiry into what people are depressed *about*, of which this survey is a part, is essential.

10. The neglected resource

This is just one instance of the kind of problem which calls for new ways of thinking, ways to which feminism of a sane kind has much to contribute. To see what is going wrong in such cases all parties need to be a lot less interested in scoring points and laying blame, and more interested in understanding predicaments. It is no wonder, however, that they have not yet become so. New thought is always hard, and thought about women in particular has always been slapdash. As Margaret Britton charitably puts it, when you begin to look into traditional teaching on this subject you are startled to notice how 'many otherwise good and wise people do not know the first thing about women, which is that they are not all alike'.[16] In most epochs this traditional teaching has consisted mainly of a very narrow set of alternatives supposed to be open to women, and an equally narrow set of opinions which could be formed about them. Yet in spite of all this – or perhaps because of it – it has often been women who, less impressed with the inevitability of the *status quo*, have shown how effective new and imaginative thinking can be.

It is worth looking at certain examples of women's work which have sprung up across the grain of the existing system. (The fact that women habitually work without getting paid makes them often less confused and hidebound than men about such possibilities.) One instance is the invention of hospices for the dying. Until a few decades ago, it was simply accepted as inevitable that those dying in hospital (as most of us now do) must die more or less alone and with little medical or personal help. When we consider how likely it is for any one of us that we shall end up in this position, the slowness in remedying this, and in applying the resources of modern medicine to it, is extraordinary. The explanation was a very common one – a sense of helplessness and impossibility. Dame Cicely Saunders and others decided to treat the problem as soluble, and produced a solution. The same sort of thing appears even more strikingly in the general invention of nursing. Florence Nightingale was constantly met by firm assurances that what she wanted to do was quite impossible, and these came most strongly from those best informed, who had officially been in charge of trying to do it (such as the medical experts of the War Office, and those running hospitals). She simply refused, in the teeth of all discouragement, to accept their views, and went on to refute them. The recent invention of refuges for battered wives by Erin Pizzey and her Chiswick colleagues seems to be another such benign and unexpected move, providing the first real inroad on an age-old iniquity. (This achievement must not be obscured by subsequent disputes about detailed policies for refuges.)

Now many of our existing problems seem to call for new thinking, and for essentially practical initiatives of this general kind. Some are fairly humdrum, but none the less life-savers for that – groups set up to help the victims of particular diseases or disasters, to diffuse small-scale but vital information through the housewives' register, or to stop some other of the gaps constantly appearing in our unwieldy, overstrained social system through which the waters of despair pour in and overwhelm people. Some, equally life-saving, are a great deal less familiar, like consciousness-raising groups. The idea that those who, for whatever reason, cannot easily express their views on what is happening to them should get together to help each other and to develop their thoughts together is an admirable one, and it is obvious that a great many women are in this position. Evidently, the project has teething troubles. It is widely reported that power structures do tend to grow up, in spite of the best intentions of being non-hierarchical, and the tendency for some groups to turn into classes with a teacher or counsellor will need watching. The problem of what the psychoanalytic tradition calls transference, and of power relations generally in the absence of forms to control them, will have to be worked out. Still, the general idea is a helpful one, and much may come of it.

Even more interesting than these two kinds of development, however, has been the Women's Peace Camp at Greenham Common during 1982 and 1983, protesting against the siting of cruise missiles. Whatever view we may take of this cause itself or of its likely success, there is no doubt that this has been a peculiarly impressive kind of protest. There has been some confusion about the point, and even the legitimacy, of having an all-woman demonstration like this – a controversy in which the word 'sexism' has played its usual obfuscating part. There are two excellent reasons for having such a demonstration. One is the purely tactical one that, if properly run, it is far more unmistakably peaceful than any demonstration containing men can be – not because the men would necessarily behave aggressively, but because their very presence symbolizes contention in a way which the presence of women does not. The other and deeper reason also turns on the symbolism of the two sexes; it is that women in a special way stand for peace, stand for life and fruitfulness and hope for the future – and if they are seen rejecting, vigorously and in large numbers, the idea that expensive and destructive hardware is any use in protecting these things, the message has a special point which men would not be in the same position to convey. Both these reasons rely on the traditional symbolism, to which some feminists object. But much feminist argument also relies on it, and it is not easy to see how we could get rid of it. In any case, Greenham Common is a notable example of the kind of thing which is possible. In fact, 'in politics, if you want anything said, ask a man; if you want anything *done*, ask a woman' (Margaret Thatcher, 1965).[17]

In order, however, to release the enormous potential of women to help to improve the quality of life for everyone, they first need certain things done for them. They need to get into a situation where they have the opportunity to use their energies for the benefit of all. Improving the position of women in our society is partly a matter of justice, but it is also a matter of necessity in a rapidly changing and demanding world.

11. Reform, revolution and rethinking

Those seriously interested in reforming any aspect of society are always faced with the problem of having to operate on three different levels. These are principle, policy and programme. The principle of a reform can be seen as the answer to the question 'what should be done?', the policy as the answer to 'what can be done?' and the programme as the answer to 'how can it be done?'.

We have to keep all those levels in mind. There are no short cuts to the ideal. Anyone who dismisses the idea of a sudden, complete revolution as senseless – which we shall argue that it is for women – must propose what is called 'piecemeal reform', that is, a programme of varying measures which are only parts of their policy and only first steps towards their ideal. But that does not mean that they must be a sell-out, nor even a job lot. The policy supplies the unity. That policy should, we suggest, here be the adaptation of women's work and pay to a woman-shaped life. This can be seen as part of a wider attempt to adapt everybody's work and pay to a human-shaped life, because the existing and supposedly man-shaped career suits many men as well as women very badly. But once we stop being obsessed with the idea of treating men and women exactly alike, the immediate aim for women will be to make it possible for them to pass in and out of the child-bearing phase of life without either penalizing children or grotesquely interrupting and distorting women's useful careers.

This ought to make it possible for the child-bearing years to be an ordinary, rewarding piece of strenuous living, not a bewildering, desolating endurance test and a sentence of exile from interesting life. It should give women a lifeline back, after those years, into every kind of occupation for which they are prepared to retrain, so that older women would be found freely in all ranks and conditions of the working world, as well as working honourably at home. It should make us find it just as natural to hear that 'the Director is on maternity leave this year' as it is now to hear that 'the Director is in America till January'. Of course this is not all that needs to be done, and radicals, as usual, will do well to keep reminding us of other aims. But it will do to be going on with. From the other side, people may well enquire whether this is a realistic aim at all. Can such changes really ever come about?

The world is always changing, yet we always tend to think of changes as impossible beforehand. Those most monastic of ancient institutions, the men's colleges at Oxford and Cambridge, now nearly all admit women. They have done this in the last two decades somewhat suddenly, because they sensibly decided that not doing so was depriving them of good students. Here, as with the suffrage, the totally unthinkable has quickly become commonplace. There seems no reason why it should not continue to do so. But to begin with we must ask how we came to find ourselves all together in a conceptual drawer marked WOMEN, and why the instructions attached to this drawer are so peculiar. Perhaps we had better start by glancing back over this odd filing system, if we want to grasp why things are so confused today.

Part Two:
False Choices in Practice

2 Choices real and unreal

> The husband wants to find himself in his wife, the lover in his mistress, in the form of a stone image; he is seeking in her the myth of his virility. ... She is also the totem set up deep in the African jungle; she is a helicopter and she is a bird. Men stretch forth avid hands towards the marvel, but when they grasp it, it is gone; the wife, the mistress, speak like everybody else, through their mouths; their words are worth just what they are worth.
>
> (Simone de Beauvoir, *The Second Sex*)

1. Destiny and decisions

Traditionally, choices for women about the pattern and content of their lives have always appeared more limited than those open to men, and, such as they are, have usually been seen as stark, inescapable and final. Throughout myth and legend, fact and fiction, women have commonly stood helplessly holding the baby, imprisoned by a choice which either they or somebody else has made, while their menfolk run away to sea or join the foreign legion or find somebody else instead.

The whole idea that most people are entitled to make or are capable of making real decisions which actually affect the way things go is, in Western culture, recent and severely limited. From ancient times to the present the notion of destiny or fate is something which has to some extent circumscribed the areas of choice for both sexes. But the ways in which it has done so, and the responses to it, have been systematically different in the case of men and women.

The primitive determinism – primitive in its metaphysics if not in its psychology – displayed by the belief of the ancient Greeks in the prophecies of the oracles seems at first glance a pretty equitable way of limiting the sphere of influence of both sexes. But a little reflection upon the circumstances of the utterances and the reaction of those to whom they spoke displays clear partiality. Though the oracles themselves were usually female, they were simply the mouthpieces of the gods. What they said was recorded, transmitted and finally interpreted by males. The Greek legends abound with stories of men who, in spite of their avowed belief in the reliability of at least the better oracles such as the one at Delphi, go to the most improbable lengths to try to stop the prophecies they do not like coming true. The story of Oedipus would probably have sunk without trace had Laius and Oedipus himself not struggled so hard and so abortively to try to outwit fate. No one tells Oedipus to lie back and enjoy it. Even in these early legends a man struggling against his fate is seen as a noble rather than an absurd, a tragic rather than a pathetic figure. A man, resisting even what he himself believes to be inevitable, is not thought to be illogical, let alone insane. But this attitude does not usually extend to women. Women are more frequently cursed and condemned by those more powerful than themselves than looked upon as agents of the will of the gods (except when they are raped and bear heroes), and any act of rebellion is severely punished by an external agency. It is Jocasta who says that the oracle is a sham and it is Jocasta who is punished by death. Implicit is the assumption that a woman must accept her destiny or die: she must see herself as a victim of it. A man, on the other hand, is entitled to behave as though he were in some sense a shaper of that destiny even if his belief is mere illusion. In general, it is assumed that men choose; women are chosen.

This simple view of fate as fulfilling what the gods ordain has never entirely been done away with, but why does it operate differently for men and women? The answers given to this question do not really flow from any theory, but from ancient custom and the deeper causes of custom. With rare and passing exceptions even the greatest theorists did not, until lately, really ask *whether* women ought to be in a position to make choices, but only why they were not. Since what is customary always tends to look reasonable to people who profit by it, there was no difficulty in producing reasons.

2. The functional argument

The most powerful and lasting set of reasons has been the one advanced by Aristotle as part of his impressive functional approach to biology. It was this great and deservedly respected philosopher who first supplied us with a definition of a woman in terms of her sexual functions.[1] According to Aristotle objects in the world are arranged in a strict hierarchy, the lesser always existing for the benefit of the greater, and each thing being definable according to its function, which in turn is always described from the point of view of the user. He assumes that women are inferior men, and defines their function accordingly. Just as a chair is for sitting in and air is for sustaining life, so a woman is for breeding from and for providing comfort to the male. Moreover, 'we should look on the female as being as it were a deformity, though one which occurs in the ordinary course of nature'. Even in reproduction, 'a male is a male in virtue of a particular ability, and a female a female in regard to a particular inability'.[2] This definition from inferiority, which has managed to remain with us for so long, has three serious and damaging consequences. First, it enables us to say what a woman *is* in virtue of her sexual nature rather than to describe simply what she *does*. Little ingenuity is required to extend the notion of her sexual nature to include her sexual behaviour, and this is exactly what happened, culminating in the virgin/whore fantasy so prevalent in Western thought. Second, it becomes possible to treat all women as if, for all purposes, they are one identifiable class of beings with the same desires, emotions, strengths and weaknesses. Aristotle classifies men into different groups for different purposes; citizens and non-citizens, shepherds and hunters, the rulers and the ruled, and devotes much time to justifying these distinctions by pointing to differences in needs and abilities and aptitudes. Of course he makes many distinctions, accepted in his day, which we may find strange, unnecessary or even cruel, but he always sees the necessity of not always treating all men as if they were clones. This courtesy is never extended to women, who appear as a single standard

39

entity, as do children and slaves. And third, it never requires us to look at things from the women's point of view.

The relation of theory to custom here is very interesting. Aristotle was not, of course, inventing a new attitude to women, but expressing habitual notions. Plato indeed had suggested that men and women might be basically similar, and argued for educating the women of his Republic's ruling class just like the men. But Aristotle did not even answer this eccentric idea. Treating the whole issue casually, he just extended his conceptual scheme to articulate the common social attitude of his day. Understandably, his attention was elsewhere. Within biology itself the functional approach was both new and excellent. By treating the parts of plants and animals as tools – 'organs' – explicable in terms of their use, Aristotle made biology possible. Plato had ruled that the whole visible, changing earth was unintelligible, mere brute confused matter. Against this, Aristotle showed a way to understand it. He thereby – among other things – made it possible for people to accept and understand their bodies. The achievement was immense. But then, as often happens to original thinkers, he was drawn on to extend his useful scheme far beyond its proper scope. Slaves and women are not in fact organs like the lungs and liver, and no disinterested biological enquirer would ever have been likely to mistake them for such. But on these occasions, where a favourite intellectual habit combines with the inertia of custom and also with self-interest, critical faculties are simply laid to sleep.

The same thing happened also with another popular and persistent Aristotelian idea on this subject, the proposition that males are essentially active and females passive. This notion is supposed to be drawn from sexual intercourse. Even there, on its home ground, it is not actually true except for necrophiliacs. In all other contexts it is a non-starter, since women do quite as many things to men – feed them, nurse them, flatter them, bring them up – as men do to women. Aristotle however seized it cheerfully and built it into his great metaphysical scheme of Form and Matter. Form, he said, is the shaping, positive, intellectual, active element in the world. Matter (the word for which happens to be feminine) is the mere blank stuff, the wood or clay on which it operates. There is a difficulty about this, because if matter actually has no qualities – if all the qualities belong to form – it is hard to see how it is real at all. Aristotle therefore gave it a sort of minimal existence, the status of something struggling out of nullity, and described this by saying that 'matter desires form as the female desires the male'.[3] This drama (which could never rightly have claimed more than the standing of a metaphor) spread itself illicitly to become accepted as a simple, literal truth about males and females. Women were thus metaphysically proved to be inferior. This piece of bad metaphysics, along with the bad biology, was allowed to remain uncriticized, though unsupported, because it really needed no legs. It simply lay on the back of custom.

3. The persistent anomaly

What happened here – and has so often happened, not only on this topic – is that philosophers who are sliding into positions deeply convenient to them and to those around them simply do not see the absurdity of their antics. Nearly every thinker, however great, has been afflicted with this sort of negligence on some topic. Nobody can be attentive about everything. This is usually not fatal, because it is the job of the next philosopher to point out the lapses. But the distinctive thing about the woman question is that nobody did this. Negligence just continued. The vested interest involved was, until recently, too strong for any real attention to be possible.

About the related question of slaves, the Stoics already had doubts. Christianity, because it arose among a class which included many toads beneath the harrow, quickly settled that matter, at least in theory, though by no means at once in practice. (When the trade in black slaves arose, the idea that they were not really human was floated as a justification – another piece of transparently flimsy theory, usable only because self-interest endorsed it.) Over women, however, as we shall presently see, theory had shifted very little by the eighteenth century. To say that Aristotelian thought remained dominant is misleading. What remained dominant was custom – an immense load of it – draped only in a small and archaic piece of Aristotelian non-thought. The sight is startling. As Mill rightly said,

> The social subordination of women thus stands out, an isolated fact in modern social institutions ... a single relic of an old world of thought and practice exploded in everything else, but retained in the one thing of most universal interest; as if a gigantic dolmen, or a vast temple of Jupiter Olympius, occupied the site of St Paul's and received daily worship, while the surrounding Christian churches were resorted to only on fasts and festivals.[4]

(Dolmens are prehistoric stone circles.)

In the eighteenth century certain bystanders, notably Helvetius[5] and Tom Paine,[6] did point out that something seemed to be wrong; but what they said cut little ice, because eighteenth-century revolutionary thought was so strongly committed to linking – almost to equating – freedom with virility. It asserted, literally, brotherhood and the rights of *man*. As Burns said, 'a man's a man for all that'. Burns, like Rousseau, drew much of his terrific subversive force from having himself been a toad beneath the harrow. But this experience, it seems, does not necessarily produce solidarity with all other toads, only with those toads with whom one can readily identify. The slogan was still 'one man, one vote'.

The gigantic dolmen, then, remained, and can be seen at its most overwhelming in the works of Rousseau himself, that great and genuine champion of liberty. It has been a constant source of amazement and indignation to feminists, from Mary Wollstonecraft on, that Rousseau's ideas about liberty never extended to women at all. Freedom, for him, was a male prerogative, and any problems about it were problems about the interaction between groups of males, or individual ones. His views on women can be found in the *Emile*. Here, after four books on the crucial importance of freedom and self-reliance in the education of boys, and just before a repetition of the libertarian manifesto from the *Social Contract*, with its red-hot denunciation of slavery and its promise that 'every man in obeying the sovereign obeys only himself',[7] he directs the education of Sophie, who is to be Emile's bride. The central principle here, he says, is that 'in the union of the sexes, the man should be strong and active, the woman should be weak and passive, the one should have both the power and the will; it is enough that the other should offer little resistance. When this principle is admitted, *it follows* that woman is specially made for man's delight.' (Italics ours.) This, therefore, must be the only purpose of her education. She should have no instruction beyond what is needed to please her husband. Obedience should be her first and effectively her only virtue. Her duty will be entirely to her husband, and since he is wholly responsible for her, she need not understand the reasons for anything which is required of her. Her life should pass so far as possible in confinement at home. Girls, therefore, 'should early be accustomed to restraint', because

> ... all their life long they will have to submit to the strictest and most enduring restraints, those of propriety.... They have, or ought to have, little freedom ... what is most wanted in a woman is gentleness; formed to obey a creature so imperfect as man, a creature often vicious and always faulty, she should early learn to submit to injustice and to suffer the wrongs inflicted on her by her husband without complaint.

It is of some interest that Rousseau himself – a disorganized man – was ruled by women for most of his life. His is the voice of seething resentment, not of triumphant tyranny. But print conceals this difference; and he could cite good authority. The reasons for this apparently extraordinary one-sidedness are there for all to see in the ancient tradition. Rousseau's political thought operated, as much good political practice must, with existing categories and concepts. What he saw clearly and correctly was that many of these categories which distinguish male groups or individuals are irrelevant when considering notions such as liberty, even if they are relevant for other purposes. For when you distinguish between men you do so on account of their actions, not their natures, and the right to basic freedoms is based on nature, not on behaviour. Groups of men can thus be compared and contrasted, since they are sufficiently alike in nature for injustices to one or another to show themselves. It is by seeing what it is possible for someone else *who is like you* to do that restrictions upon your own freedom become apparent. No freedom is absolute. But if you accept, as Rousseau did, the Aristotelian definition of a woman, you place her for ever outside the realm of possible comparison. There is no standard against which you can measure or even determine injustice done to her; and by treating all women as one class of being, you preclude the possibility of identifying relative injustices among women, and so extending the notion outwards in relation to men. This is something that radical feminists may care to ponder before they play the Aristotelian game themselves.[8] Finally, stuck fast in the functional fallacy, you become incapable of looking at the problem from the woman's point of view, since a functional definition necessitates seeing the thing under consideration solely from the point of view of the user. To justify this it is a small step to argue that the used *has* no point of view, or at best that its point of view is of not the slightest importance or interest. And once you have taken that step, literally anything goes.

What is remarkable is that this primitive way of thinking persisted in the central European tradition for so long, not only unchallenged but without serious attention. If it was true that the basic principles of the Enlightenment applied only to less than half of the human race, one might have expected the champions of that movement to find this fact an interesting and exciting one, calling for discussion and explanation even if not for doubt. They did not. Neither Hume nor Kant paid the topic any serious attention, but what little they did say shows that their dogmatic slumbers were undisturbed. Kant, that great architect of the idea of personal freedom, remarked that 'the only characteristic that permanently disqualifies any person from citizenship in the state, and therefore from the obligation to obey only those laws to which consent has been given, is that of being born female',[9] which is exactly Rousseau's position. Hegel, less surprisingly, thought that 'the family becomes one person', and that while men were like animals, women were like plants – that is, without any real individuality.[10]

Rousseau's views on almost every other subject received endless fertile discussion, but not on this one. Even Mary Wollstonecraft's shrewd, vigorous and fair exposure of Rousseau's inconsistencies in *A Vindication of the Rights of Woman* (1792) did not arouse general discussion. It was a century after the publication of *Emile* before its author's intellectual heirs got round to this part of their inheritance. Fourier raised the topic, and though Marx himself showed little interest, Engels took it up seriously in *The Origin of the Family, Private Property and the State* (1884). We shall see in Chapter 6 that he was not altogether successful, but at least he had insisted on discussing the matter. And in 1869 John Stuart Mill, to his undying credit, did the job properly in *The Subjection of Women*. But even then no other major thinker took much notice, unless we count Bernard Shaw. The topic went on being treated as eccentric – not one which people were unwilling to talk about, for everybody pontificated about it, but an unsuitable one for methodical, systematic attention. The result was an amazing conventionality. There cannot be many matters on which Freud, Nietzsche, Rousseau and Schopenhauer agree cordially both with each other and with Aristotle, St Paul and St Thomas Aquinas,[11] but their views on women are extremely close.

When women read philosophy they tend to fall into an embarrassed habit of feeling that they ought not to criticize the ludicrous views which result, that it is unfair and anachronistic to think that people of this calibre should have been able to avoid going into print with such stuff. But even with Aristotle this is not really true; he had the arguments of Plato and Euripides before him. He did indeed live in a harem society. And one can make some excuse for the Church Fathers on the grounds of celibacy; but again, this will not get them far, since they were very sophisticated thinkers who ought to have seen the feebleness of their arguments. When we get to the eighteenth century, however, all such excuses fail, and it is important to say plainly that things went very badly wrong. Unthinking conformism was replaced by positive reactionary efforts to resist and reverse change. The reason for stressing this is not, of course, vindictiveness – we all make bad mistakes – but the need to see how today's difficulties arose. No one ought to be surprised if protests on this matter, when they are finally heard, are a trifle crude and extreme. It would be extraordinary if they were not. Nobody in the central, established tradition has bothered to do the spade-work which would have made more sophisticated discussion possible.

This traditional way of defining women as actual or potential breeding machines for the use of men has of course been used to justify all kinds of treatment given to them, from denying them education and legal identity to distrusting their capacity to tell the truth or refrain from shoplifting. The insidious thing is that, like all great lies, it contains a piece of truth. The fact that women give birth really is an important element in their lives. This is something that we will need to consider later. But for the moment it is enough to remark that when a woman was defined solely in terms of her sexual functions – over which, until recently, most women have had little or no control – it is hardly surprising that her choices always seemed so much narrower than those of a man. They have been seen in relation to those functions alone, while men's choices have extended ever outwards. The main choice seemed to be whether they were good girls who fulfilled their destiny silently and obediently, or wicked women who did it angrily and resentfully. But fulfil it they had to. It does not look like much of a choice. Destiny and decision-making are unhappy bedfellows.

4. Good girls and wicked women

Choices for women have thus inevitably been connected with their sexual identity and, by extension, behaviour. The official view of the nineteenth-century bourgeoisie confirmed this. The choice for a woman was to be an angel in the house, or a castaway. Theoretically at least, as Bracebridge Hemynge put it, 'literally every woman who yields to her passions and loses her virtue is a prostitute'.[12] There is no ambiguity about that. The angel in the house[13] exemplified all the feminine virtues of silence, obedience and sexual anaesthesia, while the prostitute was raucous, wilful and randy. Any indication that the angel was attempting to think for herself was supposed to be firmly repressed before the one-way ride to damnation was begun. Much has been written about the standards of Victorian morality, and there is no need to repeat it here. The usual criticisms involve decrying the double standards employed. These are certainly unfair, but the real damage lies deeper than unfairness. In this double standard we are still stuck with the assumption that a woman, in choosing a certain kind of sexual behaviour, chooses what she *is*. When a man prays 'Lord, make me pure – but not yet', we canonize him. Not so for women. Mary Magdalen is no exception; she had to be good *now*. A woman is not allowed such a prayer in this morality. Nineteenth-century evangelism certainly gave women some comfort in that salvation became possible for a 'fallen' woman, but only at the price of total renunciation. And the salvation was not in this world. An impure woman could not regain purity; she could at best spend the rest of her life in repentance and atonement, trusting in the infinite mercy of God. The just man can fall seven times a day and remain just; the just woman cannot sin at all.

What is wrong with this is not simply that it is unfair, but that it is daft. Men always knew that there were elements of good and bad in themselves, but consistently refused to accept this as a fact about women. This refusal takes us straight out of the real world into a fantasy world peopled by creatures bearing little or no resemblance to the actual ones. People who make theories about these bogus creatures, as Freud did, or who legislate for them, as has often been done, incur only scorn and ingratitude from real women. In reality the angel in the house and the prostitute never existed at all. Housewives sometimes fancy the milkman; prostitutes sometimes fall in love. The trouble with insisting on classifying women according to polar extremes is not that it is unfair because we do not do it to men; it is that it is nonsense because we cannot credibly do it to anyone.

It is worth remarking that in general the human imagination strongly tends to dramatize, to paint characters in extremes of black and white. When, therefore, we find that some class of beings seems to be sharply divided into just these two sub-classes we should always suspect that the division is the work of our minds, not a fact in the world. Real people are all colours. About women this kind of projection is particularly rampant. As C.S. Lewis puts it,

> You will find, if you look carefully into any human's heart, that he is haunted by at least two imaginary women – a terrestrial and an infernal Venus, and that his desire differs qualitatively according to its object. . . . In the second type, the felt evil is what he wants; it is that 'tang' in the flavour that he is after. In the face, it is the visible animality, or sulkiness, or craft, or cruelty which he likes, and in the body, something quite different from what he ordinarily calls Beauty.[14]

The fact that this 'human' is male gives a clue to one reason why the power of such images flourishes more about women than about men. Since men have played the dominant part in building up the official culture, they have themselves constructed most of their own public image. Accordingly, whatever its faults it does not remain at this crude, unrealistic, projective stage. It is well known there are many kinds of men. But the women's image easily does remain there. On top of this, it is possible that Melanie Klein is right to suggest that a baby's early relation to its mother always plays a special part in developing its powers of love and of hatred, giving a special force both to the idea of the life-giving goddess-mother and to that of the evil, hostile witch. This does something to account for the ambivalence of both sexes, the tendency of both to rest satisfied with a crude pair of archetypal women. Witch-hunting and prostitute-baiting have, unfortunately, been pursuits for both sexes. Carl Jung has suggested, further, that our whole tendency to polarize experience into extremes, finding in it both ideals and terrors far beyond what our actual life has ever provided, is the unfolding of an inner programme for development.[15] We ought therefore (he points out) always to be prepared for differences between the drama, which comes so naturally to us, and the unfortunate real people whom we involve in it. This warning accords with common sense, because we are all familiar with the kind of mistakes which come from neglecting it. But it is hard to apply, most particularly in the case of women, and this effort was not even seriously made until lately.

Proletarian women in particular were not supposed to call at all for a realistic discrimination betwen fact and image. Nineteenth-century lower-class women had, if anything, less choice than the gentry, a number of whom viewed them all as actual or potential prostitutes anyway. The history of Victorian prostitution – in particular the facts uncovered by Josephine Butler – shows how widespread this attitude was.[16] In fact for such women prostitution was only another risk in their already insecure lives. Lack of legal protection, the risks of pregnancy and venereal disease and the brutal attitudes of those who exploited prostitutes were hardly great incentives to take to the streets. But they always undertook paid work of some kind whenever they could find it; for them it was simply an extra burden to be borne. The official image did not alter to accommodate these facts, however. It remained that of home or vice; the slightly tarnished angel – this time hurrying back to the house – or the whore. Peter Cominos, in his unhappily titled though otherwise very interesting article 'Innocent Femina Sensualis in Unconscious Conflict', sums up these attitudes very well:

> Victorian society and the family spawned two kinds of women, the womanly woman and her negation, the whorely whore: the pure and the impure ... they were sharply differentiated in their awareness and conduct and in the approval and disapproval and the rewards and punishments which others, especially women, eagerly conferred upon them. The pure woman was innocent, inviolate, inspirational and indulged; the impure woman (less than a woman)

was doubtful, detected, detestable and destroyed. No dialectic could join the two; a great and impassable gulf divided them.[17]

The obvious way of keeping women pure is to keep them under lock and key; to give them as little choice as possible about the pattern of their lives and to protect them, forcibly if necessary, from the attentions of other males and from their own licentiousness. The woman who, perforce, left the protection of her home was immediately suspect and at risk. In an age so dedicated to the power of reputation there could have been no more effective way of limiting the choices open to women.

5. Unreal choices

This is a common kind of problem, both in private life and politics. Ideologies often face us with alternatives which we ought not to accept. Compassion or justice? Truth or loyalty? My own country or others? My family or the human race? Men or women? Equality or liberty? This is the kind of thinking that makes confrontation politics so rife at present. It is not that confrontation, and the cultivation of extremes, has been found to be an effective way of running states. It has not. It is that a kind of desperation seizes people when they see the distance between the two extremes, and they find it almost impossible to go back and look for the mistakes in the way the dispute arose. We can do this afterwards (as for instance over the seventeenth-century wars of religion) or over other people's quarrels today. But over our own politics we are continually driven to typecasting. We feel that anything a Tory government does must be anti-egalitarian, for it is committed to the personal freedom ethic; and that anything a Labour government enacts must strike at the roots of our liberty, for it (after all) wants to make us all the same. The nonsense of this is displayed in the frequently made complaint that in the end it does not much matter which party is in power, since what either can actually do is dictated by pragmatic considerations and external forces far removed from any questions of principle. The relation between theory and practice seems then to have evaporated altogether. But the myth of confrontation between irreconcilable ideals persists. It embodies some curious notions: first, that equality and liberty are the only alternatives; second, that they are always at odds; third, that a general commitment to one principle or the other is binding for life, so that a change is betrayal; and fourth, that any action is explainable in terms of the principle or damnable if it is not.

Ideologies beget images; images beget stereotypes who are always the very picture of grandad. Left/right stereotypes are with us still. Most people vote as their parents did. Tribal loyalty prevails. The left is male, flat-capped, Northern; the right is female, flower-hatted, Home Counties. The trouble with these images is not just that they are false, but that they actually prevent us from concentrating on real issues while we agonize about choosing between them. We need to look directly at the world, which is changing rapidly. Political satirists understand the power of these stereotypes very well and exploit them to the full. Giving us a false choice about something which does not matter is a very good way of avoiding real issues and problems. Many people have been shocked to hear David Owen say that his party sometimes agreed more with the Labour Party and sometimes more with the Conservatives. Such lack of tribal commitment flouts the rules of confrontation politics, but it concentrates the mind in a way that no chanting of slogans can do. The balance achieved by the traditional kind of debate is a mere balance of prejudice. It actually engineers a situation in which the real issues cannot be discussed. What is needed is a balance of opinion, not a balance of mutual dislike. Serious separate discussion is, at least to begin with, a much better way to sort out one's views and communicate them to others than the ritualized, unreal debate which we so often witness.

For women, too, it is important that when they are trying to identify and make recommendations about rectifying injustices they should do so alone, not in relation to an identifiable enemy against whom they can direct their energies. They need those energies for the job in hand. But it is a mistake to think that that is the end of the matter. On the contrary, it is just the beginning. Men and women must in the end live together. Accordingly the notion of 'separatism' is itself one half of a false dichotomy (the other half is 'consorting with the enemy'). Separatism is not a real choice for the human race, though a few individuals might manage it. Making this the issue – will you leave the company of men or remain for ever in their power? – obscures the real problems of finding ways to live together in harmony, which in the end is what most people would prefer.

It is by concentrating on the genuine issues that progress is made, not by pointing out the funny hat of the opposition. Equality and liberty have taken on the role of the funny hats in modern political thought, and indeed they do sometimes conflict; but particular situations really do require particular solutions. More often than not it is perfectly obvious in a specific case that there is an overriding need for one or the other or for something quite different. It would be nonsense to allow people, in the name of equality, to pump toxic fumes into the playgrounds of rural schools because urban schools get them, or, in the name of liberty, to allow people not to have their children educated. And neither ideal ought to be allowed to stand in the way of other essential values, such as compassion. It is not that there is no need for principles in political life, but that those principles should be general guides rather than the modern equivalent of the oracles. And there is a real difference between having principles and having principles which require you to damn everybody else's.

What has so often gone wrong in the choices presented to women is not only that they are not genuine alternatives, but that they are not the choices that women would choose to present to themselves. The element of fantasy in alternatives like virgin or whore irritates women very much, for they know that this is not a real issue for most of them. Irritation promotes over-reaction and effectively obscures problems which are real. One of the great contributions of modern feminism has been its insistence that women have the right to identify their own problem areas and choose accordingly, rather than merely to decide between those alternatives which are selected for them.

We have looked at some of the strange habits which distort choice. In resisting these, our best safeguard is never to assume that the choice handed to us is the one we have got to accept, and to remember that not all choices are the same: they vary so much that we should look round to the widest possible horizons. Some choices are made deliberately and painstakingly, some casually, some subconsciously; sometimes we do not notice that we have made a choice until well after the event. Choices can be made between two positive courses of action – do X or Y – or between a positive and a negative alternative – do X or do not do it. They can be final and decisive and exclusive, like having the dog put down, or they can be temporary and non-exclusive in the long run, like going swimming today and making jam tomorrow. They can have consequences which are significant or not, they can depend on external circumstances or upon ourselves only. Above all they can be real or illusory; we are sometimes compelled to choose, and sometimes we create anguish for ourselves by presenting perfectly compatible courses of action as incompatible. All this is just plain common sense and it indicates that when we are faced with what looks like a choice we should always ask ourselves first what kind of a choice it is. The power to answer that question is the first thing we need in a process of rational decision-making.

6. Work and family

What choices have traditionally existed for women? Often not very many, and certainly not the choice whether to work or not. The poor, men and women, always worked for pay when they could; the rich, rarely. In the last century the expanding middle classes, with their roots still firmly in the workers' soil, but more affluent than before, had to set about creating their own identity, and this included attitudes to women and work. Inevitably, since they were balanced precariously between two incompatible traditions, it was not a single attitude that emerged. By the end of that century, however, perhaps the most prevalent attitude was the one found now amongst many young girls, much to the despair of psychologists and educationalists – that women would undertake some kind of suitable employment until released from it by marriage. Once respectable employments – notably post office work and typing – were established for women in the 1870s, this attitude probably appealed to the fathers of the women involved as much as to the women themselves. A man hauling himself into respectability by his bootstraps could not afford to maintain a large bevy of daughters in the style to which he hoped they would become accustomed. Genteel employment for them was a financial necessity for him. (This was the context of Bernard Shaw's sad remark about Emancipation – that a million women had stamped their feet and cried 'I will not be dictated to', after which they all went out and became stenographers.) Work for these women meant a job from which they expected to escape as soon as possible.

As industry expanded and wages rose somewhat, paid work became a more genuine option for women, and many of them chose it. Presumably they were grateful to be able to escape from the cloying atmosphere of confinement in their parents' homes; but marriage was still seen as the stopping-place and, indeed, the desirable stopping-place of work. This inevitably meant that women's work was regarded as unskilled, unprofessional and temporary, as in fact it usually was. 'Work' for women was in no sense interpreted as 'career'; it was a job which benefited them a little and the expanding economy a lot.

The nineteenth-century pioneers of real female success changed this. That small, courageous cohort of women who about the turn of the century invaded the seats of learning throughout Europe raised new issues about women and careers, not just jobs. They were living proof of the fallacies of the old arguments designed to show that women were actually incapable of reaching the highest peaks of intellectual achievement. How ever, rather than being abandoned, the old arguments were ingeniously changed to show that such women were not 'real' women at all, and this suspicion of the 'career woman' is with us still. Dame Ethel Smythe was a boon to the advocates of this view, Mrs Pankhurst an embarrassment. The reasoning was that it was part of the nature of women to desire above all else a husband and children. Obviously she could not have them and a career, since women were supposed not to work after marriage. Therefore if she chose a career she was rejecting marriage and thus behaving unnaturally. It could not have been simpler. The much-publicized photograph of jeering louts raising the skirts of a suffragette is a poignant reminder of these attitudes.

The few prominent, highly successful women remained. Nevertheless, with a few exceptions, these women did not marry if they wished to pursue their careers, or sank without trace upon marriage. The price of a career was celibacy; it was an enormous price to pay. The choice was interpreted as a choice between any career or job and marriage.

Successive changes in life-cycles made this particular choice look less and less plausible. As life expectancy increased and contraception became more effective and widespread, resulting in smaller families, women suddenly found that they had time on their hands at a stage in their lives when previously they might have been dead or still breeding.[18] More and more, often by way of working on a voluntary basis in the community, women began to return to work after a period of absence. This was and still is much easier for those with unskilled jobs where continuity is not important to the structure of work. They returned to the same kind of jobs as they had done before marriage, and consequently the low status of women's work was not improved at all.

The social revolution following the Second World War dealt the death blow to the simple work-or-wed alternative. After the years of enforced austerity, and with the advent of more equitable social policies, more and more ordinary people set about improving their material lot. The Pill made it possible for women to delay having children, and it became perfectly acceptable for them to work after marriage until the arrival of their offspring. This had little effect on the image of women's work; it simply pushed the terminus one stage further back. Both men and women regarded women's work as a bonus to the family income, welcome but not essential. Blatant pay differentials reflected this attitude, even within the professions.

More importantly, however, the massive expansion of educational opportunities within the school and university systems altered the expectations of many girls. In spite of the imbalance of grammar school and university places open to them, more girls than ever before were receiving education previously reserved for their brothers. They began to worry, as Mary Wollstonecraft had done before them, about the waste of their training and talents in a system which demanded that they stop work when having children, and then used the fact that they did this to justify denying them equal pay and opportunities. For some the solution was to continue with their careers throughout the child-bearing period, hiring others to care for the children. But the system could and did forestall this as a genuine possible option until very recently. Many women were simply sacked from their work at the diagnosis of pregnancy; the luckier ones received minimal maternity leave. Only the very stalwart and determined, however, could face the prospect of a return to work after a mere six weeks of leave. They therefore left work when they had their children. But once out of the job market in this way, women found that their position had hardly improved at all since their grandmothers' day. When they tried to return they could only enter the lower ranks of the hierarchy. Their work was still considered to be secondary and inferior. The choice that women were being presented with had not changed very much: previously it had been work or marriage, now it was work or children, and this still goes with an obscure but persistent impression that women's work is never quite real. Sometimes it is made to sound like a hobby, a luxury.

7. Careers and children

These attitudes die hard. It is true that most men now talk less about 'allowing' their wives to work, but it is also true that for a large number of people the pattern of a young wife following her husband from post to post, finding such work as she can, is still the norm. The presumption is that her work is secondary and, preferably, temporary. She takes a 'job' until he is sufficiently established in his 'career' for her to be able to give it up. And it is still the case that women who do achieve high positions in their own careers are regarded as aberrations, viewed with an inordinate amount of suspicion. The somewhat unsubtle language of work in terms of jobs and careers led to the great marriage myth. According to this, jobs are nasty, dirty things that we would all much rather do without. Careers, on the other hand, are desirable, interesting, status-making, self-fulfilling occupations. So when doing the little woman out of a job you only have to explain to her that marriage is a career, and back she goes to the kitchen with all her ambitions fulfilled. Now for some women this was, and is, very near the truth. The wives of diplomats, clergy, small shopkeepers and, until very recently, doctors and schoolmasters all play, or have played, essential, recognized and unpaid roles in the economy. And it is true that the image of the successful career man could not be what it is without the women who make the image a reality. The problem, exposed by Betty Friedan in *The Feminine Mystique*, is that for most women it is a lie. Marriage is not a career for them, in the sense that being a doctor or a diplomat is for a man. And, anyway, why should it be a career for women only? Imagine telling a man that even though he is unemployed he can always make his marriage his career.

The early feminists saw through this story easily enough. Many of the real functions which some wives fulfil, like entertaining or answering the phone, could just as easily be done by paid assistants. The rest come nowhere near the ideal of a career. Realizing the dishonesty of the old arguments, women have recently rebelled against the idea of having to make a choice. Men, after all, have both; why should women be different? Of course, there was always the knotty problem of the children, and what would be done with them. But times had changed; women spent much less of their lives in child-bearing and rearing than in previous ages, and these no longer provided a compelling reason for choosing between work and family. Many women bravely tried to cope with both. The solutions to the children problem ranged from the state-organized kibbutzim model to the piecemeal nursery school and baby-minding provision well known in Britain. None of these solutions seems to have worked. Much to the consternation of those reared on the militant feminism of the sixties, Israeli women started to demand the right to have their children at home, at least to sleep, while Russian women refused to breed and the Swedes wanted the right to stay at home with their pre-school offspring. In Britain the provision was so inadequate as to be of not the slightest use to most women, and an added source of anxiety to others.

There are here two sets of confusions and bad arguments which are common to both sides. The first concerns the notion of work. It seems perfectly natural to talk about work as opposed to domestic life, but, as many writers have pointed out, this is both insulting and unhelpful. By 'work' is nearly always meant 'paid employment' and these two things are not at all the same. Remembering to pay the milkman is just as much 'work' as remembering to pay for the last batch of rubber ducks from the wholesaler. Looking after the children is as much 'work' for a mother as it is for the dinner lady. A 'job' is something you would rather not do; men, when defensive, always claim to be the ones who have to get out and do a job to provide for their voracious families, but on official forms they state their 'occupations'. But it is a woman's 'job' to look after the children. The whole language of work is a dead give-away as to the true esteem in which the noble career of wifing and mothering is actually held. The work/family antithesis is a false one because these two things are not, and could not be, alternatives.

The second concerns the difference between the supposed necessity of choosing between paid employment and marriage and between paid employment and raising children. The first is patently a nonsense. Men, however much they might enjoy being waited on and cosseted, do not actually need continuous care. However they may behave sometimes, when sick or fed up with the office, they are not children. But children are not spoilt men either. Having exposed the work/marriage dichotomy for the myth it was, the early feminists were a shade too hasty in assuming that the work/children dichotomy was a simple extension of this myth. Children really do have needs which are quite special and which somehow have to be considered and met. It is when we come to consider them that the notion of choice seems to have some real application. We will look at this in the next chapter.

Today we are witnessing an interesting new limitation of choice for women. Some of those who are not economically compelled to work outside the home are beginning to complain that it is becoming more and more difficult to admit to a preference for staying within it. This is usually attributed to the attitudes of other women who further diminish the status of domestic life by making those who live it feel that they are 'letting the side down' or being unacceptably vegetable-like or parasitic. The glib answer is that of course women should not do this to each other, and that of course women should be able to stay within the home if they so wish. In fact this is not as simple as it sounds. It can work well in a stable relationship where a woman is content to be financially dependent on her husband and he is prepared to take total financial responsibility for her. There is nothing shameful about that. But we cannot afford to ignore the fact that in Britain the number of marriages that break up is rapidly approaching the current American level – one in three – and that security of employment for men is no longer something to be taken for granted. These social and economic factors are already combining to make a lifelong choice of commitment to domesticity less and less plausible. These facts, rather than the superiority complexes of other women, are likely to make such a choice a non-starter for most of our daughters. A woman who may very well find herself obliged to earn her own living in her mid-forties is at least imprudent if she does not make some prior efforts to equip herself for such an eventuality. At the risk of sounding callous, it may strike men as a good idea to encourage rather than discourage their wives' independence in these matters. At best they will lose nothing; at worst it could save them years of alimony.

8. Models of work

There is no doubt that in today's world women are obliged to play an ever-increasing role outside the home. The vast numbers of women bringing up families unaided, the thousands of two-parent families which would fall beneath the official poverty line without the woman's income, the avowed preferences of the women themselves all point to this as a trend which will continue to increase.[19] Whether or not it wants to, the labour market is going to have to adapt itself to the pressing needs of a huge element of its work-force.

The first need is to accommodate within its structure those women who wish to continue with some form of paid work during the period when they have demanding family responsibilities, as well as those who wish to return to work after a relatively short absence. Solutions to the problem of how women can be accommodated in the work-force began with the demand that women should simply adapt to the *status quo*. In spite of the fact that they were attending to other equally time-consuming and important aspects of social life, they were expected to work on the same terms as men if they were to be regarded as employed. The traditional view of work is that those who are employed are expected to devote most of their time and energy to that employment. Those who do not are allowed, when it suits the employer, to work part-time (part-time in relation to the norm), but at the price of security, decent pay and fringe benefits.

The present high level of unemployment, coupled with the

advent of the era of microtechnology, has made modern writers question this model. But many of them make only a limited attack on the tradition that work should be divided into the largest possible bundles for the few. Their equalitarian view is that it should be divided into smaller, but still equal, bundles so as to enable women to work on equal terms with men. Anna Coote and Beatrix Campbell recommend thirty-hour weeks for public sector workers;[20] the 1979 TUC Congress recommended working towards a thirty-five-hour week. Deirdre Sanders and Jane Reed go further: 'As microtechnology really gets under way, we should be thinking in terms of twenty-five-hour and probably twenty-hour working weeks for everyone'.[21]

Moves such as these would certainly suit women better than the present forty-hour working week, but they would still be too long for many, and they would in no way improve the situation of women relative to the situation of men. Of course a twenty-hour week is better than a forty-hour week; a five-day week was an improvement on a six-day week, but justice has a relative as well as an absolute face. And such moves would not help to overcome the problems of being obliged to move in and out of the labour market. It seems likely, too, that overtime would restore the men's advantage. In any case, the need is for the present.

What we need to get away from is the idea that there is only one proper way to work, an all-or-nothing choice. As employment becomes more precarious for men, they are learning what women have always known – that their needs and situations are not static but are constantly changing. In a world which is becoming less and less labour-intensive, we shall need to break away from this single model and begin to think in terms of much greater flexibility in patterns of work which can be adapted to the needs of employees as well as employers. This ought to be one of the great bonuses of the microtechnology age; but it requires initiative and imagination to make the break.

In all attempts to deal with these questions, we are continually stubbing our toes on a vast and ancient anomaly between the idea of reward directly proportioned to work and the idea of maintenance proportioned to the needs of a household. This clash makes nonsense of the ideal of a simple, arithmetical equality. But both ideas enter deeply into our customs. We cannot hope to adjust them together at one stroke. The important thing is to be constantly aware of their conflicts. Looking at past history, our impartial, newly arrived third sex, if called in as arbitrator, would, it seems, see reason to agree with feminists that there has been a constant tendency to use whichever of these ideas favoured men, forgetting their effects on women and children. Thus the quite numerous men – not only in the working class – who still see their pay as entirely their own, and any subsidy to their families as a matter of favour, are operating solely on the first model. (This way of thinking is found persisting even in the case of state payments such as unemployment benefit, which are calculated for whole families but are paid to husbands. There is a real case for paying the wife's and children's benefits directly to the wife.) Officially, however, wages in our society are supposed to be calculated on the second model, as a single 'family wage'. The objection raised to women's going out to work assumes that this wage supports the whole household. In fact it often does not, even when the housewife can lay hands on it – and she may herself be the chief breadwinner. In fact the standardized 'family wage', adjusted only to full-time work, is a confused compromise, with little to recommend it apart from its convenience for trades union bargaining – something which unions both in other European countries and in the United States seem to manage to dispense with.

Many other ways of arranging work are possible and would be convenient for many men, as well as vital for women. There is much to be said for job-sharing and for working flexi-hours, as well as for part-time work in general. There is no need for these systems to be treated as ghetto alternatives, excluded from the decent conditions which attach to full-time jobs. From the point of view of the work itself, it is often an advantage that two people understand it. Obviously not all jobs can be so divided, but the idea that only the least responsible ones can be treated in this way seems unrealistic. Managers as well as secretaries get ill and go on holiday and to conferences and on trips abroad, without disastrous consequences.

The importance to women of taking part-time work seriously is clear. In 1981 there were nearly three and a quarter million women working part-time outside the home for an average of approximately twenty hours per week.[22] When one considers that such work is relatively poorly paid, insecure and lacking in status and fringe benefits such as eligibility for company pension schemes and long service awards, it is reasonable to conclude that many women undertake part-time work because they simply cannot manage to find the time to move into the full-time bracket. Below sixteen hours per week workers receive no normal job protection. Between sixteen and thirty hours per week there are certain protections, but no rights to benefits and no comparability of pay with full-time workers or pension schemes or holiday pay. Many women, particularly, are obliged to work in situations which are frankly exploitative of their time and effort. They are deliberately kept just below the number of working hours which would give them certain rights, but the low number of hours worked ensures maximum productivity from them.

Can they be given job protection? In a period of economic depression and alarm such as we have at present, there is a natural tendency for anyone who has advantages to hold on to them and kick those who aspire to share them off the ladder. But this is not necessarily even in their own interest. At such a time, job protection is in general a problem. It can dry up the supply of work, since employers dare not take on workers for a temporary need if they can never get rid of them, and if they do take them on and go bankrupt their workers suffer along with the rest. When so many businesses are in fact closing down this is no idle spectre. It could be worthwhile for workers in general to allow more flexibility here. But the point about part-time work is distinct from this. Whatever claim long service gives it surely gives to part-time workers as well as full-time ones, even if some discount rate may be used in calculating it.

The project of encouraging women to work part-time, rather

than either competing for full-time work or dropping out of economic activity altogether, is not just a charity and certainly not a luxury. It may well be an economic necessity in times of industrial contraction. Many people, not just women, may find that their work is part-time, intermittent and sometimes changing, so that retraining and lateral movement may be much more common. To see this as a disaster is surely naive and narrow. The predicament of the worker who stuck at the same bench or desk for the same hours all his life has long been a subject of entirely proper horror and anxiety, and miners in particular used to vow that their sons should not spend all their working hours underground. For those approaching retirement, too, there is an obvious advantage in making the change gradually, and often much to be said for some part-time overlap to train their successors. If industrial contraction continues – and there seems less and less reason at present to think that it is just bad weather which will go away – then a realistic use of part-time work seems necessary to take us with the least possible injustice towards the situation which will be inevitable anyway.

What happens, however, if we get a little more ambitious (as the spirit of the age demands that we do) and ask not just about earnings which will boil the pot, but about careers? Here the interruption which almost inevitably attends the rearing of children still affects women's prospects drastically. Changing technology quickly puts old skills out of date, and this, coupled with the loss of youthful confidence, gives the returner a double handicap in seeking employment in what is now a desperately competitive market. Government has shown signs of taking the problem seriously by some investment in retraining programmes, though these are usually geared to the supposed needs of men. What many women – and indeed some men too – need is a more general refresher course, designed to stimulate their minds and rebuild their confidence in their power of thinking, at the same time as advising them about job opportunities and more detailed retraining possibilities. (Many university adult education departments have worked out such courses, which were pioneered by Hatfield Polytechnic.)[23] These courses, where they operate, are always over-subscribed; they are relatively cheap to run, and are plainly very effective. The combination of academic study with advice on jobs and – as only a third factor – deliberate attempts to help students gain confidence is a healthy one. It suits many people who have absolutely no wish to present themselves as cases for treatment, nor to undergo an ideological conversion, nor to put the heavy emphasis on personal relations that may seem central to the enterprise of 'consciousness-raising,' but who simply need help and practice in tackling again the world outside their homes. By such simple means women can get through the stiff but movable revolving door of diffidence, which at this point holds back many who are capable of long and useful careers.

This, however, is only one part of a programme of unpretentious activities which is needed, not only to lead women back into wider circulation after the years of child-bearing, but to take them through those years without unnecessary and wasteful damage. These activities can be thought of as substitutes for the village green. But they are no unreal piece of nostalgia; they are essential. The slum street used to do the same job. Any normal human community provides places – usually just around people's homes – where women can meet while their children also meet and play together. But our streets are now far too dangerous for this, and our communities too large and fluid to let it happen naturally, so we need special efforts to arrange it. Many such devices are cheap and call only for initiative. Much can be done, quite modestly, merely by a better distribution of notices and leaflets at places which women must visit anyway – baby clinics, hospital maternity wards and above all during the intolerable and senseless boredom of queues at ante-natal clinics. Personal canvassing at such places can be better still, though of course it must not be importunate. At present any information which does get around tends to be confined to a single aspect of life. Thus the baby clinic will have leaflets about diet and vaccination, but not about pottery classes or the townswomen's guild or the local women's group. Conversely, the women's group may not have information about the other activities. If that group is separatist in tone, or exclusively devoted to cultivating personal relations, it may even discourage interests which lead back into the ordinary two-sex world. But it should surely be a first priority for everybody dealing with women with a new baby – in a situation which tends constantly to narrow their lives – to let them know as much as possible about every kind of activity. On a more ambitious scale, of course, a great deal can be done by changing the design of housing estates, flats and other buildings, and, in principle at least, architects and planners do now seem to know that their brutal and dehumanizing products have been a monstrous error, and have possibly done more damage in this century than any other item whose causes lay purely in folly and vanity rather than actual vice. But remedying this is really hard, and we shall have to watch closely what is happening in order even to avoid making things worse. One worrying tendency at present is the steady disappearance of small shops under competition from supermarkets. Shopping is often the last lifeline which connects lonely people with the rest of humanity, and nearly always the first which people establish in the stressful process of moving to a new district. Any move which can be made towards, say, allowing small shops in new housing estates a reduced rent, or arranging tax concessions for already existing ones, would probably pay off on a large scale in lowering admissions to psychiatric wards and other expensive final resorts of despair.

9. Conclusion

In looking at the choices so often presented to women we have noticed a strong element of fantasy in the way in which they are stated. Offering choices to a person about the whole pattern of their lives is not like offering them a choice of pie or pasta for lunch. If they are there for lunch you can reasonably assume that they expect you to choose the dishes you will offer, that they will be prepared to accept one of the available meals, and that they will not be so ill-mannered as to demand both. But if you offer a woman the choice of being a virgin or a whore, she may quite sensibly suggest that she would rather just be an ordinary woman with an ordinary sex life, and that she has her own individual interests. Or if you offer her work or a family, she may ask you to convince her that she cannot have both. Anyone who offers anyone else a choice does so against a whole background of assumptions which themselves stand in need of justification. In discussing the choices offered to women we have seen that they often rest on assumptions about her nature, some of which have been wild. Similar assumptions about men's nature exist too, but they are mainly wider and more general, and considerably less wild. It does not necessarily follow from this history that – as many feminists have thought – women's 'natures' do not affect their behaviour and the choices open to them (we shall discuss this point in Chapter 7). But what does emerge is that many of the beliefs held about women's natures have been baseless, and many of the choices derived from them unreal and dishonest. Others look more plausible and deserve further thought.

What, however, in general needs to be dropped is the notion that women's choices (unlike most of those made by men) must constitute a once-for-all commitment to a particular way of life. Most serious choices do indeed have serious consequences. But people's lives are not a series of static, frozen tableaux; they are moving pictures with developing plots, which always leave room for the main character to produce an unexpected twist.

At a deeper level, we need to notice that the presentation of false choices tells us more about the person offering them than about those to whom they are offered. There is a horrid story about the French Resistance, concerning a French woman whose two sons had just been taken to be shot in a reprisal for anti-German activities. The distraught woman begged the officer in charge not to take them as her husband had recently been shot in a similar reprisal. The officer agreed to spare one, on condition that she chose which should live and which should die. The reason why this story is loathsome is not just that it describes the death of innocent human beings, or the bereavement of a woman. It depends on the phoney element of choice which is supposed to exist, on the travesty of freedom. To give her *this* choice is to mock her freedom. An element of this mockery is present, more often than we care to realize, in the painful choices which we offer people.

In so far as men offer women the crude choice of being good or bad, angel or devil, muse or millstone, they display their own fantasies about the way in which they would like to be able to see and treat them, rather than reacting to them as they actually are. In offering the traditional straight choices between work and marriage or work and children, they display confusion about the nature of work and the difference between the options they offer. Dazed by the old images, they do not ask how these choices relate to the real women who have to make them now. This is of advantage to no one. Unreal choices can be made only by unreal people. Real people need other real people around them, and need to make real choices about real issues. Fantasies are for fun, not for directing the pattern of our lives.

3 Choices concerning children

Why should the generations overlap each other at all? Why cannot we be buried as eggs in neat little cells with ten or twenty thousand pounds each wrapped round us in Bank of England notes, and wake up, as the sphex wasp does, to find that its papa and mamma have not only left ample provision at its elbow, but have been eaten by sparrows some time before it began to live consciously on its own account?

(Samuel Butler, *The Way of All Flesh*)

1. Eat or be eaten?

Here, again, the theorists do not like to give us much choice. In general, both from feminist and anti-feminist writers, women still get a fairly sharp ultimatum: either (1) have kids and give up your life for them, declining into an irreversible domestic Nirvana which (according to taste) can count either as death or fulfilment; or (2) fulfil yourself and have no children – not, that is, real children, the sort that make demands and do not evaporate. Do not attempt both assignments. It is known that a few specially lucky women do get away with some sort of compromise, and that the best way to do this is to be extremely rich. But this is held to be a fluke that the multitude should not presume to aspire to. In general, woman's lot still tends to be seen as splitting with elegant simplicity on this irremovable rock.

Those of us who suspect that only bone-headed bad habits prevent other options from being properly developed for all will therefore have to get on with the work ourselves. In this chapter we shall start by surveying some of the rather extreme and melodramatic proposals which have been put forward. We shall look for the bits of truth which they contain, and try to move towards a more realistic view.

The idea that women ought to find their whole fulfilment in

sacrificing themselves for their children is of course an old one, which was sharpened up and reformulated in the nineteenth century as a crushing answer to any proposals for their taking up other activities. John Stuart Mill therefore rightly complained that questions about, for example, divorce were usually discussed 'as if the interest of children was everything, and that of grown persons nothing',[1] and that this was a hollow piece of humbug, typical of the unreal arguments used against every attempt to emancipate women. All the same, with that maddening honesty which makes him so great, Mill also pointed out the piece of truth that lay behind the humbug. To have called somebody into existence does, he said, put you under an obligation to them. So far as you act freely in producing a child, that act makes you responsible. Your claim to personal liberty is indeed strong, but it is no stronger than theirs. And if children are to develop into free beings, as they have the right to do, they may need a good deal of help. 'To bring a child into existence without a fair prospect of being able, not only to provide food for its body, but instruction and training for its mind, is a moral crime, both against the unfortunate offspring and against society.'[2] Thus, for instance, if Rousseau did indeed leave his five children on the steps of the Foundling Hospital as he himself claims,[3] he was not just exercising the normal rights of a free citizen. The freedom of parents does not include the privilege of writing off their children.

The clash of interests that emerges here raises a real problem. Later history has not made it much easier to look at fairly. Anti-feminists have kept up the provoking habit, which Mill noted, of using children's claims wholesale, as general arguments against any demand for a wider scope for women, without checking in detail how grave a conflict of interests must really arise. Feminists, naturally, have often replied in kind, by equally wholesale claims that there would be no such conflict. Sometimes, of course, this is really true. But not always. Some conflicts are real.

Where the interests of adults and children really do conflict, has the issue become a political one in the sense of a contest for

power? Are we to handle it by somehow weighing the importance, or the muscle, of the contending groups? There is something odd about the idea of treating children as one political
group among others. In the first place, of course, there is a
psychological difficulty. It is not easy to think realistically about
children in a political context. They arouse non-political emotions, and those emotions are not all of one kind.

Like women, they provoke strong ambivalence and give rise
to fantasy. Sometimes – in fact on most public occasions – we
idealize them, speaking of them not only as delightful, but as a
treasure to be approached with awe and reverence. This is not a
lie; the reaction is genuine. But at other times (and this more
often in private) we see them as exasperating nuisances. They
take up a great deal of time. And it is true, as many people have
remarked, that there is no sound so maddening to a parent's ear
as the crying of a small child. Nobody doubts that this reaction
too is genuine; the interests of children and adults can indeed
conflict.

All this is not surprising. Our relation to children, like all our
other close relations, can bring out in us the whole range of
emotion, both positive and negative, of which we are capable.
Mere closeness always brings trouble as well as joy. But this
relation is also peculiar in that the directness of the child's
contribution tends to make for an equal, and rather frightening,
directness in the adult's. We get the impression, then, that we
are dealing either with angels or with devils. That impression,
however, as we well know, has to be a mistake. We need in all
such cases to balance out our reactions and somehow reach a
more realistic estimate. Feminist thinking has helped here by
emphasizing on the whole the nuisance or devil aspect of children, in reaction against the excessive idealizing of the main
educational tradition. Women do, after all, have a great deal of
experience of the nuisance aspect. There is nothing like being
shut in a small flat on a rainy day with a set of whining toddlers
for distancing the angel story. And people who are being asked
to make sacrifices for an important purpose are quite right to
point out what those sacrifices involve. But the nuisance aspect

is still hardly the whole account. How should we arrive at a reasonable, impartial view of the claims of children? Can the theorists help us?

2. Are children equals?

When the interests of children do conflict with those of adults, is the issue a political one or not?

Children are altogether rather an awkward case for political theory. Theorists have usually treated their interests as firmly enclosed within those of their families. And of course there is good reason for doing this. Parents and other relatives are the people who normally see to a child's needs. But suppose they fail? As we now realize, political theory was a bit hasty in taking this same line about women. Rousseau excepted women from the social contract, seeing them merely as appendages of men.[4] The idea that they might really have separate interests, needing separate protection, has taken a long time to develop; the political business of modern feminism is to get it finally expressed in institutions. But while we are doing that, we also need to consider the similar problem concerning children. Are they, too, an oppressed class? In certain obvious ways the cases are very similar. Many children also get beaten. They get beaten, in fact a good deal more than women do, not only because they are smaller but because they are beaten by women as well as by men. (This is one of many upsetting cases where the oppressed can themselves also be oppressors.) They often suffer from poverty, aggravated by the irresponsible behaviour of those who are supposed to be supporting them. Their voices are not easily heard. Ought the notion of equality be invoked for their protection too? Is what is sauce for the goose also sauce for the goslings? Are children one more 'minority' to whom the basic rights of citizenship need to be extended?

Strange difficulties arise about this. Children, looked at in one way, are indeed a minority, and a substantial one. But looked at in another way they are simply all of us, including women, at a particularly crucial and vulnerable stage of our lives. In this they are like the old. But children are also the *future* of all of us, the ship that carries our hopes. We cannot see them just as competitors. The idea of citizens banded into competing interest-groups, each organized to assert the interests of its members, and forced only by prudence to acknowledge each other's claims, fits very badly here.

Have children the same right to liberty as adults? Common sense will probably give this odd question quite a complicated answer, running perhaps something like this: 'Children and adults have the same basic right to such generalities as safety and respect. But, because their needs are different, what they ought actually to get is different. On the whole, children need more care and attention, and less liberty, and this is more true the younger they are. That, therefore, is what they have a right to.' We shall see reason to suspect that common sense may be right here. But if this common sense answer is reasonable, quite awkward conflicts of interest can sometimes arise between children and the adults who have to give the care. That, however, seems to be a reason for working on those conflicts and trying to reconcile them, not for giving up in despair and accepting an unrealistic solution.

Much more extreme approaches to this problem have been suggested. The idea that children are entitled to less liberty than adults causes alarm. Can it be right? Even theorists deeply dedicated to the importance of liberty have hesitated about it, and no wonder. Mill, after flatly saying that adults must never be interfered with for their own good, either physical or moral, adds that this cannot apply to children because 'those who are still in a state to require being taken care of by others, must be protected against their own actions as well as against external injury'.[5] On the face of things he seems to be right. It is not obviously the duty of parents to let nine-year-olds ride motor bikes, even when there is no one else around to be injured; nor to refrain, with Sartrian dignity, from giving an opinion on whether they should join the Mafia. The charge of 'paternalism', which tends to inhibit all direction today, looks out of place here. Normally protective parents do not strike us as paternalistic, merely as parental. Certainly there are kinds of freedom which children do need right from the start, and certainly these increase as they grow older. But, especially in early childhood, care and attention seem quite as important as freedom, often more so. A baby or a toddler needs a good deal more than the freedom to scream unanswered for as long as it likes.

3. Atomistic Utopia

People disputing about education have usually taken this background of parental care for granted, as a necessary context for the greater or lesser liberties which they wanted to arrange for children. Even theorists inclined to anarchy have commonly done this, because the obvious institutional alternatives appealed to them even less. Feminists, however, have begun to challenge the idea, and their challenges are interesting.

For instance, Shulamith Firestone – certainly an exceptional extremist of the early American vintage, but one who has left a lasting mark on feminist thinking – wrote in *The Dialectic of Sex* (1970) that the whole institution of parental care was nothing but a device for the joint enslavement of women and children. No such care, she said, is really needed at all. What is needed instead is full political autonomy, based on economic independence, for both women and children. (Economic difficulties are to be met by 'cybernetic communism'; all work is to be automated.) Each individual will then be a totally free unit. Nobody will know who their parents are. *In utero* pregnancy will have been abolished; reproduction will be impersonally conducted in the lab. 'Child-rearing will be so diffused as to be practically eliminated.'[6] The remaining 'minimal responsibility for the early physical dependence of children would be evenly diffused among all members of the household', a household which is a large, voluntary grouping formed for a decade or so.

In this way, once the cybernetic Utopia has been set up the concept of childhood has been abolished, children having full political, economic and sexual rights, their educational/work activities no different from those of adults. During the few years of their infancy we have replaced the psychologically destructive genetic 'parent-hood' of one or two arbitrary adults with a diffusion of the responsibility for physical welfare over a larger number of people. The child would still form intimate love relationships, but instead of developing close ties with a decreed 'mother' and 'father', the child might now form those ties with people of his own choosing, of whatever age and sex. Thus all adult-child relationships will have been mutually chosen – equal, intimate relationships free of material dependencies.[7]

In case anyone feels that something is missing, she adds 'the right of immediate transfer; if the child for any reason did not like the household into which he had been born so arbitrarily, he would be helped to transfer out'.[8]

We might ask, where does he then go? Is somebody else compelled to have him? How in fact, was *mutuality* built into those love relationships? What happens to a child whom nobody likes very much? Or to one who attaches himself to people whose lives are too full already? Can we really ensure that nobody ever has to give any services which they do not feel like giving? ('Since there would be many adults and older children sharing the responsibility – as in the extended family – no one person would ever be involuntarily stuck with it'.[9]) But the well known trouble about such shared responsibility is that somebody always does get stuck with it. The idea is to get rid of all dependence: 'all relationships would be based on love alone, uncorrupted by dependencies and resulting class inequalities'. But the dependent nature of children – and probably the nature of love itself – makes this a scarcely intelligible demand. Love normally and naturally includes service, and service is not serious unless it is really needed – that is, unless there is some dependence. This does not have to lead to class inequality, which is another kind of relation altogether.

The interesting thing about this extreme proposal, however,

is not its details but the confidence with which it is put forward as the *only* alternative to slavery. Again, the choice offered is amazingly narrow and drastic. Suggestions for other options are dismissed with contempt:

> Proposals are imminent for day-care centres, perhaps even twenty-four hour child-care centres staffed by men as well as women. But this, in my opinion, is timid if not entirely worthless as a transition. ... Day-care centres buy women off. ... At the other extreme there are the more distant solutions based on the potentials of modern embryology, that is, artificial reproduction, possibilities so frightening that they are seldom discussed seriously.... To free women thus from their biology would be to threaten the *social* unit that is organized around biological reproduction and the subjection of women to their biological destiny, the family.[10]

But she urges us to turn those frightening possibilities into reality, and eliminate all traces of the family. Until then, she says, no change can have the slightest value. We have only two choices: we must either accept this extremely singular Utopia as our goal and move towards it as fast as possible, or remain stuck in our present slough of corruption for ever.

Of course the book is extreme, and of course its continued popularity rests on its being the expression of a mood – a mood which men as well as women sometimes feel – rather than on its argument. All the same the argument is there, and as the parallel case of Plato's dehumanizing arguments in the *Republic* shows, such arguments can be influential. We need to notice what has gone wrong. It is not, we see, just that the argument 'goes too far', but that it is going the wrong way. It is wholly unrealistic. It combines optimism about the untried with even stranger pessimism about everything familiar. The pessimism is quite comprehensible while it operates within realistic limits and simply criticizes existing attitudes to families. It shows up admirably the dangers infesting a small and isolated family, where dominance over children compensates the parents for the lack of a wider social life, and where an obsession with property poisons the parents' attitude, leading them to treat their children primarily as status symbols and mechanisms for self-assertion. Such parents obviously do exaggerate their children's dependence, and try to preserve it by preventing the children from forming outside bonds. The main strength of these early, wild feminist books like *The Dialectic of Sex* lies in this kind of criticism, which is long overdue, and which was not fully and explicitly made until recently because of the opposite notion that 'the family' was itself so transcendent a good that the way it worked was immune from criticism.

The criticisms are often powerful and some of them have wide application, although each author's local roots are usually obvious and determine the emphasis. Just so, Nietzsche captured shrewdly exactly what was wrong with his pious, cosy Lutheran upbringing in a small German town in the 1840s. Everybody knows their own corner of hell; but when it comes to propounding universal remedies, this gimlet-eyed obsession with the evils one knows has its drawbacks. The miseries of children without stable families tend to be brushed aside as minor troubles, mere by-products of a society which mistakenly treats families as the norm. And since misery has innumerable shapes, an argument really is needed for the decision that certain vices (which indeed can poison families) are an essential feature of the abstract 'family' as such, or even of the abstract 'nuclear family', rather than just human failings. These vices – possessiveness, avarice, ambition, cruelty – can crop up in other, alternative institutions for rearing children. They can also poison other forms of human associations, such as friendships, artistic partnerships, orchestras, schools or the crews of boats and aeroplanes. This leads sensible people to denounce the vices, not the forms of association. Why is 'the family' to count as an abstraction of a different order?

4. Childhood, real and mythical
The answer lies in a special theory about human nature, which sees pregnancy and childbirth as essentially corrupting and

degrading conditions. According to this view, humanity's best and highest side is chronically at war with, and threatened by, what is called its 'biology' – that is, primarily its reproductive system, though apparently, and rather oddly, not its purely sexual one. We shall have to deal with this more fully later, in Chapter 7. But a few words about it are needed here to explain the strange way in which, in the Firestone Utopia, children have suddenly ceased to be children at all as we know them, and have become indistinguishable from adults, needing no extra care and no distinct occupations. The story which supports this convenient change is a stretched version of a historical theory (itself, as most would now agree, stretched well beyond the evidence) that childhood as we know it is not really part of the human condition at all, but only an artificial institution invented in the late eighteenth century.[11] Before then children did not, it is claimed, show the special characteristics which we now attribute to children. They were not emotionally linked with their parents. They did not go off on their own to play with other children. They had no toys and no special interests, but were virtually indistinguishable, except in size, from the adults around them.

Now it is true that the sophisticated view of children held by intellectuals did indeed change a great deal around that time. Childish characteristics were no longer held beneath serious mention, but began to be studied with some interest. Their relevance to educational theory was suddenly seen, and, as does happen with sudden and delayed discoveries, was no doubt over-emphasized. The resulting theories did give rise to an official, theoretical, view of children which no doubt differed a good deal from that held before and which did have practical consequences in our institutions – notably in the extent to which we set children apart from adults to be educated, rather than simply apprenticing them to whatever is going on around them. This habit is indeed distinctive of our culture, and de-schoolers may well be right to criticize it.

It cannot follow, however, that the more general dependence of children on adults is unnecessary, nor that children do not naturally need their own distinct world of play among other children. No small patches of evidence from the history of one culture could establish this, since both these things are found throughout the whole range of known cultures. If it really were possible to bypass children's period of play and dependence altogether, obviously many peoples would be likely to choose this option, which would notably increase their labour force. This does not happen. Observers of different cultures regularly include accounts of children's distinctive games, interests, toys, attitudes and special interactions with adults, centring on parental affection. It is true that in many cultures children do more work than they do in ours, but even this is not universal. And it never eliminates special childish activities.

The only plausible exception is the forced one, where (as in the early Industrial Revolution) parents have no alternative but to make children work like adults. The cost in misery is well known. Even at a more comfortable level, the occasional prodigy who does get treated almost as if he were an adult often suffers a great deal by it, and says as much afterwards – as John Stuart Mill did. And even for these cases, the extent to which the adult treatment was actually carried is not, and cannot be, clear. Anyone who has dealt with small children knows that it is often simply impossible to give them undiluted adult treatment, and that attempts to do so cause them every bit as much annoyance and confusion as the misplaced over-childish advances of which Shulamith Firestone complains.

This whole notion that children do not really need looking after is in fact far too weird and implausible to be accepted only on the historical evidence which is brought in to support it, even if that evidence were more impressive than it is. What supports it, in fact, is not the evidence but the hope which it seems to give of eliminating the special demands of children, and thus abolishing parents. If one takes normal parental attitudes to be a mere perversion, a bad habit of bullying possessiveness springing from the child's physical weakness and the trauma of childbirth, the apparent chance of establishing everybody on a new, antiseptic, independent footing looks like the only hope for mankind. But that hope is wild, and there was no need to accept the alarming premiss in the first place. However grave the corrupting effects of capitalism may be, the range of parental habits over the world certainly offers plenty of hope for arriving at better ones without ditching the dependence which is in fact essential to children's position. And Firestone's impossible general project cannot fail to hinder us, because it distracts our attention from the particular circumstances which are the real source of our trouble – for instance, the strange isolation of today's mothers, along with their children, on which the authors of a much more helpful book comment: 'Evaluating anthropological reports on child-raising in many other cultures, sociologist Jessie Bernard reports that the isolation and exclusivity with which American mothers raise their children is both historically new and culturally unique.'[12] It might be worth trying to do something about that before concluding that the whole business of personal mother-hood needs to be abolished.

5. No child is an island

If this is true – if children really are, and must continue to be, children – it seems reasonable to accept and develop something like our suggested common sense answer to the question of their equality with adults. Basic rights, such as the right to liberty, cannot, except at the most abstract, general level, be considered apart from particular needs. Children's needs really are different from those of adults, and moreover change profoundly through the various stages of childhood. Children are therefore not op-pressed by being given, at each stage, a range of choices limited to what they can at that point handle. Motor bikes and the Mafia come later. It is indeed important that a child should, as it develops, become increasingly able to control its own course and eventually to throw off many parts of the life-style that its parents provided. But just in so far as someone can do that effectively, he or she is no longer a child. Full personal liberty is the aim, and it carries with it political autonomy. But it is not a condition of childhood.

The needs of children are, in fact, in some ways radically different from those of adults, and those of older children from those of younger ones. The younger children are, the more care and protection they need, and the less liberty they can use. Accordingly, it may turn out that the notion of equality, important and useful though it is, cannot be applied to them directly by demanding equal treatment for all at each stage. Perhaps we shall need to conceive of it instead in terms of whole lives, saying that, as far as possible, people ought to get what they need at each stage, so that their life as a whole makes sense when they come to look back on it, or to compare it with other lives. The notion of somebody's interest must then be considered over the whole range of their life. If young children have needs which are in some ways specially strong and specific, it is then reasonable that others should make sacrifices at that time to meet those needs. What equality demands is not that there should be no sacrifices, but that they should be fairly distributed, honestly recognized and not allowed to become outrageous. This calls for sharp and perceptive observation of changing problems, and willingness to alter customs which concentrate the burden unfairly. Danger signs, such as the high number of housewives who are on tranquillizers, have to be taken seriously, not accepted fatalistically as a matter of course.

A political question does, therefore, arise, even though it is not a clash between articulate adult citizens. The interests of parents and children can indeed conflict, and the notion of equality can to some extent be used to arbitrate these conflicts. But the aim cannot be to standardize everybody's civic status at every moment, nor to make sure that nobody is at any time better off than anybody else. It should be to achieve a reasonably fair distribution over a whole lifetime. It is not necessarily wrong that our parents sacrificed a great deal for us, nor that we do so for our children. What is needed is just that those sacrifices should be properly controlled. They should as far as possible be voluntary, necessary, used to good effect, justly distributed and balanced by suitable satisfactions.

This looks pretty obvious; but it has been obscured by individualistic political and psychological thinking that has sometimes gone to extraordinary lengths, making it seem outrageous that anybody should ever be called upon to make sacrifices for somebody else at all. Competitiveness has been seen as the law of life, and self-fulfilment as the only value. This arid and negative ideal is a very strange one for a social animal which finds most of its fulfilment in joint activities. Indeed its chief use has been as a solvent to get rid of unsatisfactory social bonds, and its positive proposals have remained obscure. Nietzsche, who promoted it, was vague about the occupations open to the Superman; but even he saw it was not an ideal likely to appeal much to women. His solution was emotional specialization: 'Man's happiness is: I will. Women's happiness is: He will.'[13] Yet this is not a very intelligent idea for men either. Emotional solitude is no condition for a human being. The Superman story, which has been built into even our more educated ideals for men, is still doing a good deal of quiet damage.

6. Weighing the claims of children

What, then, can our children reasonably expect of us? Traditional feminist thought has tended either to take little notice of this question, or to answer it in a somewhat abstract and negative way by saying 'at any rate, not the family'. This neglect is not surprising. Enlightenment thought – which has been the chief model for feminism – concentrated strongly on the political right of responsible adults to assert their own interests, and usually excepted children from its discussions, treating them as passengers. Feminism's first job was to resist the mean and narrow conception of this right, which dismissed women also from the political scene as being only wives and mothers, and therefore as pure cases of self-sacrifice whose separate interests need not be represented or considered at all. Feminism asserted the rights of women within this framework of conflicting interest-groups without seriously questioning the framework itself much.

When we look at the case of children, however, we have to question it. Not being articulate, nor in any position to judge what is wrong with their situation, children can never form another interest-group to assert their rights against those of adults. And as we have seen, they are in any case not really a separate, competing group at all. Clashes of interest between them and adults are real and sometimes harsh, but they take place against a background of real community and common interest. In particular, the interests of women and those of their children are typically not in any straight conflict, but continually converge and overlap. They do so very simply in the first place, as we have noticed, because women themselves start life as children and more than half the children at any time will be women. But they are woven together still further because sooner or later most women want to have children themselves, and want their children to live well and happily. The same is true of men. A purely competitive model, setting all these interests against each other, is of little help. The simple ultimatum 'abandon your children or be eaten by them' does not fit the case at all.

The natural feelings of women are therefore often in conflict over the clashes which do arise. Demands on behalf of their own lives sometimes clash, and sometimes converge, with ones made on behalf of their children; and the children's demands, as well as the adults', have solid backing from our political principles. Enlightenment individualism cannot take sides; it is sauce for goose, gander and goslings alike. It allows no exceptions. That has always been its strength in combating slavery, racialism and other forms of systematic injustice. When it was expressed in terms of 'the rights of *man*', an arbitrary and irrelevant injustice was indeed temporarily built into it.[14] That wording obstructed for a couple of centuries the full perception that women too are people. (It is very remarkable how resistant the obstruction was, delaying for instance until 1882 the Married Women's Property

Act, which finally gave British women a legal right to their own earnings and other possessions.)[15] This bias, however, is just as glaring when it restricts consideration to the claims of adults. Children's needs are different, but their claim to justice cannot really be less.

7. The problem of the unborn

To determine what justice really demands in cases of conflict can of course be very hard. Here, as elsewhere, the language of absolute rights, to which Enlightenment thinking inclines us, leads to deadlock and often to a useless shouting match. Nowhere is this clearer than with the delicate and complicated issue of abortion. Here one party credits all embryos with an absolute right to life, so that all abortion is mere murder. The other has replied (not surprisingly) by crediting women with an absolute right over their own bodies, which results in absolute liberty to abort, and indeed an absolute right to be given an abortion on demand.

Unfortunately, this language of absolute rights is unusable. In many spheres clashes arise between rights which have been seen, separately, as absolute. We are forced then to adjust our ideas. We have to treat these supposed rights simply as claims – claims which may be very strong, but cannot be known to be stronger than all which might conflict with them. The idea of an absolute right over one's own body is never a very clear one, because our bodies act on each other in so many ways. In cases where someone else's body is as deeply involved as one's own, or more so, it really cannot be used at all. Typhoid carriers and other infectious people get restrained. Siamese twins presumably have problems about enlisting or committing suicide. To exclude pregnant women flatly from this class of case is to rule that foetuses are not people in any sense at all. This seems strange if we think that they become people the moment they are born. On the other hand, to treat all foetuses as completely full-blown people seems equally bizarre, if we deem that a sperm and an ovum did not constitute a person the moment before they were united, or perhaps implanted. In both cases, an instantaneous change on such a scale is more or less unimaginable.

There really is a grave difficulty here, not to be abolished by the insistence of either extremist party on settling things with a definition. Our thought can scarcely take in the genuinely gradual way in which a human being arises out of physical matter which clearly was not a human being. Our imagination demands a single, definite starting-point, but the facts do not supply one. We are called on, therefore, to allow for a gradual transition. We have somehow got to treat foetuses as beings which are *partly* people, and which become entitled to more and more of human consideration as they develop. In fact, this is one of the very common, though worrying, cases where we have no choice but to draw a line across a continuum. It is not, and it cannot be made into, one of those rare cases where the job is already done for us. (Other similar examples, also involving life and death, concern such questions as the amount of aid which we should send to the victims of various disasters, the number of animals we kill and the way we treat them, and the level of support which we give to the sick and elderly.) We cannot avoid these hard decisions by using dramatic 'wedge arguments' designed to show how each criterion, if used alone, could be distorted to justify evil. Wedge arguments are demands for simple solutions, but these are not available. We have to use a number of mutually correcting criteria to draw lines as best we can. It is our job in doing so to avoid these distortions.

In the case of abortion, then, our present system is surely right to make it available in principle, but to give the factors surrounding each case very careful consideration. Since these vary widely, they can call for very varying treatment. For instance, variation during the normal course of pregnancy is much more dramatic than either extremist case would lead one to suppose. A very early foetus is a simpler creature than many animals (such as rats) which most of us kill without question, while a late one can of course be more fully developed than some babies which are already born. These and other considerations give reason for discriminating between the stages of pregnancy. There is also a great range of factors which can affect the woman's position, attaching serious evils to alternatives other than abortion. Those who counsel women on these occasions report that what commonly occupies them is not any question about abstract rights, but pressing practical dilemmas over how to reconcile the care of an expected child with their existing responsibilities. Many interests can clash here, and it seems impossible to rule in advance that any one of them has an all-conquering right. Such simple rules and simple attitudes cannot help us. Besides this, women range in their emotional attitudes from those who would never willingly abort at all to the few but real individuals who have a positive horror not only of pregnancy and childbirth but of rearing children. And the creeds they live by can vary almost as widely. Some creeds simply forbid abortion, and for their adherents this settles the matter. But not everybody holds such creeds.

On such a difficult and sensitive subject, the assumption – shared by both sets of extremists – that morality imposes a single unvarying solution seems strangely unrealistic. Issues like this are not battles, to be won wholesale by campaigning. They are real dilemmas, choices of evils, to be painfully worked out by those concerned, with such help as society can give. (In this way, the question has something in common with that of divorce.) People not currently involved in such difficulties tend to hope that they can impose uniformity in accordance with their own principles, but this is scarcely possible. People's views about such things as the nature and standing of foetuses relative to the beings around them are not just factual ones, nor legal ones to be settled by a convenient ruling. They are moral ones, growing out of and expressing whole views of life. The ill effects of an imposed uniformity have long been seen in the prevalence of illegal abortion, with all its dangers, which resulted from failure to grasp the difficulties endured by the women to whom legal methods were denied, or to respect their views on whether they were entitled to this relief. If the contrary kind of uniformity were imposed, and women were given total freedom to abort at any stage without consultation, there would certainly be trouble (though of a different kind) from the protests of those who do not accept such casual disposal of foetuses.

It is very unfortunate that this matter should be so complicated, and still more so that it should have become such a popular disputing ground for those who favour simple solutions. It is, however, only a specially awkward corner of a larger problem, that of the rights of children. On the whole, political theorists are inclined to deal with these somewhat hastily, in a parenthesis. Old-fashioned hierarchical thinkers do this because they are satisfied that children should be subject to their fathers, and modern libertarian ones do it because they concentrate all their attention on fully responsible rational agents, and it looks as if these cannot be children. It is one of the many good by-products of feminist discussion that the matter has now been properly raised. What has feminism got to say about it?

8. Can children be mechanized?
Until lately, the attitude of feminists to it was somewhat casual. While domestic servants remained, the upper classes did not find the matter pressing. Long-term nannies could save mothers – as well as fathers – the trouble of seriously weighing their children's claim to attention and deciding on its true force. And well before the nanny supply failed, the behaviourist view of child-care came forward to support this rather curious habit of inattention. Child psychology was developed in a way which made such questions look unimportant. Rearing children was seen as being essentially an impersonal process guided by scientific principles. It was held not to matter who gave the baby its four-hourly bottle, provided that that person was properly trained. And proper training was thought to centre on a professional detachment from all traditional and natural tendencies to direct emotional response.

The reasoning behind these policies is none too clear, but

87

there is no doubt about the vigour and confidence with which they were proclaimed. Thus John B. Watson, the founder of behaviourist psychology, lays down 'the sensible way of treating children':

> Treat them as though they were young adults. ... Let your behaviour always be objective and kindly firm. Never hug and kiss them; never let them sit on your lap. If you must, kiss them on the forehead when they say good-night. Shake hands with them in the morning. ... Remember when you are tempted to pet your child that mother-love is a dangerous instrument. An instrument which may inflict a never-healing wound ... may wreck your adult son's or daughter's vocational future and their chances for marital happiness.[16]

In the same spirit, an official *Infant Care* manual of 1917 advised: 'The rule that parents should not play with the baby may seem hard, but it is no doubt a safe one.'[17] Not surprisingly, the difficulty of ensuring this treatment lined Watson up, along with Plato and Shulamith Firestone, as an opponent of family upbringing: 'It is a serious question in my mind whether there should be individual homes for children – or even whether children should know their own parents. There are undoubtedly more scientific ways of bringing up children, which probably mean finer and happier children.'[18] The term 'scientific' here does not mean, as one might expect, that there is a solid range of empirical evidence showing that Watson's preferred methods had been tried and were specially successful. It seems to mean just that they accord better with his preferred methods for psychology. Nor does the word 'objective' mean 'free from personal bias'; to this Watson clearly remained subject: 'When I hear a mother say "Bless its little heart" when it falls down, or stubs its toe, or suffers some other ill, I usually have to walk a block or two to let off steam.'[19]

The weathercock of psychological fashion has veered round several times since these confident pronouncements, and leaves them now looking strangely arbitrary. What was really supposed to be the danger of responding normally to small children? All that comes through clearly is a powerful fear and disgust at parental intimacy. Again, this is an all-or-nothing approach. Because natural sentiment is not enough – because it needs to be informed and supported by understanding – and because it has been overpraised, it was to be entirely excluded. The experts were therefore to take over from the parents, particularly mothers, who could be dismissed as discredited amateurs.

This bizarre phase passed, as fashions eventually do. But the dream of the up-to-date, mechanized, labour-saving infant that it expressed continued to haunt controversy, and ideas of it certainly seem to have delayed feminists in taking seriously the problems, already evident to mothers working in factories, of fitting proper child-care into the modern world. When the nannies eventually faded away (except among the richest), women who did not want to stay at home looked anxiously for ways to dodge some of the burdens which were rolling onto their shoulders. These often centred on the thought that 'children do not really need us; what they want is to be free', or that 'anything is better for them than being at home with a discontented mother' (what, *anything*?).

The 'liberation' or 'emancipation' of women was often seen as meaning chiefly the cutting of the web of personal ties in which they lived. To some people it seemed obvious that this should mean detaching them from children. Men, after all, did not necessarily have this special attachment; why should women do so? Without it, would they not at last be free to pursue their own individual wishes?

9. Without committal?
The really simple and infallible way of solving the problem is of course the one Mill suggested – not to have children at all. The wish for children is, however, remarkably deep and widespread. Many people feel that solution to be a terrible deprivation, especially as they grow older. And because the wish is such a

personal one, they may well feel that it would not be satisfied by institutional solutions like those of Plato and Watson. The knowledge that you have probably got a child somewhere in one of the communal nurseries is coldish comfort. Besides, feminism often contains a vigorous element of anarchism, to which the thought of these institutions is repugnant anyway. What is to be done? Germaine Greer did us all a service by putting on paper the ideas which she had on the subject – a scheme for an 'organic family':

> I hit upon the plan to buy, with the help of some friends with similar problems, a farmhouse in Italy where we could stay when circumstances permitted, and where our children would be born. Their fathers and other people would also visit the house as often as they could, to rest and enjoy the children, and even work a bit. Perhaps some of us might live there for quite long periods, as long as we wanted to. *The house and garden would be worked by a local family who lived in the house.* ... Being able to be with my child and his friends would be a privilege and a delight that I could work for. If necessary the child need not even know that I was his womb-mother, and I could have relationships with the other children as well. If my child expressed a wish to try London and New York or go to formal school somewhere, that also could be tried without committal.[20]
>
> (Italics ours.)

At an obvious level, this solution cannot be serious because of the words italicized. It concedes that children need a family, but proposes paying somebody else to provide it. Plainly, the fact that there are people rich and lucky enough to do this does not undermine children's general need for families, nor does it make it any easier for most women to find someone prepared to do what they do not want to do themselves. Naturally Germaine Greer knows this, and the Italian family, though it gives the scheme its faint air of plausibility, is not, on her principles, supposed to be necessary. To explain those principles she hazards some remarkable views about child psychology:

> A child must have care and attention, but that care and attention need not emanate from a single, permanently present individual.

Children are more disturbed by changes of place than by changes in personnel around them, and more distressed by friction and ill-feeling between the adults in their environment than by unfamiliarity. . . . The point of an organic family is to release the children from the disadvantages of being the extensions of their parents so that they can belong primarily to themselves. They may accept the services that adults perform for them naturally, without establishing dependencies.[21]

This is to say that children, unlike adults, do not really become attached. Love, for them, is just a nutritious substance, not a relation. They do not distinguish between individuals. If properly brought up, they are emotionally independent and make no demands. They do not want to be owned or to belong to anybody. If this were true, it would simplify life no end; but it does not happen to be. (The point about people and places can be tested by having a familiar person carry a small child around in a strange place, and then a strange person do it in a familiar place.)

Rousseau said that 'the child knows no other happiness but food and freedom',[22] but that, like many other things, just shows his ignorance about the subject. This same strange idea of love as a standard, impersonal commodity, to be doled out in quantities, appears when Shulamith Firestone meets the objection that her Utopia is no better than a vast orphanage. Orphans, she answers, are at present 'those unfortunate children who have no parents at all in a society that dictates that all children *must* have parents to survive. When all adults are monopolized by their genetic children, there is no one left to care about the unclaimed.'[23] But this is plainly false. Many adults are childless, and these include most of the young nurses etc. employed in orphanages. The trouble is not that all the love, like all the treacle, has flowed elsewhere. It is that even as small babies, orphans, like other people, want to attach themselves to *particular* adults – and in the nature of the work most of such attachments cannot be permanent, or mutual, or have time to become deep. She goes on, however: 'if *no one* had exclusive relationships with children, then everyone would be free for *all* children. The natural interest in children would be diffused over all children rather than narrowly concentrated on one's own.'

This is exactly the hope which Plato expressed in making similar arrangements.[24] And if love, like water or treacle, were a liquid which could be made to flow one way simply by being prevented from flowing another, the project would be quite a reasonable one. As things are, however, love seems to be much more like a plant, which can be cultivated and helped to spread once it has a first secure root, but which, if it is suspended from a string and told to diffuse itself all over the field at once, will not grow at all. Children need, and insist on forming, particular, exclusive attachments. They can then go on to wider ones. But the project of totally impartial, impersonal affection is one which only the religious have attempted, and which they report to be scarcely within human capacities at all.

These schemes, then, cannot seriously be taken to apply to children in general, and especially not to small ones. They become intelligible only in their original context – as expressions of protest from adolescents anxious to leave home, and from mothers whose lives are too isolated. Here, no doubt, they are important and deserve attention. But the long-cherished idea that children could skip the dependent stage and *begin* life as adolescents is a scholar's pipe-dream. From Plato onwards, it has had immense attraction for theorists who fear and distrust the intimacy, the real emotional and spiritual interdependence, which early childhood carries with it. None of them, however, has found a way of engineering society so as to dispense with this stage. There really is attachment, and it has to be mutual. Nor will it even be possible, as Germaine Greer hopes, to make it one-sided by concealing from the child its real parentage. This is something that children insist on knowing about. Of course they can often be deceived, but – as many adopters, including Oedipus's family, have discovered – not without paying a heavy price. They are not passive little sheets of blank paper on which we can write what we please. They make their own demands, which often astonish us, and the game must be played from there. None of it will be 'without committal' – that is, without consequences for which somebody must be responsible. Certainly you can keep making changes. But that has consequences of its own.

10. Conclusion

Both the Greer scheme and the Firestone one are designed as devices for bringing up children without bothering anybody to become involved with them. It seems likely that this cannot be done. That, however, does not mean that the responsibility has to be crushingly concentrated on one person. The parents hold the baby, but they can be given solid ground to stand on and plenty of people round them to back them up. In the first place, there are usually two of them. (Where there is only one, extra help is certainly needed.) Rather than accepting the old view of men as being free from all responsibility, and competing for the same status, feminists need to stress that fathers should share that responsibility with mothers. They are in fact now often taking this line, and fathers are often responding well.

We still need a considerable effort to change attitudes, however. In a recent television debate the following question was put: 'Which ought a woman to put first, her duty to herself or her duty to her child?' How would that question sound if asked about a man? If it were so asked, anyone trying to answer it would quickly see that they needed to know *which* duties (in both cases) and why there had to be a conflict. There is no general answer to such questions. But in the case of women people are still inclined to think that there is, because they still tend to suppose that *all* a woman's duties to herself (however central) should come after *all* her duties to other people (however trivial). As Mill pointed out, this is the surest way to make all those around her, and particularly her sons, into arrogant and selfish oafs – a policy that nobody can really favour.[25]

It is important to notice, next, that the close interdependence of parents and children does not actually last very long. It is not a life sentence. With today's small families it usually lasts no more than a decade, often less. And a European woman's expectation of life is now about seventy years. What seems necessary is to develop all the paths leading in and out of this intense phase, and, while it lasts, to provide support systems which will prevent it from seeming like (and sometimes becoming) a sentence of life imprisonment in futility.

This notion of a futile imprisonment in the home has been the keynote of modern feminist protest. The imprisonment is real, but it is not incurable. The solitary confinement of an unwilling woman with her children is quite evidently bad for all concerned, not only for her. The question is not one of a ding-dong battle between women's interests and men's or children's. Everybody suffers, and that suffering is expensive and wasteful to the community. All kinds of things can and should be done to mitigate this sense of imprisonment. Playgroups, nursery schools, housewives' registers, better housing design, neighbourhood schemes, consciousness-raising groups and many other things that have already been devised can help. Part-time work (sometimes for both parents) may well be the most central of them. But many others ought to still be invented.

Feminists were, however, for some time particularly devoted to a single solution to this problem, namely full-time crèches combined with full-time paid work for all women. This is a strange choice. Russian women, who have long been provided with crèches and paid jobs, have become intensely dissatisfied with a system which prevents them from making a home for their families. So strong is their distress that it has resulted in a sharp fall in the national birth rate, and has finally led to a change in policy on the part of the Russian government, which has lately begun to allow a year's maternity leave after each birth, and various similar concessions. The Russian feminists who have been demanding this sort of change, in the face of the usual appalling difficulties, have as their cult figure the Virgin Mary, the idealized mother. The difference between their view of this figure and Germaine Greer's is illuminating. It is terribly hard to know what you need until you have had to do without it.

Whatever may be thought about this Russian experience, however, and about the rather similar Israeli one, the point which no doubt chiefly moves these feminists seems a sound one. As far as the welfare of children goes, nobody supposes that an institutional upbringing is actually better than a normal family one.[26] To be left to the hands of professionals – even kind ones – is recognized as a misfortune. We do not find a crowd of autobiographies in which people rejoice at their particular good fortune in having been brought up in this way. The demand for crèches is not motivated by consideration for the children. But neither, it turns out, does it really suit the women. It may be the simplest way to live like men. But that is not necessarily the aim.

The moral emerging from this sort of experience seems clear enough. Women's typical life has a different shape from men's. Different does not mean worse; it means different. It has to be organized so as to leave room for what to a crude-ish man may seem like a long interruption, but to a woman (and to a more perceptive man) may seem more like the culminating experience of her early life. The details of this experience are highly educative. With reasonable support and normal good luck, they should leave her much wiser and more capable than they found her. When she wants to return to the official labour force, this ought to be considered. She ought not to be received at this point like some kind of village idiot without qualifications, trying to crash the barrier into serious work. She can be very useful. The proper reply to her at this point if she asks for work is not 'you decided to do without it, Mrs Dandin' but 'here are the programmes for the retraining courses, and we look forward to taking you in this time next year'. This answer might often be a very good one for men too, when they want to change direction. But for women it is absolutely vital.

4 Choices concerning men (1): war

[Radical feminism requires] the determination to wrest power
from the ruling group [men] and to end their domination.
(Sheila Jeffreys, *The Need for Revolutionary Feminism*)

The rationale which accompanies that imposition of male authority euphemistically referred to as 'the battle of the sexes' bears
a certain resemblance to the formulas of nations at war, where
any heinousness is justified on the grounds that the enemy is
either an inferior or really not human at all.
(Kate Millett, *Sexual Politics*)

As for the issue of whether or not to continue to reproduce males,
it doesn't follow that because the male, like disease, has always
existed among us he should continue to exist. When genetic
control is possible – and soon it will be – it goes without saying
that we should produce only whole, complete beings, not physical defects or deficiencies, including emotional deficiencies, such
as maleness.
(Valerie Solanas, *SCUM Manifesto*)

We and our whole community of canons, recognizing that the
wickedness of women is greater than all other wickedness of the
world, and that there is no anger like that of women, and that
the poisons of asps and dragons is more curable and less dangerous to men than the familiarity of women, have unanimously
decreed for the safety of our souls, no less than for that of our
bodies and goods, that we will on no account receive any more
sisters to the increase of our perdition, but will avoid them like
poisonous animals.
(Abbot Conrad of Marchthal, fourteenth century)

Women, you are the devil's doorway .... It is is your fault that
the Son of God had to die; you should always go in mourning
and in rags.
(Tertullian)[1]

1. What kind of conflict?

Opinions of the kind quoted above set us rather a grave problem. The rhetoric of sex war and sex revolution is certainly one of the chief obstacles preventing those outside the women's movement from grasping what it stands for. Not all feminists use this rhetoric; an increasing number reject it flatly. Probably most can see how much it slows down the spread of their ideas even among women. Yet to many it seems bound up with important truths about the real defects in women's position. Writers therefore almost inevitably oscillate between appealing to it and disclaiming it. It is one of those ways of thought which seem to demand a kind of *gestalt* shift, appearing at one time as self-evident, at another as unthinkable. Women who reach the movement by way of a transforming crisis in their personal lives do not find this shift surprising. (This is where the parallel with revivalist religions is so striking.) They have accepted a general change, and find it natural to see those who have not made it as simply deluded creatures, wallowing in outer darkness. By staying in the society of the converted, they can easily forget how numerous these outsiders still are, and how unlikely they are to be converted by people who treat their present lives and opinions with total contempt.

In this kind of emergency it becomes necessary to break down the alarming doctrine into its various elements – to translate the rhetoric into concrete terms and consider the various parts of what is being said one by one, on their own merits. Hard-line feminism of the kind shown in the first three quotations above is unworkable for most of us, because it presents men with no choices at all, and women with only a single crude dilemma – grovelling, conventional submission or war. This is exactly the same choice which the misogynist tradition gave them; only the recommended alternative has changed. It is arbitrary and lazy-minded. No obvious reason emerges for accepting it. In particular, the wholesale dismissal of all men as damned because of the faults committed by some of them is an impossible position for those who have rightly rejected the similar wholesale dismissal of women. Certainly there are things badly wrong with the customary relations between men and women. But many men, as well as many women, already disapprove of these, and more can always be convinced that they ought to do so. Both sexes, indeed, need liberating from many confusions and bad habits.[2] But to write any part of the population off as unable, on genetic grounds, to share in this liberation is an extrordinary piece of arrogance. Anger which is directed so widely carries no political meaning at all. There seems no way in which it could work to improve the situation.

Is it even meant to do so? It is not always easy to discover whether writers are recommending anger simply for its own sake, or as a means of changing the world. Thus Dale Spender answers the charge that she is 'portraying men as the enemy' – a charge which should surely be taken seriously, since it touches one's power of convincing outsiders, and therefore one's sincerity – merely by saying: 'As no equivalent "good manners" are required in relation to race and class, as no similar concern is shown in these contexts, to refrain from calling the oppressor the enemy, I see no good reason for making sex an exception. Objection overruled.'[3]

This common but empty argument shows the harm done to the women's movement by the chance that made it emerge, in the USA, under the shadow of disputes about race, and particularly of the (now largely superseded) militant black power movement. Even if unmitigated enmity had been able alone to resolve racial disputes – which it was not – nothing would follow about sex, a case so different that comparison collapses. For racial disputes there are in principle at least three possible solutions which do not depend on the parties understanding, accepting and learning to live with each others' distinctness. They are assimilation, apartheid and emigration. For sex, there are none.

Because the prospects are wholly different, they call for a quite different range of tactics. Women are not honorary blacks; nor are the causes of trouble any more similar than the prospects. What brought the blacks to America was for them a historical accident – the monstrous and unnecessary crime of the slave-trade. They have really had little or no choice about their social position. What brings men and women together, by contrast, is their deepest affectional nature, and it has always done so; as groups they have never lived apart. The terms on which they live therefore result from mutual interaction and compromise over untold centuries. Of course this is no guarantee that they are fair or satisfactory; but it does mean that women have had a considerable say in them. To suppose that they have had no voice at all – that all cultures are, as is often said, 'entirely man-made' – is to treat women as really being the wholly passive, will-less, vacuous creatures which feminists so rightly insist that they are not. It is to write off, with startling contempt, their immense contribution to our culture. Had they really remained up till now inactive and, so to speak, socially transparent, there could be no hope at all of changing that condition today.

What, then, is this violent language actually saying? Two main abuses are in question, and the war can accordingly be either hot or cold. Socialist feminism directs our attention to the economic oppression of women, and sees the conflict between the sexes simply as part of that already raging between the classes. It is therefore to some extent continuous with ordinary politics, and is prepared to use its methods. But radical feminism sees this trouble as only one aspect of a more general oppression extending through all sex relations, an oppression which has its roots in private life and is therefore not vulnerable to political methods. It draws attention to such things as rape and wife-beating, and to the attitudes which not only produce them but protect them. It is inclined to propose that there had better be no relations between the sexes at all until men have mended their ways, if ever.

2. The property war

Let us look first, then, at the socialist feminist idea in relation to the Marxist tradition of class war. Feminists certainly make a most interesting contribution to this by pointing out the enormous disparity, world-wide, between men and women in pay and the ownership of property. It is not hard to argue that, if those richer than oneself are necessarily one's enemies and oppressors, then men are the enemies and oppressors of women. Might it follow, then, that this is the real break between the classes, rather than that between the proletariat and the bourgeoisie, and that revolution needs to break out here rather than where it has so far been expected? A recent United Nations survey reports that 'women, while they represent 50 per cent of the world adult population and one-third of the official labour force, perform nearly two-thirds of all working hours, receive only one-tenth of the world income, and own less than one per cent of world property'. Moreover, 'poverty and under-development have sharpened and continue to sharpen these inequities'.[4] In Britain the difference is smaller, but it is still alarming, as we shall see in Chapter 6.

This economic picture is our first topic. How should we read this evidence? To treat it as simply showing a conflict which amounts to enmity has some odd consequences. For instance, similar reasoning will equally prove parents to be always the enemies of their children, and the middle-aged to be enemies both of the young and of the old. Like many other models, this gives us only one way of looking at the matter. Still, it is one that calls for real attention.

How true is it, in general, that those richer than oneself are always one's enemies and oppressors? Marx, following Proudhon's idea that 'property is theft', extended the idea of robbery to cover the withholding of wealth by the rich from the poor. This is a conceptual move of enormous power, an insight built into modern notions of social justice. But it seems essentially a thought about real, distinct economic classes. It is not easy to apply to a group whose members are not united by absolute poverty, but only by being individually somewhat poorer than their partners in another group.

Middle-class Western women are indeed on average poorer

than their husbands, but that still leaves them richer than the proletariat. From the ground level, the claim that all women are oppressed or underprivileged, and therefore equally comrades in the class struggle, tends not to look very convincing. Women, just as such, are not honorary proletarians. These women's position is in some ways like that of old people compared with the middle-aged, or of younger brothers where the eldest gets the main inheritance. There is always the possibility of injustice in such inequalities, and it is very important to have a defence ready against it. But that does not make them necessarily unfair in themselves. It is in fact impossible to read off the actual fairness of a system from statistics of ownership, since everything depends on the spirit in which daily business is handled, and the extent to which people understand each other's needs.

Is this oppression? Certainly the greater the disparity becomes, the easier it is for actual oppression – which is not just power but the abuse of power – to develop. But to call inequality of power, economic or otherwise, in itself oppression is to widen and weaken the sense of that useful word. In its natural, everyday sense, oppression means the abuse of power. Not all invalids or old people, for instance, are oppressed; some are oppressors. So are some wives and mothers. Not all administrators are oppressors, nor are all children oppressed. The widened sense of the word, though it quickly comes to sound natural to its users, has three rather serious disadvantages. By sounding like an exaggeration, it puts off the unconverted. By putting all women in the same category it distracts attention from the ones in most need – from those who really are oppressed in the strong, everyday sense. And by dividing the world into two distinct camps, oppressed and oppressors, it can generate a dangerous, self-righteous drama. It enables even the most privileged women to see themselves as bearing no responsibility for the way the world is, and drawing no profit from it. This chronic bad faith is a heavy price to pay for a clear, rousing, simple conceptual scheme.

Simone de Beauvoir does an excellent job in pointing out the inescapable joint responsibility of women and men. She never forgets that locating social causes is one job and describing personal choice is another. She is clear that it is unrealistic for a whole sex to disclaim responsibility for the goals which its society adopts, and that women do not in fact want to reject all the values so far proclaimed by their society. As she puts it, 'Woman also aspires to and recognizes the values that are concretely attained by the male. .... In truth women have never set up female values in opposition to male values; it is man who, desirous of maintaining masculine prerogatives, has invented that divergence.'⁵ The values, in fact, belong to all, and have been shaped by both sexes. Any unevenness in this process is of the usual kind – the sort of defect which can be found in the value-system of any society, reflecting defects in its shapers, and needing repair work from anyone who notices it. It is not like the sort of trouble that would arise in a culture formed by left-handed, deaf, carnivorous midgets when it came to be taken over by right-handed, blind, vegetarian giants.

Unless one is prepared to forswear all the achievements of the human tradition so far – as some feminists seem to demand – on the ground that they are man-made, some such admission seems necessary. And the uncompromisingly honest refusal to make excuses which is the best part of existentialism made this point very clear to Simone de Beauvoir, in spite of her deep understanding of women's social handicaps. Like Virginia Woolf, she could see both sides. (Today's feminists officially honour both these prophets, but are often unprepared to follow them here.) Simone de Beauvoir herself did use the word 'oppression', but took care not to fall into the traps which it offers. The wholesale orgy of dramatization which has gone on since she wrote makes this much harder today. It may now be better to avoid the word, not to claim that women, simply as such, are, in this part of the world, oppressed. Claiming that they are seems like insolence to the real sufferers. Some women, however, really are oppressed, here and now, to an extent that is not commonly grasped. Help for them is an urgent priority.⁶ And many more women – perhaps most, at some time in their lives – suffer to some extent from certain specific and chronic injustices, which are good deal more serious and less necessary than is commonly noticed.

It is not too misleading to describe this as oppression, as long as we know that, by these standards, very many men are oppressed too and that some women are oppressors. There is not a solid block of oppressors, all males and none of them themselves oppressed, sitting elsewhere and profiting by women's troubles. Any extra strain on relations between the sexes hurts everybody. The fact that men are in general so placed as to come out of conflicts less injured does not show that the conflicts are in their interests. They do get injured too, sometimes seriously. And the whole thing is wasteful. The distortion of reality – the confused view of our own and other people's lives – which produces a lot of the trouble cannot really benefit anybody.

3. Putting money in its place

In any case, this rather grandiose political claim does not seem necessary to express what is really wrong with the economic status of women in the West. Its defects are chiefly of two kinds. There are unfair legal arrangements, covering such things as income tax and unequal pay and the division of assets after a divorce. And there are more general social slants which have economic effects, such as difficulty in getting paid employment at all, and obstacles to promotion, to education and to training. Both these troubles can be very serious, and may urgently need reform. But they do not amount to war. In our part of the world the margin by which men's effective wealth exceeds women's does not come near that radical divide between the 'two nations' in nineteenth-century England which convinced Marx that co-operation in reform was impossible, and bloody revolution the only option. There are certainly parts of the Third World where it may look more plausible. There many women are in absolute poverty, and are therefore oppressed. But, where this happens, many men too are almost or quite as badly off. They cannot therefore be named as the oppressors.

There is, moreover, always a gap between knowing the economic statistics and understanding how they work out in practice. In some cultures, especially simple ones, women seem to have a thoroughly free and independent position, even though a formal census of property would record them as poor. On the other hand, of course, it is possible for a rich Western person to become a pawn in the hands of those who wish to exploit his or her wealth. It is also possible for someone – man or woman – who officially owns the whole family property to feel morally and socially bound to use it all for the support of the whole family. In cultures where the extended family is a strong unit (as for instance in India), it may often be hard to see who is being sacrificed to whom, and men can certainly be as firmly bound as women. Property does not necessarily confer freedom of action.

The immense emphasis which our society places on money tends to obscure this point. And much dishonest use of the argument has of course worked to discredit it. The poor, including women, have too often been told by the rich that they do not really need help, because money is not everything.[7] All the same, it is true that money is not everything. In particular, money is not a proper measure for esteem. People ought not to be valued according to their pay-packets. Therefore, if any set of people living together choose freely to arrange that some of their number will earn money for all, while others work for the general good in other ways, there is nothing disreputable about that arrangement. Non-earning members have no reason to feel guilty or dependent. So the traditional household division of labour is not in itself unjust or oppressive, so long as it is genuinely voluntary on both sides. It goes wrong only where one party begins to exploit the other, because consent has lapsed. Since people do not understand either themselves or each other very well, it is perfectly possible at this point for both parties to be exploiting each other unconsciously, in a violent and painful see-saw. Each has a grievance; each is amazed that the other does not see it.

The division of the sexes on economic grounds into oppressors and oppressed does, then, show us an important aspect of life, but a limited one. The time when this aspect becomes really important is when other things have already gone badly wrong. And, of course, precautions for the times when things do go wrong are essential. Murphy was right; as his law says, if something can go wrong, sooner or later it will. John Stuart Mill was also right to stress this.

> Laws and institutions require to be adapted, not to good men, but to bad. Marriage is not an institution designed for a select few. . . . It would be tiresome to repeat the commonplaces about the unfitness of men in general for power . . . were it not that hardly anyone thinks of applying these maxims to the case in which above all others they are applicable, that of power, not placed in the hands of a man here and there, but offered to every adult male, down to the basest and most ferocious.[8]

Much of this is right. The grotesque imbalance of power licensed by the marriage laws of Mill's day could not be excused by the belief that it was rarely abused, even if that belief had been true. Where it was not abused, it was not needed. While it remained it not only allowed iniquity, but endorsed and provided for it. Nothing could justify this. But when the wild and arbitrary parts of that imbalance have been removed, we have to deal with inequalities not produced by law, but by circumstances.

It is scarcely possible, when any set of people live together, that some will not have more power than others, or that custom will not sometimes increase that difference. If laws and institutions are adapted *only* to bad men and women, decent ones are going to be unduly hampered. It suits households which are getting on well together to treat their property as common. When they break up there is always trouble. There is no simple solution, whether over wills, divorces or ordinary quarrels. And it is important not to be obsessed with just one possible abuse, like Schopenhauer, who said that women 'should not have the guardianship of their children under any circumstances whatever' because he thought that his own mother had been a bad guardian. Even if she was, and some others would be, this is a cruel and pointless rule. For the sake of preventing occasional wrong such rules stand in the way of everyday, normal right.

4. The limits of competition

Here we run into a more general difficulty about the use of confrontation models. The simple, competitive view of society as essentially a device for striking a balance between competing interests is meant for cases where things have already gone wrong, where co-operation no longer works. Because it is often hard for people to see and admit that they are dealing with such emergencies, this competitive model tends to be introduced with noisy and misleading claims as a universal truth. Thus Hobbes said that the state of nature was a state of war, and a war, at that, 'of every man against every man'.[9] But co-operation is actually just as striking a feature of human life as conflict, and if co-operation were not the deeper and the more widespread the species would have died out long ago. Hobbes did not know that we were descended from social animals, to whom co-operation comes naturally. [10] Of course we, like they, are capable of conflict. And of course it is possible for us to extend it deliberately until it seems to take over the whole of life. But that is a choice. We are not forced to do it. Using negotiation instead is not falling back on a secondary growth, devised to cover or mitigate an underlying conflict. It is an independent process, quite as natural and quite as real. The competitive model does not have a deeper, more privileged metaphysical status.

Marx, like many political theorists, took this innate human sociability for granted when building his theory. The appeal to the emotional solidarity of the working class is an essential part of his message. But to generate this appeal it seems necessary to have a genuinely cohesive class. For Marx, this meant one bound by a common economic predicament. Those who are really bound in that way are not going to accept women as comrades just because a rather different kind of misfortune has befallen them. And as for the women themselves, it is not clear that what binds them is economic at all. It certainly is not primarily economic.

Feminist uses of Marxism involve, indeed, a rather grave paradox. Marx thought it crucial to locate the class struggle at a particular point – between the proletariat and the bourgeoisie – and went to some trouble to show that other classes were irrelevant, and other analyses of existing conflicts a dangerous distraction.[11] Since the sex difference crosses this divide, feminists like Shulamith Firestone,[12] who claim to use Marx's analysis, but say that the oppression of women is a far deeper problem, a problem whose neglect accounts for the failure of proletarian revolutions to date, may seem to be sawing off the branch they sit on. Why use Marx at all if you distort him so far?

Their line of thought seems bound to lead away towards separatism of some kind. The alternative is to stick closer to Marx, to concentrate on the oppressed proletariat, and to point out what has not even yet been fully grasped – how regularly women tend to be among its most deprived members, and how little attention they have had from mainstream revolutionaries. This very urgently needs to be done. But it does not separate the cause of these women from that of the men with whom their lives are bound up, nor does it concern women who are better-off. So on the puristic view of feminism, it is excluded from the canon. The question of equality with men distracts attention entirely from inequalities between women in different classes.

Anna Coote and Beatrix Campbell discuss this dilemma very well. As they say,

> One characteristic which has distinguished the British from the American women's movement is the strength of the organized left. In Britain there has been a mass-based Labour Party in government, and a trade union movement which constitutes the biggest working-class assembly in the country. British feminism has always been more socialist than its American counterpart.[13]

British women, and Europeans generally, had, in fact, somewhere to go within the existing political spectrum, which the Americans did not. (Accordingly, it has usually been Americans who have explored the wilder shores of separatism.) Socialist feminists, the authors continue,

> were convinced of the importance of understanding economic forces, and of Marx's analysis of class conflict. For the committed Marxists especially, the radical feminists' sex-class analysis, with its inversion of Marx's analytical methods and rejection of Marx's own prognosis, was unacceptable. In their view, the pro-woman line raised awkward questions about the role of women who reaped the privileges of capital and strove to uphold its power. They rejected separatism both as a strategy and as an end in itself.

5. The problem of ambivalence

Apart from this question of consistency, there is a further difficulty for feminists about using the Marxist appeal to class solidarity, with its accompanying call to revolution. This call can only work where its predictions of possible success are found convincing. In order to believe that war is our best or only option, we must have reason to think that it actually can improve our lot, and that nothing else is so likely to do so. In really bad political situations people often do have reason to believe this. They have no other hope. Revolt may really be their best option. But it is most obscure how this could ever work for women and men, who live together and continually give each other hostages. The act of faith always required for Marxist policies seems in this case an exceptionally wild one. Given determination, we might indeed be able to destroy all goodwill between women and men. Like some strange cactus, we could cultivate the female equivalent of Tertullian and Rousseau everywhere. And we could easily ensure – what is essential to the notion of war – that the process was not just one-sided; that men for their part returned the compliment. But how would we live then?

The trouble is that inter-sex hostility has a very different meaning from the hostilities which arise temporarily between tribes, classes or nations which have got into a dispute with each other over a practical issue. That hostility, though it may be complicated by various kinds of projection and symbolism, is essentially external. But hostility between the sexes is not. It has an emotional basis in the ambivalence generated by life-long intimacy. Perhaps, on top of that, it dramatizes profound conflicts between aspects of our own natures. Inter-sex disputes draw on and revive deep, ancient pains and resentments in all of us. They cannot be contained within the limits of their nominal occasions. In the ordinary way, the bitterness is countered by equally deep and ancient loves. With goodwill on both sides it becomes possible and delightful to work together, in spite of the differences. But when the dark side of the ambivalence is deliberately detached and cultivated we are in trouble indeed, as misogynists have frequently shown. We do not want to take them as our models. Marx believed that his violent revolution was a sure means to triumphant and final peace. Even on its political home ground, this is a lot harder to believe now than it was in his day, and every revolution that we see makes it harder still. But with a sex war it becomes almost inconceivable.

6. Violence, servitude and immunity

We need to consider, however, a range of cases, more sinister and harder to come to terms with than the economic ones, which explains more clearly why terms like 'war' have seemed appropriate in this context. These concern actual physical violence towards women and the background out of which it grows. The opening of refuges for battered wives during the 1970s, and of the rape crisis centres that followed them, has taken the lid off problems which our official thinking scarcely admitted to before. It turns out that the prehistoric temple which Mill spotted not only still stands, but still houses fairly frequent blood-sacrifice.

What is instructive is to notice the lengths to which civilized people have gone to avoid facing this ugly fact for what it is. It has long been held that this is not a serious issue because these things only happen to women who deserve them, consent to them or ask for them, and that this makes it both unnecessary and futile for the state to interfere. Recent experience shows that these beliefs are in general simply false.[14] As soon as the harsh alternative of the refuges became available, the women took it. Before this they often had no alternative at all, especially if they had children. But, beyond this falsity, it is essential to see that these excuses are simply a string of red herrings. Even had they been true they are not the kind of considerations which, in any other context but marriage, could be used today to justify beating people up, and could put the beater-up outside the scope of the law.

In the case of desert, this is obvious enough. A Glasgow Conservative councillor, opposing the establishment of refuges for battered wives in 1975, declared 'Anyway, some of these women might well deserve the batterings they get from their husbands'.[15] But citizens are not supposed to take physical punishment into their own hands, even when culprits do deserve it – a fact which he would doubtless have remembered had he been set upon afterwards and beaten by exasperated women. Nor does consent justify crimes. Killing and wounding by consent are not legal. This is doubtless because it has been noticed that consent in such cases is rather unlikely to be free. Suttee was forbidden, even though it contains an element of consent. People do sometimes consent to terrible things when all their alternatives are worse. As for provocation, or 'asking for it', this is not a justification at all. Motorists are not allowed to knock down provocative pedestrians, nor schoolteachers to break the arms of provocative pupils, nor employers to tear out the hair of provocative shop-stewards. We all provoke each other, and are all supposed to be able to deal with provocation decently. Certainly, strong provocation can mitigate an offence. But it does not put it out of the reach of the law altogether, which is what, by an extraordinary anomaly, has happened for so long over domestic violence.

In general our law now goes to remarkable lengths to protect most people from the trouble they continually ask for. Employers are supposed to make factories safe for rash employees, as well as for careful ones. And even the most suicidal behaviour by, say, motor-cyclists is not held to justify garages for neglecting their machines, nor lorry-drivers for flattening them when they invite it. The law, in fact, usually recognizes the complexity of human motives. It knows that people are not always prudent, and that danger can confuse their judgement and even fascinate them. But it rightly treats these confusions and fascinations as misfortunes, not as declarations of policy, and does not allow others to take advantage of them.

Against this background, it is very remarkable that domestic violence is still treated as an exception. Discussion of it still focusses almost entirely on the motivation of the victim, still seems to treat this as the determining cause, and, when it does glance casually at the offender, still deals mainly with personal causes such as his 'inadequacy'. An inadequate person certainly can do many violent things. But of those open to him, this is the only one he is fairly certain to get away with. Until the last century domestic violence was not even illegal, and though it is supposed to be so now, police practice still makes interference rare and usually ineffectual. He would be a strange fellow indeed if this difference did not affect his actions. What little information has now been collected about wife-beaters makes it fairly clear that they are mostly not people who are generally deranged, or who beat up everybody in sight. They commonly do not even beat their children, only their wives. The special factor here, as Mill pointed out, is that not only are they secure, but this security has a message for them. 'The notion that the law has delivered her to them as their thing, to be used at their pleasure, and that they are not expected to practise the consideration towards her which is required from them towards everybody else'[16] is in itself an invitation to contempt:

The legal slavery of the woman, and something in the merely physical subjection to their will as an instrument, causes them to feel a sort of disrespect and contempt towards their own wife, which they do not feel towards any other woman, or any other human being, with whom they come in contact; and which makes her seem to them an appropriate subject for any kind of indignity.[17]

Accordingly there lies behind the violence a general habit of enslavement, of denying the wife any life of her own, as the evidence amply confirms. Many motives combine to produce this oppression, but the remarkable self-righteousness that often goes with it suggests that among the strongest of them is the pleasure of having somebody to blame and punish for whatever goes wrong. The wife's function is to make everything perfect – here some confused notion about angels seems to be at work – and since she continually fails, she ought to be continually punished. There are many people whom the wife-beater would like to punish, but she is the only one whose punishment is permitted. This naturally confirms his suspicions that she is actually the one whose fault it all is. Never mind her motives, this alone is enough to decide the matter.

This belief in the servitude of wives, and to some extent of women generally, is a fragment of the old hierarchical institutions; it is still active in the lives of many who know that they cannot today hope to get away with bullying anybody else so crudely, and provides the main explanation of their conduct. It still gets public support from the attitudes of many of those professionally involved, as is shown by remarks like this from a judge: 'It is well-known that women in particular, and small boys, are liable to be untruthful and invent stories'.[18] It needs to be finally shaken out of the public mind by a very different official attitude. And those who suffer from it can rightly be described as oppressed.

7. The dilemma: socialist or radical?

How can we understand, and how remedy, this range of oppression? The common-sense approach suggests that it has two main strands, the public and the personal, and that we can attack both at once without needing to worry first about which is the deeper. On the public side we can demand things like changes in the rules for police and other professionals, and an increase in refuges; and also, at a deeper level, better economic opportunities for women, in order to prevent their becoming so helplessly dependent in the first place. The economic inequality should not be such as to set this trap. On the personal side, at the same time, we can work to expose and to civilize, through all the usual channels, this pocket of crude hierarchical thinking which devalues women, and does so all the more dangerously today because of its comparative isolation. Where men no longer view themselves as being under the judgment of their God, their king or their employer, any remaining licensed serfs are in special trouble. A lot has already been done to civilize this kind of attitude, but there is still a great deal that needs doing. What does not seem obvious is why we have to choose between this social and psychological change and the public measures just mentioned. They seem to complement each other. Why does the split between socialist and radical feminism call for this choice?

The difficulty here lies in understanding what is really meant by radical feminism, and it is a difficulty largely caused by unsuitable terminology. The word 'radical' tells us little because it simply means extreme. To interpret it we need to know in what direction things are supposed to be moving. In politics it commonly indicates a more drastic programme. Radical feminism, however, differs from the socialist kind in recommending complete withdrawal from ordinary politics, not a more vigorous spasm of it. In literal Marxist terms this ought to mean withdrawal to the use of physical force. Marx, with his memories of 1848, knew what he was talking about and meant what he said. He meant that there must be shooting in the streets, and this time it must not stop until the revolution has succeeded. Feminists, however, obviously do not mean this. With the sole and scatty exception of Valerie Solanas, they reject physical force as not just an impractical but a despicable method. A great part of their moral case against male rulers, and males generally,

WOMEN'S CHOICES

rests on this rejection. But since the Marxist language is retained, we are continually puzzled to see where the withdrawal from politics is now supposed to take us.

Feminist authors, when they occasionally condescend to help us with this puzzle, explain that they mean only to 'withdraw their labour'.[19] But this gets us no further forward. Strikes are effective only within an organized context of employment. Even there they have to be carefully calculated and can achieve only limited results. They call for a united labour force whose sharply defined objectives must include staying in their present positions once they get improved pay and conditions. But this is just what radical feminists do not want. Again, the language of traditional left-wing politics misleads us. What they mean is much closer to what used to be called 'dropping out' than to any sort of industrial action.

In fact, despite the Marxist language, this kind of feminism is surely best described not as radical but as anarchist.[20] Its real ancestors are people like Blake, Bakunin, Nietzsche, Kropotkin, Tolstoy and Berdyaev. This is a rich and honourable intellectual lineage which has no need to become mired in the problems of Lenin and Chairman Mao. Its strength lies in its honest and unbridled criticism of all existing systems. Its weakness, generating its own problems, is its difficulty in relating to practice, in escaping a universe of pure rhetoric. That so many of its prophets have been Russians, shut off from influence on an almost hopeless political system, is significant. Most of us today are not helpless in quite that way. We are, however, desperately confused, and the question of how to use what little power we have can be overwhelming.

Radical feminists propose an answer to this problem, namely 'concentrate solely on the injustice of sex relations', and a policy, namely 'women of the world, unite and leave the men'. The answer is certainly a possible one with a good deal to recommend it, but not, to the unconverted, any more than many other answers, and less than some. As for the policy, that is much more puzzling. How does it help the injustice? Why should no relations at all be better than faulty relations? Certainly you can get rid of a wart by chopping your finger off, but most of us prefer other forms of cure. There is an awkward uncertainty, too, about whether the withdrawal is supposed to be temporary or permanent. If temporary, it is conceived as a device to give both parties time to re-educate themselves, to fit them for a better reunion. But, unless this re-education is a joint enterprise, there is no reason to expect that they will be any more able to live together at the end of it; indeed, quite the contrary. If it is a joint enterprise, common political activity is needed to organize it. But if it is permanent, how will life go?

This really is not obvious, and it is rather surprising that separatists have not explained it in the most obvious way, by composing Utopias. We have only found one – *The Wander-ground* [21] – which is a colourful and instructive fantasy, but does not touch the real difficulties at all. It solves all practical problems by giving the women vast psychic powers and the magical help of the earth. And psychologically, while talking a great deal about love and tenderness, the book crackles with hatred, not only towards all men (including homosexuals) but towards non-lesbian women, who are dismissed wholesale as vacuous bits of fluff.

It is interesting to turn from these vague, confident pages to the deeply worried discussions currently appearing in the women's press about how radical feminists should actually live. The papers from a conference on 'The Women's Liberation Movement and Men' provide a lively and thoughtful example. [22] All the writers here expose with devastating shrewdness the unreality and inconsistency of rival solutions to their common problem, and all are also very worried about their own. All houses are glass; all stones strike home. Only the thought of complete revolution gives them hope, and, not surprisingly, they sometimes express despair. A project whose only live example is apartheid can scarcely be a hopeful one.

Among many unrealistic elements in their discussion, one which strikes a bystander strongly is the contradictory set of demands made on men, who are doomed to be wrong whatever they do. Their offers to mind crèches for feminist conferences are

treated as a sinister bid for power. The wish of male homosexuals to meet alone together is not seen – like the women's
similar wish – as legitimate bonding, but as a vile assertion of
maleness. And so on. Against these demons, therefore, tribal
loyalty is still demanded as imperative. But the tribe to which
this loyalty is owed is not actually the whole group of women,
most of whom would dismiss this stereotyping game as childish.
It is a 'movement', a loose grouping that is becoming increasingly
mixed and divided. Tribal chauvinism and common hatred,
which are never attractive qualities, become quite out of place
here. Unanimity cannot be expected, and it is contrary to the
standards of anarchist thinking even to demand it.

The anarchist's real problem remains. It is always possible for
rebels to withdraw temporarily into small groups, and often to
bring back from them an influence which profoundly changes
the world. But it will only do so if the problems of the world are
realistically faced in the first place. And a withdrawal that never
soils its hands by returning at all is either barren or belongs
altogether to the world of the spirit.

Separatism, of course, need not have any of the extreme
meanings frequently suggested by its rhetoric. In practice it often
seems only to mean that women should have a chance to be
alone together, that they should have some institutions of their
own, and that some of them (like some men) prefer to live almost
entirely with each other. This is an excellent idea, and a highly
traditional one, which was only eroded from common practice
in the 1950s and 1960s, largely by the propaganda of the sexual
revolution. The destruction of single-sex schools, in particular,
seems to have been a real loss for women. Girls clearly find it
hard to gain confidence in mixed schools; they do better on their
own.[23] A high proportion of the successful women of this age
were educated at single-sex schools. The move to co-education
seems to have been unduly influenced by concentrating on
boarding-schools, which are a special case.

More generally, ordinary social life certainly does not have to
be conducted on Ark principles, always two by two. This admirable notion, however, will worry some feminists because it

is 'sexist' in the sense of recognizing sex differences as important, and of sometimes building them into institutions. Moreover, while it can make a real change in ordinary social life, it does not provide a complete alternative to it. It is not, therefore, going to justify pronouncements like that of the Leeds Radical Feminist Group, who say 'we do think that all feminists should be political lesbians' – that is, should boycott men entirely. Why on earth should they if they do not want to? This moralistic attitude is part of the rhetoric of war; one must not fraternize with the enemy. But war (as has frequently been pointed out) is a bad thing, and one of the notorious bad points about it is that it makes warring groups abandon all charity towards one another, view each other unrealistically as stereotyped villains, and lose touch altogether with the complicated facts about life behind the enemy's lines. The use of bombs and guns may indeed demand this attitude. But guns are not being used here. And since they are not, there is no question of a sudden instantaneous revolution imposed from without by a conquering proletariat on a prostrate bourgeoisie. By revolution, feminists can only mean a great but gradual educational change produced by persuasion and consent (as in 'industrial revolution' or 'green revolution'). To produce this without keeping in close touch with the group to be persuaded is impossible. Lenin is a bad model. Politically, separateness is a seductive distraction.

8. The personal and the political

In what way, however, should the political part of the feminist enterprise relate to the personal one? This is a most interesting question, calling for a lot of hard work both in thought and experiment. It is unfortunate that at present discussion of it tends to be cut short by the apparently simple ruling that 'the personal is the political'. This obscure and tainted Marxist tag does no work and needs to be cleared out of the controversy. If it means anything, it means that there is no such thing as private life. This was apparent in its original use, which was to explain why Party members must always murder their friends when directed to, or be written off and executed themselves as traitors – as in Koestler's *Darkness at Noon* and Sartre's *Les Mains sales*. Its past history might not matter if its present sense was clear and useful, but it is not. The tag does not express at all the reasonable point for which it is often used – namely, that personal troubles are not *just* personal, but can have a social and political aspect which is sometimes crucial, as in the case of wife-beating. To make this point, we need a clear distinction between the two sides of life in the first place. We cannot point out this important relation between them unless we can distinguish them. But this tag apparently equates them. It is one of those trendy, deep-looking paradoxes, so much more impressive in French than in English, which cannot actually be used at all.

On top of this confusion, there is trouble about the meaning of 'politics'. Kate Millett gives a clue here.[24] She rejects the dictionary definition – 'methods or tactics involved in managing a state or government' – and rules that instead 'the term "politics" shall refer to power-structured relationships, arrangements whereby one group of persons is controlled by another', adding that, as things are, this is just about what politics in the first sense amounts to. She thus telescopes a fairly crude and hasty view of politics into an impossibly crude and hasty view of individual motives, and entirely drops the notion of large-scale public activity that is so central an element in the normal meaning of politics. After this, 'the personal is the political' simply means that personal life is nothing but a power contest.

Apart from the inconvenience of leaving us with no language for what is ordinarily called politics, this Hobbesian view has the disadvantage of being, in its literal sense, obviously false. Certainly it is only being applied to relations between the sexes – a restriction which will need explaining. But, even there, it goes far beyond her modest official point that 'sex is a category with political implications' to a sweeping generalization that it is only a relation of one-way dominance. What this has to mean is that this is the *right* way to view it. Among the many things we see, we ought to concentrate selectively on male dominance as the central element in sex relationships, dismissing everything else as superficial or misleading. Since anybody who looks for occasions when they or their group are being put down can always find them, and since one's own domineering behaviour is usually invisible, this is an easy programme, and one that is not likely to run out of material.

The probable effect of this selective scanning on anyone's personal life is obvious. And its bearing on the prospects of real political activity can scarcely be less disastrous. Any actual attempt to improve the world for women must involve working alongside men, however necessary it may also be for women to do much of the initial planning on their own. And it is impossible to work with people whom one insists on regarding as tyrants plotting to dominate one.

What, however, about relations between women, which are excepted from this generalization about dominance? Feminists often balance a generalized distrust of men with an amazing confidence in the solidarity of women. This confidence cannot be justified by drawing general conclusions from the degree of harmony that is reached in the tiny, highly select women's groups, which meet for special agreed purposes and devote themselves particularly to the business of bond-forming, which are the core of the women's movement. It is clear that these groups meet a tremendous need, and are the scene of very important experiences. But this does not necessarily mean that the bonds can be indefinitely extended. In fact it can make that extension impossible; the background of a hostile, uncomprehending world gave the original bond much of its force.

Sisterhood, if it merely means a common gender, is not powerful at all. It means something to us, but not much more than mere shared humanity. Where other powerful factors divide us, it counts for very little. It does not unite feminists with the ladies at the Conservative Party Conference. Like brotherhood, it is not powerful without the further bond of common views and experiences. And these bonds do not always coincide with it. For instance, in the churches women really could bring proceedings to a halt by withdrawing their presence, if that was what they chose. But, even where they feel strongly on such questions as their admission to the priesthood, they do not use this method because the unity of the church is more important to them.[25] Again, violent disagreement can be seen among women in (say) the Labour Party about their place within it. This kind of thing is usually explained as being due to the fact that a male framework is still in force; the women not on one's own side (whatever it may be) are not real women at all, they are pseudo-men, collaborators with the enemy. Anyone old enough to remember the daily working of single-sex schools can testify that there is nothing in this; even with no member of any other sex on the horizon, being female does not make people get on together any better than being male does. Deep disagreements are common to both.

9. Rediscovering history

All these gloomy remarks about practical possibilities are not, of course, meant to deny the imaginative force of the idea that women can unite to overthrow and reverse male folly. Symbolically, it is true. Presented in works of art – most notably Aristophanes's plays about women, especially the *Lysistrata* – it is persuasive and magnificent. And the more our age loses the strange confidence which it had until lately in a narrow range of values identified as specifically male, the easier this message is to see. People need to stop being ashamed of the female side of life. Any hope that there may be for our civilization surely demands this; but the change cannot possibly be made by conquest.

The fact that feminists have used this imagery to represent it may really be due, at least in part, to a misunderstanding of history resulting from the rather selective way in which the history of women's progress is now being written. Feminist historians, quite reasonably, stress the achievements of the pioneer women of whom they write, and tend to say little about the men who worked with them. This is fair, because the men's lives have often been recorded elsewhere, and the women's have been neglected. But it can mislead readers who do not know the historical background into supposing that all that was needed was for these women to point a gun at their cowardly oppressors, who then fell back foiled and could do nothing to prevent their power from being wrested from them.

This view of historical possibilities is expressed, more generally, in the belief that no powerful group ever does abandon a privilege until it is forced to. In relation to large, distinct, political groups this idea contains a lot of truth; but about social relations it is false. This can be seen in the case of children. The regular beating of children, along with a great deal of other unwarranted punishment and restraint, has been abandoned in the last hundred years – not because the children united to crush their oppressors by force, but because the parents themselves came to see that it was unnecessary and objectionable. The enormous improvements in women's conditions which have been made since Mary Wollstonecraft's time have depended on a similar gradual change in public opinion, brought about by reasoners and campaigners of both sexes alike.

This misconception is a stage in an interesting change in the attitude of modern feminists to history. Many members of the current women's movement, including some of its prophets, have recorded that when they began their work they thought they were breaking entirely new ground. They did not know they had predecessors at all, and were often delighted to discover them. Dale Spender, among others, attributes this ignorance to a deliberate conspiracy by men to conceal these potent ancestresses in order to neutralize their influence. She asks why she was never told that there were women like Aphra Behn and Mary Wollstonecraft, and replies that this news was carefully kept from her:

> While education remains under male control ... every generation has to begin again from the beginning. ... It is a mark of our sexist education system that ... three hundred years at least of women's

protest and struggle could be kept out of the record without our knowledge and consent.[26]

Out of what record? It is all there in plenty of popular books, and is collected in the most convenient manner in *The Second Sex* (published in 1949), which is commonly regarded as a kind of bible of modern feminism. In that book Simone de Beauvoir, who takes history very seriously, cites and discusses all her predecessors of note, including Aphra Behn. She deals with both male and female writers, British and American as well as French. Her references are full, and she pays special attention to Virginia Woolf. Any reader who is at all interested might be expected to follow her directions as far as *A Room of One's Own* (1929), and would find there full and fascinating details about many earlier figures, with plenty about Aphra Behn. *Three Guineas* (1938) contains a lot more, and has particularly entrancing notes. There has also been an unbroken stream of biographies and social histories, retelling various parts of the story with further historical detail. Besides all this, what about Charlotte Brontë? Most English-speaking schoolgirls seem to read at least some of her novels. And anyone who can read them without noticing the blazing feminist feeling is not the victim of a conspiracy, but simply asleep.

It is quite true, however, that modern feminists did manage for a time to miss these clues. The reason for this is simply that these feminists were part of the revolutionary movements of the 1960s. And those movements were dedicated, with peculiar fervour, to concentrating on the future and ignoring the past. They distilled to the last drop that strange doctrine, brewed early in the century, that salvation lies essentially in being modern, that one's predecessors are always a clog and never a guide or an inspiration. This idea, along with the bogus exaltation of youth which accompanied it, caricatured itself after a time to the point of collapse, so that even fashion has now turned away from the future to a bizarre patronizing of the past.

At a deeper level, the rediscovery of roots was a real emotional gain. Alex Haley's celebration of black American roots, reaching right back through the slave tradition to Africa, expressed a renewed openness to the past that was badly needed. The widespread welcome it received showed this. Something rather similar seems to have happened over feminism. Once the pioneers were noticed, it seemed incredible that they had been neglected before. But it was true. No conspiracy was present or needed; the spirit of the times did the job. It is not true, however, that this neglect was a cyclical phenomenon, that earlier women had also had to rediscover the story from scratch. Previous feminists, if they were serious, took the trouble to find out about their predecessors and to learn from them, as Virginia Woolf and Simone de Beauvoir did. Lack of curiosity about the past was a peculiar phenomenon of the 1960s, and it has fortunately proved a passing one.

It is, however, true and important that this knowledge has never been widely enough diffused. It did not reach uneducated people, and was therefore not usually available to encourage the working-class women who needed it most. And even for the educated it remained something of a special topic. It is not that women were, as Dale Spender puts it, 'invisible', but that their visibility remained fitful; now you see them excessively, now you don't at all. Virginia Woolf, looking them up in the index of the British Museum Reading Room, exclaimed in amazement: 'Have you any notion how many books are written about women in the course of one year? Have you any notion how many are written by men? Are you aware that you are, perhaps, the most discussed animal in the universe?' 'No age', she commented, 'can ever have been as stridently sex-conscious as ours.'[27] She concluded that men were on the defensive, and she may well have been right.

The effect is still to isolate women, to emphasize their distinctness and to make it hard to put in the ordinary, undramatic, female half of a proposition which should apply to both sexes. A striking instance is John Stuart Mill's excellent little book, *The Subjection of Women*. Although it had a *succès de scandale*, it has never been widely read or discussed. Had it been printed as part of his *Essay on Liberty*, to which it really belongs, it would no doubt have had more attention. It is in no way inferior to the rest of that book, and extends its argument in important ways. But discussions of the *Liberty* do not usually mention it. People interested in liberty did not necessarily want to read what they thought of as a book on women. Often they apparently did not notice that it was also a book on subjection, and that that was part of their topic. They thus often failed to apply Mill's principles to this intriguing case. This is not Mill's fault; he simply wrote the book later. But it underlines a lasting difficulty. Had he included this discussion in the *Liberty*, that already much-attacked book would have been dismissed by even greater numbers as merely a feminist tract.

There is a real problem here, which cannot be solved just by the current expansion of 'women's studies' as a distinct discipline, particularly where that discipline is taught only to women students. The wall separating this interest from mainstream general history needs to be breached. The past is not divided into two distinct parts, *his* and *hers*, like bath towels. The neglect of *hers* has actually caused alot of distortion in the view of *his*. The separatist response to this is to suggest expanding *hers* until it forms a separate domain as large as *his*. ('Perhaps when women's studies is as old and established as men's studies is to-day, it too will have as many sub-branches, variously compartmentalized and named.')[28] But this seems wild. The stories simply are not sufficiently separate, whether in history, anthropology, psychology or any other area. They have to be considered together. What is needed is to do this in a new way, so that a history of 'the Egyptians' does not suddenly reveal, by a belated footnote about 'their wives and children', that it was actually only a history of male Egyptians all the time. History ought not to take the reader into an unreal world; and a world in which the human race consists, for all serious purposes, of only one sex, is an unreal world.

The historical record, when we do turn to it, shows us plainly that co-operation between men and women is indeed possible, and that it is what has produced the immense widening of women's lives over the past two centuries. (In the neglect of

history, the mere extent of that improvement has itself sometimes been forgotten. This confuses the issues still further.) Of
course women's own efforts have been crucial. They always
must be so in any campaign for emancipation. And of course
there is a place for extremism at times, both for extreme doctrines and for the direct expression of indignation and fury.
These are needed to shake prejudice; they make change possible.
But they cannot make a revolution on their own.

The only feminists who tried these methods seriously were the
suffragettes. Their personal heroism is undoubted, but it is not
at all clear that their campaign had much effect. (The employment of women in the First World War, which shortly followed
it, seems to have been the main cause of further developments.)
Apart from their efforts, virtually everything that has been
achieved was brought about by the one method which separatists
rule out – by dialogue, by joint consent and co-operation between men and women. This is what fuelled the hard slog of the
Victorian age – the early suffrage campaigns, the Married
Women's Property Act, the founding of schools and colleges, the
repeal of the Contagious Diseases Acts and the entry into medicine – and also the final gaining of the suffrage, and the gradual
penetration into the trades and professions in this century. The
record needs to be put straight about this. If it is not, the next
generation of feminists will exclaim in amazement 'Why did
nobody tell me that it is possible for men and women to work
together? Why was it concealed from me that there were men
like Henry Sidgwick and John Stuart Mill and Bernard Shaw?
There has been a conspiracy to hide my birthright from me and
mislead me here.' And this time they will be right.

Anger has a role, but it has to be a limited one. Even where it
is initially well justified, anger is terribly habit-forming, and
grows with being indulged. The harm done in the world by
corporate hatreds is startling, but most of them have grown out
of justified anger. The trick of generalizing resentment is deadly.
Victims of injustice tend, like the genie in the bottle, to brood on
the wrong done to them to the point of taking it out on those
who try to release them, and thus they tend to get shut up all

over again. In this particular case, too, there is the special problem that any sort of war declared on men would also, perhaps primarily, have to be a war on those women who would not line up with it. Valerie Solanas, drawing attention to this inconvenient fact, asks plaintively 'Why should the fates of the groovy and the creepy be intertwined? Why should the active and imaginative consult the passive and dull on social policy?'[29] But unfortunately there is an answer to that one. Feminist tyranny, if it ever became possible, would still be tyranny. And that is just what we are supposed to be moving away from.

In this chapter we have been considering the language of full-scale sex warfare, and have not found a lot of sense in it. Yet behind this language there obviously lies a serious set of complaints about the difficulties of positive harmony at an ordinary personal level. Talk of sex war is an exaggeration, but it expresses a real uneasiness about the problems of sex peace. Our culture has a deep, perhaps unrealistic, traditional investment in the idea of romantic love, and of personal relations generally. Our expectations from these sources are very high, so high that it is perhaps inevitable that reality disappoints us. In the next chapter we had better consider how drastic this disillusionment needs to be in the case of sexual love.

5 Choices concerning men (2): love and sex

> Each of us then is the mere broken tally of a person, the result of a bisection which has reduced us to a condition like that of a flatfish, and each of us is perpetually in search of his corresponding tally. ... Love is simply the name for the desire and pursuit of the whole.
>
> (Aristophanes, speaking in Plato's *Symposium*)

1. All or nothing?

Here again those who love dilemmas hold their usual pistol to our heads. Women, they say, must either have nothing at all to do with men sexually, or abandon all personal independence and accept chronic humiliation. Plainly, this sort of thing would not be said if things were not really difficult. It is not a complaint picked out of the air. If we look round at the range of human cultures and see the immense variety of complex, often seemingly pointless, customs which have been set up to regulate relations between men and women, we can probably conclude that there are real, inbuilt difficulties in the enterprise. The idea that a cheerful anarchy here is the natural human condition is not convincing. And in our own culture the problems it raises are very serious. But are they so grave that we have to part company altogether? What does the trouble amount to?

We will begin by assuming that certain things, for example rape, wife-beating and sexual torture, are simply wrong, and are therefore not part of a discussion of normal problems. However often these things happen, however angry they make us, they are not the primary causes of discontent in ordinary life. We take it as read that such things should be prevented if possible, and punished if not, in any civilized society. Of course they are real problems. But we can at least recognize them for the evils that they are, even if our institutions are culpably sluggish in dealing

127

with them. These are areas for action rather than discussion. By contrast, it is the things which upset and confuse and irritate women – and indeed men too – without doing them visible and obvious damage which will occupy us here. These poisonous seeds, which are reaped as anger, depression, estrangement and resentment rather than injury, arise in that great twilit area where we are not sure what is evil and what is not.

2. The dream of freedom

The history of the last two decades, both in general and among feminists, is one of steady progress from certainty to doubt. In the 1960s sexual freedom was widely and confidently accepted as the obvious aim, and, for the first time, efficient birth control seemed to offer a sure means of reaching it. There can seldom have been a clearer demonstration of the old truth that freedom is not just a matter of multiplying your options. It is striking now to see the confidence with which the liberating feminists of that day accepted both these ideas. Their lack of doubts about the Pill is itself remarkable. Along with their unhesitating recommendation of *in vitro* pregnancy and universal automation, it shows an uncritical reliance on technological magic which is scarcely credible today, though it was common enough at the time. And it goes particularly oddly with their anarchic tendency to propose breaking up machinery and withdrawing one's labour so as to smash the system. This mistake, however, affects only means, and is less serious than the confusion about aims, the heavy and sometimes almost exclusive investment in the idea of sexual freedom. This freedom, as often happens, proved to be chiefly a new burden of responsibility. The story is like that of being given magic powers; the problems of decision quickly become unbearable. Apart from its physical drawbacks the Pill, being treated as infallible, made women entirely responsible for contraception, and removed at a stroke their most obvious ex-cuse for saying no. At the same time a whole set of new reasons for saying yes appeared in the emphasis laid on the female orgasm as an easy and obligatory experience, a necessary diploma in self-fulfilment, obtainable by persistent practice, enlightened attitudes and reading all the right books. This literature tended (and still tends) to treat orgasm as an isolated end in itself, ignoring the more lasting relationships which, for most women, are needed to give it meaning, and ruling that women in fact did not need such relationships, or that if they did there was something wrong with them, since men did not. Instant bliss, then, was said to be on offer, yet people did not find it. Both men and women were deeply disillusioned and looked round for someone to blame.

Separatist feminism now came forward, blaming the men and recommending a lesbian life (and masturbation) for the women. But such recommendations are usually just idle breath. We do not choose our emotional responses, and cannot produce them to order. However, the notion of orgasm as a detached event, like an explosion, which might as well take place in one situation as in another made this proposal sound plausible to many, and the end of the rainbow was moved one field further off. But dissatisfaction continued. And since (as was to be expected) most women did not move into a separate lesbian paradise, it was still chiefly focussed on the difficulty of relations between women and men. It crystallized, from about the mid 1970s, on the accusation that men treat women 'as sex objects'. With startling suddenness the demand for more sexual congress had given place to an apparent demand to abolish it altogether.

3. What is a sex object?

The charge of 'objectifying' is not a very clear one. It can cover anything from a whistle to multiple rape. The word *object* is of course ambiguous. It can mean a mere lifeless thing, such as a table, as opposed to a person, and in that sense to be treated as an object is always offensive. But it can also mean simply some-one on the receiving end. People can be the objects of the deepest awe, veneration, wonder, respect and love. Nobody minds this. It is not offensive in itself even to be the object of less welcome feelings, such as anger, fear, resentment or curiosity. These are feelings which people must expect to arouse sometimes; they involve their objects in no indignity. Only when the feeling is itself an offensive one, such as hatred or contempt, do we resent being its object. Is sexual desire to be grouped with these as an emotion which is essentially and inevitably degrading to its objects?

When the question is put like this, most people today do not say that it is, whatever Tertullian might have thought. And the feminist complaint about male sexual desire is not usually ex-actly that it is itself degrading, but that it is accompanied by feelings of hatred and contempt, which are. Now where this happens the mixture certainly is offensive, and we shall have to look at this kind of case very carefully. But the phrase 'treating as a sex object' simply does not describe these cases. The trouble here lies in treating someone as an object *of contempt*. Where this does not happen, where the feeling is simply sexual attrac-tion, it is hard to see why there is anything wrong, whichever sex feels it. The complaint may, of course, be the slightly differ-ent one of being treated *only* as a sex object. But even this is not always wrong; in some contexts it can be appropriate. We do not go to bed to discuss monetarism or the ontological argument. Anyone who wants to be a sex subject must surely agree to be a sex object as well.

What is the real complaint expressed by this phrase about sex objects? It seems to have two main aspects. Publicly, there is in our culture an enormous commercial exploitation of women's bodies. And in private life there is a string of connected troubles. There is the unpleasantness of being treated as *only* a sex object all the time, or at times when something else is clearly called for. This may well be largely a negative point, a protest about what is not happening and ought to be. But since there are usually some positive reasons why it is failing to happen, this merges into a positive complaint about attitudes like contempt and hatred which are accompanying the sex feeling and which change its quality so as to block other responses, rather than about the mere fact of sex feeling on its own. It is fairly important to clarify this point, because women who seem to be complaining of sexual interest merely in itself and at all times are liable to seem unconvincing and, if they are believed, unreasonable.

Turning to the first real charge – the commercial exploitation – we should surely recognize at once that it is a real evil, a widespread fault in our culture. Stimuli which would be all right in their natural place, as part of personal life, are continually canned, repeated and forced upon us impersonally for commercial reasons in a way that batters our sensibilities and cannot fail to distort our emotions. It is not that there is anything wrong with adornment and visual admiration in itself. Certainly, as Janet Radcliffe Richards points out, there is nothing sinister about beauty,[1] and the kind of puritanism which insists on everybody wearing boiler-suits for fear of looking attractive is senseless. But exclusive, obsessive concentration on the visual surface of things (which is what the publicity techniques of our age produce) is bound to distract our attention from other aspects of life, and it exhausts our responses.

Beyond this, and more peculiar to the case of women, the immense artifice that goes into fabricating visual fantasy images produces a female stereotype, a kind of bogus ideal, a new phantom with which ordinary life cannot possibly compete and which is bound to make it disappointing. Just as real country, unlike that on television commercials, contains mud and flies and smells, so real men and women have defects. In spite of deodorants, they too smell, they grow old and fat and have colds and do not dress perfectly and are sometimes not pleased to see us. That indeed is how we love them. But unless we sharply resist the false image, it can sometimes come between us and those we love, like a chill and dreadful succubus, and can spoil them for us. That it does do this is clear from the amount we spend on cosmetics, and from the fearful anxiety expressed in all those magazine articles on how not to lose your youth. This is what sends processions of sad, rich ladies continually to the plastic surgeon's office.

In these cases, however, the right complaint is surely not of being treated as a sex object. The complaint really runs: I am *not* your sex object. You look at me only as a reminder. That object is Miss World, or the latest model. And what she is being treated as is something which, however objectionable, cannot be described just in terms of sex. It brings in the whole wider social and commercial scene. For instance, she is also a status object, and a means of advertising other status objects. She is a piece of conspicuous expenditure, an occasion for competitive displays of wealth. The chief deities to whose worship she contributes are success and Mammon, not Aphrodite, who tends to turn a somewhat sardonic eye on these goings-on and can sometimes visit their devotees with impotence. Straightforward sex would be a much less harmful thing.

4. Fantasy takes off
Here the public aspect has an important impact on the private one. Institutions like pornography and prostitution, and the attitudes taken to rape and sexual abuse, affect ordinary life. As we have said, undoubted injuries like actual rape are not in question at this point. They are agreed to be injuries, and there-fore wrong. But there are many who argue that nothing short of actual injury is a matter of general concern. Women, they say, have no reason to mind anything that goes on by consent. On this basis, defenders of porn tend to take the line that it is all harmless fun. 'Sexual experimentation is delightful and should be encouraged – pictures of pretty girls are nice – all women like the idea of being raped – we ought not to be narrow-minded about "perversion" – and anyway nothing must interfere with individual liberty.'

This line has some obvious sense in it, and tends to look impressive if one assumes that the only alternative is a joyless concealment of everything sexual. But clearly there are other possibilities. This, again, is a false dilemma. The point about civil liberties is a red herring. We are not involved in trying to forbid things, but to find out what is wrong with them. The law is a crude weapon. There are a thousand bad things in any society, from boredom to hypocrisy and bad temper, which cannot be made illegal, but whose badness needs none the less to be recognized. We need to understand what is amiss, and to locate its influence on our lives.

The real difficulty lies in understanding properly the very subtle relation of fantasy to reality. The line between them is not at all as clear as we might like to think. Our lives are a continual mixture of both. Complete fantasy and stark reality lie at the two poles. In between is a large area of overlap. Indeed, virtually all our experience combines elements of both, for of course fantasy is not all illusion. We need imaginative activity to make sense of the scrappy data we receive, to fill in gaps, and to work out our own attitudes to what is happening. It is also the seed-ground of art. Personal relations need a great deal of this kind of imaginative attention, and sexual ones above all are quite in-human without it.

Fantasy only becomes illusion when it takes off, abandons the attempt to make sense of the data and becomes an end in itself. But the welter of contrived images in which we now live is designed to make it do just this. In that way people can be influenced, notably to spend money. This is dangerous in many ways, but especially to sexual life, because here strong, simple, standard responses are available which make manipulation particularly easy. Those who manipulate fantasies naturally prefer to work with an efficient stereotype of this kind. But what works in a real relationship is by contrast highly individual. It cannot be discovered by following a fantasy script. Pornography, even when it is not actually sadistic, is a real menace because it is so stereotyped. It distorts perceptions beyond the bounds which people's shaky sense of reality can handle. What offends is not the sight of a pretty girl, but a cosmetic creation which is produced as an *aim* for all women, and a condition of their figuring in somebody's life. Pornographic pictures are distorted to bring out the 'releasers' – the configurations directly adapted to produce particular sensations, in isolation from their living context – and suppress the background of characteristics which make a complete person. Those who respond to them are like Tinbergen's sticklebacks, which are placed in tanks looking out on a courtyard and respond with threats to the red post office vans that pass, because the colour of a rival male fish is the releaser for their anger.[2]

If men do much of this, the fragmenting of their reponses has to distort their reaction to real women. This distortion is immediate. The objections to it cannot be properly stated by those who, obsessed with consequences, look only at people's later conduct to see whether they have been depraved and corrupted. The trouble is not that this sort of thing causes corruption; it already *is* corruption. No doubt one corrupt experience is likely to lead to others. But it does this as part of a continuous process, all of which is already evil. We do not have to wait for certified external disasters before judging cruel or contemptuous or inhuman states of mind as bad, any more than we have to wait for statistics of the impact of affection on the population before judging it to be good. The utilitarian yardstick is senseless here. There are many kinds of vile situation (such as that in Aldous Huxley's *Brave New World*) which can subsist without ever causing disaster or even distress. It is quite unrealistic to pretend that we cannot make value-judgements about such things. We know that we cannot dwell lovingly on a brutal idea – such as the cannibalistic one that man is the hunter and woman the prey – without first distorting our attitudes to real people.

When we turn to consider attitudes to such things as rape, this complex relation between fantasy and reality is crucial. The idea that all women want to be raped is pure fantasy. What gives rise to it is the interesting fact that both women and men can enjoy taking part in games which involve mock pursuit, conquest and submission. But the difference between play and earnest is enormous. Pretending to resist is not resisting. Fantasy itself does not incorporate real pain and fear. Moreover, day-dreams constantly deal in experiences which the dreamers would be quite appalled to find realized. An obvious example of this is the popularity of disaster movies. No doubt those who see them develop the script in their leisure moments afterwards, performing daring rescues and so forth. But it is never supposed that this indicates a hidden wish to find themselves really trapped on the fourteenth floor of a burning skyscraper. Again, someone might well cherish bold dreams of what he would do if only he were President of the United States. He would not be at all pleased to be woken up afterwards by the words, 'Good morning, Mr President. Here is the red box. I'm afraid we're going to need a quick decision ...'.

'Rape fantasies' cannot really be fantasies of rape, because rape is by definition what you do *not* want. Both sexes may indeed fantasize about episodes of being carried off by the right person – say on a milk-white charger into the desert. But these scenes are supposed to culminate in the dreamy look of adoration in her eyes when all is done. They do not involve genuine threats with knives, real black eyes, teeth being knocked out, multiple lacerations or internal injuries, which are the sort of things that happen in actual rape cases. Novelists who want to use rape in their stories while retaining their readers' sympathy for their characters do not usually represent it in detail, and this leaves readers free to conclude that consent was in fact arrived at, even if by unorthodox methods. If it was not, there is nothing for anybody to be pleased about. In Galsworthy's *Forsyte Saga*, when Soames actually does rape his wife Irene, her reaction is to leave him, and most women would see the sense of that. This is one dream that is not supposed to come true, a game that must never degenerate into earnest.

In rape cases it is often argued that this ambivalence between play and earnest is so confusing that men cannot be expected to follow it ('my client honestly thought, m'lud, that she just enjoyed screaming'). But it is not unreasonable that they should be expected to make this distinction. It is one of a kind which all of us learn to make in countless contexts extremely early in our lives. Children very quickly grasp the difference between play and reality. They sometimes pretend that they do not know it when they do ('we really thought they were enjoying the game'), but their bluff can be called and they can always learn to abandon it. They get continual practice in this skill, and any adult who has had anything like a normal childhood knows how to go about it. The main thing that tends to block intelligent discrimination over sex is a kind of folklore about the opposite sex, which rules that women – or men – all have tastes which cannot be read off at all from the usual common-sense formula, 'what would you think if that was done to you?' nor from a knowledge of their characters. To read the signs of someone else's preferences correctly we need to attend directly to them, not to any such general doctrines, and to put the particular act in the context of their whole life – not to isolate it, as is so often done with sex. Since pornography is a crude and powerful disseminator of male folklore, it is liable to be a real menace on this matter. It can produce a singular confidence in one's own insights. Men who, like Sweeney, already know the female temperament,[3] tend to be fairly impervious to actual information on the subject.

This piece of folklore, however, is currently being echoed by another, which is now appearing widely as a graffito: 'all men are rapists'. What do the writers mean? Is it just that all rapists are men? The usual reply is that they are all *potential* rapists. If this is just a piece of physical information it is not true; some men are impotent. Nor is it even true that all those raped are women; men and boys can be so too, though somewhat differently. What follows from the physical differences? Like other differences of physique and capacity, they certainly do make some people vulnerable in a special manner. But we are all vulnerable to each other in numberless ways in any case. Our security rests entirely on trust and goodwill. We are all, for instance, physically capable of poisoning each other, and many of us could get away with it. What is so special about rape?

Two answers are given. One is a perfectly sensible objection to the current dangers of the city streets, for which this language is a bad expression. Walking alone at night, anyone who is not physically stalwart may well regard all others as potential mug-gers. In a sense they are. But that sense reflects only ignorance. It says that we do not know who is harmless, not that nobody is. One real mugger among hundreds of harmless people can well make this a sensible attitude. Just so, on an alien planet every food is a potential poison. This is a fact about our ignorance, not about the food.

That the streets should be safer is a political demand which it may well be very important to make. But it gives no support to the other interpretation of the phrase 'all men are rapists', which makes it a psychological claim, much like 'every man has his price' and 'we would all be murderers if we thought we could get away with it'. This kind of cheaply cynical stereotyping ought to have no place in feminist thinking. It is sometimes given a different, rather scattier, sense when it becomes physical rather than psychological. Sexual penetration, even when it takes place by consent, is considered as necessarily an aggressive act, so that intercourse itself has to constitute rape. If this made sense, it is hard to see what could be done about it. All the higher animals do it this way. We cannot become as the codfish and scatter sperm in the sea. Even snails, which are lucky enough to be hermaphrodite, shoot little pellets at each other and interpene-trate. In spite of all the warlike imagery, we are adapted to it and consent is genuine.

Here again, feminists who regard intercourse as essentially aggressive are echoing exactly those men whom they should be most concerned to expose as mistaken. The retreat to the labor-atories and the hospital glassware is not only repulsive, it is wholly unnecessary. The idea that intercourse is an outrage on individuality expresses the same misguided worship of solitude which found pregnancy and childbirth so scandalous. Certainly, billiard-balls never get penetrated. But we do not have to aspire to the condition of billiard-balls. We are organisms, so we are lucky enough to lie open to the world.

5. The private prison

The isolation of sexual acts from contexts is a part of the peculiar negative conception of freedom as isolation and fragmentation of life – as simply not being bound – to which the libertarians of the 1960s were dedicated. If individual self-fulfilment and self-expression are private aims, not concerning anybody else, it follows that each person must concentrate on their own sexual experience in a vacuum, and that a partner is only a sex aid which happens to prove effective. People cannot normally treat each other like this, however, and the idea that they ought to try to is merely a confused expression of a mortal fear of intimacy. Where more than one person is involved, each must take up some attitude to the other. The attitude of deliberately depersonalizing them, of treating them as a sex aid, is not a way of avoiding this direct encounter. It is a way of handling it, it is one personal approach among others, and a very objectionable one. It really is a case of treating someone as an 'object' in the sense of a thing – that is, contemptuously. There is no possible impersonal attitude to persons. Attitudes affect behaviour, and systematic indulgence in fantasy has consequences for behaviour which can be disastrous in reality.

It is notorious, of course, that there can be a clash of fantasies. A woman can be treating a man merely as an appendage to the beautiful home she has or hopes for, as a meal-ticket, or as a minor character in her own personal soap opera, while he sees her as a minor character in his. If things have not become too bad, life usually proceeds by the steady mutual adaptation of these scripts in the light of real interactions – a development which can be reasonably satisfactory if both parties have some self-knowledge and some humour, but painful and bumpy if not. Since we cannot instantly remove the electronic dream-factories from our world, but are likely rather to see more of them, the main lifeline for everybody here is increased self-knowledge and an understanding of the dangers. What fairly certainly will not help is the demand which some feminists make to *share* the kind of fantasies that men have by asserting an equal right to beefcake. This seems to be one of the many places where equality is a bad guide. Women do not tend to want beefcake much for a start; and, if they do cultivate a taste for it, it seems likely that the special affinity which cheesecake certainly has with sadism might come along as an unwelcome consequence. People are not things, and it seems fairly important not to start treating them as such.

Sexual freedom, then, is not best seen as the isolation of partners' personal lives from each other. Neither is it best seen as the isolation of acts from consequences. But this too has been another aspect of the 1960s fantasy. Since the effects of sexual activity on both birth and venereal disease were supposed to have been done away with, people had the impression that they were at last free to act without consequences. Yet interaction, like all real action, always has consequences. (Even the Marquis de Sade dreamed up a potion which was magically able to remove whip-marks before returning Justine to circulation.)[4] The exaltation of pot-smoking showed a similar view of freedom as essentially an escape from reality, from involvement in consequences.

Since fantasies themselves really cannot be shared – since all sharing brings us back into the real world – anyone who does not want solitary confinement for life has in the end to adapt their life to other people's. No doubt most people taking part in the 1960s jamboree discovered this fairly quickly, and it was only the more extreme gurus of the age who denied it. But the less ambitious notion of mere exemption from personal ties in sex relations had a much stronger influence, because it was a traditional male ideal. Women have had great problems in dealing with it. So far as they accepted the ideas of the time they found it hard to avoid agreeing that the men were right in blaming them for being frigid ('she won't'), a charge which did not prevent their also being accused on occasions of being nymphomaniacs ('she will when I don't want to', or 'with somebody else': jealousy had not been abolished). It has proved virtually impossible to do right, and this has greatly upset both sexes.

Could this trouble have been avoided without abandoning the individualistic notion of freedom and self-fulfilment as involving exemption from personal ties? It is hard to see how. In its original, grander, form this notion was an exaltation of actual solitude. Writers who are solitary in their personal lives, such as Nietzsche, can give it great dignity. Zarathustra is an impressive figure. If, however, the solitary still wants the enjoyments of sex as well (like Sartre and Schopenhauer), there are real difficulties. Can both sexual parties be emotionally independent? Sometimes this works, but it is impossible to ensure it; and women do tend to find total disengagement harder, just as men tend to find it harder to accept bonds. Even if this difference were produced only by culture (which it pretty certainly is not), it still poses a problem. Who has got to control their existing tendencies? Which party is to change its ways? In an age devoted to extreme individualism it seemed obvious that this duty fell on women, because their preference was less worthy in the first place. Their wish for a joint life counted as a weakness to be conquered, while men's wish to remain uncommitted counted as honourable independence. Hence the startling self-righteousness of writers like Henry Miller and Norman Mailer about the sexual aggression of their heroes, a trait neatly exposed by Kate Millett.[5] The ground for this moral cockiness is not too clear. On the face of things it seems that some human activites – for instance quartet playing, or football, or producing tragedy – cannot satisfactorily be carried on in isolation by egoists, and that most sexual activities may fall into this class. However that may be, the demand for detachment often could not be met, and the fact that men still felt that they were entitled to be jealous showed that they were not even always sincere in making it. On the men's side, the savage misogyny which we have noticed from writers like Miller and Mailer expresses the resulting resentment, to which the women's explosions of the early 1970s are a not unnatural response.

The nature of the disillusion needs to be understood. People had, it seems, believed that only conventional restrictions stood between them and total fulfilment. But it emerged, when those restrictions were lifted, that the main trouble had all along been something quite different – namely genuine conflict between the wishes of different people, and also between each individual's own discordant wishes. Disappointment was very sharp, and took shape as resentment. Somebody had to be blamed, and the obvious scapegoat for each sex was the other. The effective remedy would have been to try seriously to understand both one's own conflicting motives and those of others, especially one's sexual partners. But this is hard, and moreover the cast-iron self-fulfilment ethic makes it unthinkable. It therefore seemed to the characters in Miller's and Mailer's novels – and no doubt to some others – that the only proper course was to secure agreement of wishes by walloping and raping the misguided women into knowing what was good for them. Even when not actually being beaten raw and rubbed with mustard, the best the women get there is: 'I just didn't give a fuck for her, as a person, though I often wondered what she might be like as a piece of fuck, so to speak. I wondered about it in a detached way, but somehow it got across to her, got under her skin.'[6]

This attitude is no doubt what is often meant by the charge of 'treating women as sex objects'. But this is far too charitable a description of it. Much of it is nothing more than commonplace selfishness, meanness and petty conceit. The root of this special kind of selfishness is not hard to find in the fear of intimacy, the unwillingness to let anyone come close enough to one to express an opinion on one's merits. This is, indeed, the same fault that is in question when women are accused of frigidity, though in men it can do much more immediate damage.

6. The meaning of obscenity

When, however, we turn from this squalid character defect to consider the whole field of obscenity – which often seems to be brought under the same heading – we see at once that we are dealing with something quite different, much larger and more mysterious. In an immense range of societies the business of sexual mockery, scurrility and dirty jokes plays an important social role, often an essential and sacred one. Athenian comedy arose from the ceremonial worship of Dionysus, which consisted in shouting scurrilous abuse at prominent citizens and had the important function of protecting them, and through them the whole city, from the danger of divine wrath, which might otherwise strike everybody. The worship of Priapus served a similar function at Rome. (These rituals persisted in classical times, and it was considered important that their obscenity should be strong, vociferous and genuine.) In a rather similar spirit, Nepalese temples display on the ends of their roof-beams small naked figures engaged in sexual activity, whose role is to ward off the lightning. The goddess of lightning, being a virgin, is repelled by them and strikes elsewhere. Serious public ritual obscenity of this kind is quite common; but its uses in private life can be very important too. Margaret Mead tells how in Manus, where things are in general very solemn, they liven up when

> ... sons of the brother and sister become formal traders. ... These business-like cousins are permitted to jest with one another, to refer lewdly to each other's private life, to break every convention of sobriety of speech, to shatter every reticence. Thus the strain of economic antagonism is ceremonially broken. A man who is receiving advance payments from his cousin of ten thousand dog's teeth, payments which it will take him years to meet, is permitted to dance an obscene defiance to his creditor.[7]

And phallic gestures are widely used to ward off the evil eye.

It should be clear by now that we are not dealing merely with the passing perverse fancies of a few Americans. Just what we are dealing with it is much harder to say. Laughter itself is a puzzle; it might greatly surprise visitors from another planet. Why sex should so universally provoke it is a further question. What does emerge, however, is that laughter relieves tension. Certainly this is a metaphor – no real strings are stretched – but it is a very clear one. Tension is a familiar state, arising out of unresolved difficulties and conflicts, and preventing ease. Sex undoubtedly provides plenty of difficulties and conflicts, but it can also discharge them, and has a strange power of discharging also ones which it did not originate in the first place. The relief seems to consist in a sudden, mysterious shift into the mode of play. But this shift can take two forms. Shared by both parties it is innocuous, and may be called straight or playful laughter. Aggressive or mocking laughter, by contrast, occurs where one individual or group relieves its own tension by expressing contempt of another. They are still playing, but now their play has an 'object'. And the object is not invited to become a subject by sharing in the laughter, any more than a football is asked to kick back. The Miller-Mailer female is a football which only occasionally becomes so far conscious as to murmur its thanks and admiration. It is a wish-fulfilment image that shows the compensating, darker half of the angel and phantom stories. The mockery and contempt directed at it have nothing amiable about them at all.

In general hostile, contemptuous laughter is one of the most savage weapons in the human emotional armoury, and it is particularly virulent when it is used between the sexes because the good opinion of each is so important to the other. To be really mocked by women is an appalling experience for a man, and it is no more pleasant the other way round. Mockers can always deceive themselves on this point, and it is notorious that children often do so. But adults are supposed to know when this will not wash. Men who find it humourless of women to object to porn might like to wonder how they themselves would feel if obscene, mocking pictures of men – or even exaggeratedly handsome ones – were widely displayed and laughed about, or gloated over, by women. They would probably feel the display itself to be an attack, and one that touched them personally, even if it did not threaten any further injury. The difference between laughing at others and laughing with them can be discovered by facing such examples. And the offence, where there is one, is related to those we have discussed earlier. Porn and mockery substitute a fantasy object, a typified figure (this time an obscene one), for the real one without regard to the feelings of real ones or recollection that they may have a point of view. The

distorted image is meant to represent them, and it cannot fail
to injure.

7. Language, dominance and anxiety

It does not follow, however, that this is happening with every
dirty joke or rumbustious cartoon, or with every artistic use of
obscenity. Some very great comic art – Aristophanes, Rabelais,
Chaucer – operates in this area, and so does much great and
sombre satire. The difference between offence and no offence
seems to lie in a certain impersonal largeness and fairness of
approach, which replaces the mean tribal vindictiveness of misogyny. With Aristophanes the joke is on all of us; with Swift the
horror is on all of us. This is not the case with the cheapies. But
in order to grasp this difference properly we need whole contexts;
it can be obscured by capricious quotation.

The game, currently popular among some feminists, of collecting what seem to be insults to women from all kinds of
sources without placing them in context is misleading and senseless. In this game all usages which favour women are treated as
hollow shams, while all which can have a black interpretation
are given it. This is specially disastrous where language is concerned. There is now a whole industry afoot of finding ways in
which language denigrates women, from putting them second in
phrases (men and women) to the distressing fact that 'although
Lord still preserves its initial meaning, *Lady* has undergone a
process of "democratic levelling" and is no longer reserved for
women of high rank'.[8] Some of these are of real interest because
they have actually been used to distort political debate, as in 'the
rights of man', or to reinforce more general prejudice, as in the
effect of masculine agent-words on the exclusion of women from
trades and the professions ('we can't have a woman barrister
because she would have to be called a barristress'). Language, in
fact, crystallizes usage and can impede its change, and it is
worthwhile calling attention to this so as to explain that some of

the sense of strangeness is merely verbal. Thus surnames descend in the male line because men used to have a special legal status, but this usage does not force us to think of women as secondary now.

Yet the complaints go far beyond this mere indication of social tradition to a general contention that the language used to refer to women is designed to be systematically degrading. This argument is naturally made easier by the idea that merely showing a difference is itself degrading – an implausible view. (See the next chapter. In Chinese, by the way, pronouns show no gender difference; this does not appear to produce a particularly liberal treatment of women.) Word lists are then compiled to show, for example, that 'not only were there more words for males but that there were more positive words'.[9] That there were more words is of course just a consequence of the fact that language is old and grows slowly; the wider variety of male roles is a historical fact which the words only reflect. When more words are needed they are evolved. There is no room here for the conspiracy which seems to be suspected.

What is meant by *positive* words? Words are not like magnetic poles, with a single charge. They are far too versatile for that. There is hardly any word so complimentary that it cannot sometimes serve as an stinging insult, or so rude that we shall not sometimes greet it with delight. In any case, conversation contains an amazing amount of irony, ambivalence, understatement, euphemism, innuendo, double meaning, friendly abuse, barbed compliment, ritual and celebratory swearing, magical precaution and general emotional conjuring. Words are the complex tools suited to this game, so if one cares to pick single meanings for them it is not hard to prove all sorts of strange theses.

It is only by this selective manipulation that words can be made to take sides in the sex war. Thus Dale Spender complains that 'courtesan' is negative, while its equivalent 'courtier' is not. But isn't it? Which of us would be pleased to be described as a thorough courtier? Certainly the two words have drifted apart, but that often happens. Dale Spender further complains that 'courtesan' is one of a large number of near-synonyms which have come to be used to describe various grades of kept women or prostitutes, after originally having a different and more general meaning. She takes this tendency to indicate contempt for women. But, like other accumulations of near-synonyms, it is surely just the result of euphemism and politeness. (Compare the many words for 'death' or 'money'.) And, as is usual with euphemism, it seems to spring essentially from fear. This group of women had a suspect and equivocal position which was both alarming in an everyday way (they might confer disease or scandal), and at a deeper level symbolically disturbing, because they represented a female force that was powerful in society but by no means integrated into it. Among this group of words 'courtesan' is of course an honorific title, suitable for describing women like the Greek hetairai, or like Skittles, who held a distinguished and secure, though informal, position in late-Victorian London society, and for marking them off from street-walkers as much as from married women. We may well deplore the moral confusion which complicates the meaning of such words, and may want the institutions they represent to be changed. But this is a social point, not a linguistic one, and it happens with all sort of words, not just with those denoting women. If we expect to class all words as positive or negative we had perhaps better start with some simpler and more general examples, such as 'politician', 'academic', 'authority', 'family', 'conservative' or 'Marxist'.

The simple accusation of a conspiracy to degrade distracts attention from some very interesting and little-understood differences in the way we both speak and think of the two sexes. Another point which Dale Spender complains of bears on this; words and indeed clothes or other gear, once used for women, cannot afterwards easily be used for men. She reads this as indicating contempt for women.[10] But again, this seems superficial. Contempt may sometimes be present, but it is certainly not the whole explanation. What seems much more important is the relatively fragile male sense of identity. As Walter J. Ong puts it, in a very interesting discussion:

Accusations of 'effeminacy' normally strike the male heart with terror ... [but] masculinity does not hold the same fears for women that femininity does for men. ... Women regularly appropriate masculine accoutrements in many if not all cultures with no threat to their feminine identity. ... In these cases, when something masculine enters the feminine world, it is immediately subjected to that world. ... The feminine simply takes over the masculine style, subtly feminizing it and thereby expropriating and appropriating it. ...[11]

This difference in security accounts, he suggests, for many of the asymmetries of gender usuage. It does not bother women to be frequently subsumed under masculine pronouns, but the converse arrangement would bother men a great deal. Language therefore avoids it. Ong concedes that

Overspecialization in masculine forms as common gender forms (such as 'he' in English for both sexes) can be distasteful and needs to be counteracted. But the psychodynamics with which one is working in making adjustments here have a life and pattern of their own, not unconnected with male insecurity, of which both females and males are at least unconsciously aware.

In the same way, he adds, women can take names formed from those of men without feeling threatened, while 'it would endanger the ego structure of most males to take an adapted name of a woman; they cannot appropriate a woman's name to the male world. Femininity is too powerful.' Obviously in so complex a matter it will not do to treat this idea as a complete explanation either; but it serves at least to balance the startlingly simple-minded suggestion that universal and absolute male dominance accounts for all the asymmetries of language. Among other matters, it does seem to clarify the asymmetries of humour. Ong suggests: 'Humour lies closer to the male world, especially gross and boisterous humour, for it relieves conflict, particularly as caught in father-son relationships. There have been few female clowns [because] clowns have normally been disabled father-figures.' Seen in this light a good deal of male rodomontade, which feminists tend to treat as the brutal exultation of a triumphant tyrant, appears in the much more appealing light of a relief to anxiety, and ceases to offend. And this often seems to be the most natural way to take it.

8. Harassed or not harassed?

With this general background we may be able to go some way towards sorting out the question of sexual harassment, which has lately come to the fore as a clarification of what it means to be treated as a sex object. The simplest cases of it seem to be those which occur at work, and which are made possible by the relative positions of the men and women concerned. Here again, extreme cases are relatively easy to deal with. It is wrong for anybody to use their superior position to impose on someone else familiarities which would be resented and rejected if that superiority did not make rejection impossible. That goes for bottom-pinching as well as rape. It also goes with still more force for blackmail, overt or covert, such as the casting couch. There is something doubly offensive about the use of sexual approaches here, over and above mere ordinary insolence, because it can constitute a deliberate humiliation, a degradation of someone's personal life designed to show their subordinate position. (Again, it is not the sexual motives themselves which are the most offensive, but the power-centred ones in whose service they operate.)

What, however, about milder cases, and ones where the position at work does not settle the matter? How do we decide the borders at which familiarity becomes legitimate? Once more, attitudes have polarized. On the one hand, everything is defended on the grounds that men cannot treat women as if they were men, that all men flirt with women, and that most women can handle it even if they do not secretly like it. On the other, everything is denounced on the grounds that everybody, equally, ought to be treated only as a person – no one, therefore, should be treated differently as a woman – and any word or action with a sexual implication is in itself insulting and diminishing.

Clearly, this includes a very wide range of actions. Some of them are aggressive in intention, and we have considered the meaning of that aggression. But others are not. Some are simply expressions of friendliness, ordinary social overtures which have no particular sexual meaning, but which are still – as in any society – differently put when they pass between people of different sexes. Some are indeed expressions of sexual attraction, but not only that; they are overtures of friendship. An invitation to eat together need not be an insult; it is not even exactly a compliment. It is a way of getting to know someone.

Now if there is indeed an element of sexual attraction here, it would be nice to know what the man is expected to do about it if he may not express it. No means exists of moving from bare acquaintance in the direction of love without passing through ordinary friendship and courtship. If people are forbidden to make the opening moves, they are left with no alternative to a sudden onslaught. Unless they can approach one another in situations which are primarily non-sexual, they are either excluded from sex (which does happen to very shy people) or reduced to inventing some engineered social situation, such as the Saturday night dance, which is known to be just a pairing-off device. This makes sense only with the depersonalized attitude to sex whose drawbacks we have discussed. Women who do not like this must surely accept, and not be offended by, ordinary expressions of sexual interest. If they take a form that displeases, it is possible to point out why. A man who asks 'do you like my Pirelli calendar?' can be given an answer which need not take the form of flinging furniture at him, nor even a serious remonstrance. It may genuinely not have struck him that this was not a conciliatory move. The point can be explained. Mere lack of mutual understanding in our crude and confusing society may cause more of the trouble than we think.

There is a quite extraordinary self-consciousness developing at present among some feminists, apparently involving the conviction that any man who looks attentively at them, let alone speaks to them, is insulting them by viewing them as prey or merchandise. In general this is certainly just a mistake. A census of men's thoughts, were it possible, would be likely to reveal a disappointing proportion of answers like 'where have I seen someone like that before?', or mere absent-mindedness. But even if they do feel a passing attraction, this is no more than we all do to some people and things we see: it does no harm to anybody. A cat may look at a king. It may even mew at him. Whistles need not be offensive. Mild cases of anything are mild.

It is important to clear this sort of paranoia out of the way, because it obscures the real difficulties. It is a genuine problem of our age that our social signals are confused and hard to read. This is the price we pay for our vast, mixed, interesting culture. We do not have the clear glossary of meanings attached to all the clothes and gestures permitted to a lady or gentleman that our ancestors had. We are, therefore, sometimes misunderstood, and have to get out of scrapes which our protected forbears never got into. What is most needed is that everybody should recognize the problem, and should not suppose that they know just what everybody else means by their every action. This applies strongly to men who think that they know all about women, and therefore think that the particular women they are dealing with really like their insolent behaviour even when they say they do not – and equally, of course, to women who hold as an article of faith that all men are rapists.

It is this kind of attitude in men, particularly in the workplace, which gives rise to the current protests from women. It needs to change sharply. The law, however, is in this case rather a blunt instrument for changing it, because proof of this attitude is usually hard to find where it has not involved witnessed assault or blackmail. There has, moreover, already been at least one case in the USA of an accusation of harassment brought against a female boss by a male employee – and, given the problems of proof just mentioned, there is no reason why there may not be more. A change in manners, rather than in the law, is likely to be needed to remedy this evil.

For this to happen it seems absolutely necessary that women should avoid being paranoid, and should sort out the things that are worth protesting about from those that are genuinely inoffensive or trivial. The demand to be treated merely as a 'person', meaning a sexless item, is scarcely intelligible. No culture yet found fails to make a wide difference between social reactions to the two sexes. To do so would be like treating people as if they had no particular age or background. Whether or not this feat is eventually possible, it is not possible today, nor is it needed. Demanding it is therefore a mere displacement activity, distracting us from the real problems. Worse, it accepts what must certainly not be accepted – that to be treated like a woman involves being treated with contempt. It does not. We are not forced to choose between the world of Miller and Mailer and an androgynous science-fiction Utopia which has not yet even been designed. Both fiction and real life give us far more choices than these, and no doubt if we keep at it we can invent better ones yet. But it really does have to be a joint enterprise.

Perhaps it is best to end this chapter with Virginia Woolf, looking out of her window as she concludes her reflections on women in *A Room of One's Own*:

> The taxi stopped; and the girl and the young man stopped; and they got into the taxi. . . . The sight of two people coming down the street and meeting at the corner seems to ease the mind of some strain, I thought, watching the taxi turn and make off. Perhaps to think, as I had been thinking these two days, of one sex as distinct from the other is an effort. It interferes with the unity of the mind. . . . The obvious reason would be that it is natural for the sexes to cooperate.[12]

It would indeed. And if, added to that, there is as she speculates the balance of two elements within one's own mind, that seems to be another reason. Sexual apartheid really is not an option.

Part Three:
False Choices in Theory

6 Difference and equality

That man over there says that women need to be helped into carriages, and lifted over ditches, and to have the best place everywhere. Nobody ever helps me into carriages or over mud-puddles, or gives me any best place! And ain't I a woman? Look at me! Look at my arm! I have ploughed and planted, and gathered into barns, and no man could head me! And ain't I a woman? I could work as much and eat as much as a man – when I could get it – and bear the lash as well! And ain't I a woman? I have borne thirteen children, and seen most of them sold off into slavery, and when I cried out with my mother's grief, none but Jesus heard me! And ain't I a woman?

(Sojourner Truth. Former slave.)

1. Inequality

In 1975 the Equal Opportunities Commission began work in a blaze of publicity and a deluge of silly jokes. In *Sweet Freedom*, published in 1982, Anna Coote and Beatrix Campbell were to describe its record of achievement as 'abysmal'.

The duties of the Commission included the monitoring of the Sex Discrimination Act (1975) and the Equal Pay Act (1970) and the investigating of allegations of sex discrimination. It was supposed to be the instrument which would finally turn the dream of male and female equality into a reality, particularly in the world of work. For all but a handful of women the dream and the reality remain as far apart as ever.

Coote and Campbell report that between 1911 and 1971 women's share of the skilled manual jobs halved while their share of the unskilled manual jobs doubled, and that this is a continuing trend. They produce figures to show that the gap between average earnings of men and women has narrowed by only ten pence in so many years, so that the present average woman's wage is 63.6p for every pound earned by a man. And this when there are 10.4 million women in a total labour force of 26 million.

It may be that they are slightly exaggerating their case when they state: 'Far from making progress towards equality, they [women] have found it slipping away from them'.[1] But it cannot be denied that these and other comparisons are disappointing, to say the least, and a very long way off the ideal of equality in the labour market.

The Acts and the Commission itself were introduced presumably to try to improve the lot of women in general and in particular to secure for them equality in the workplace. This seems straightforward enough, but it is not.

It was no accident that improving the lot of women should be conceived as the attempt to secure for them equality with men. Men get a much greater share of the goodies on offer than women do. At the simplest level, in demanding equality with men, women are simply asking for their fair share of the goodies. But that is not the whole story. What angers Coote and Campbell so much is not just that women earn less than men, but that a society which offers them equal pay for equal work and then makes it impossible for them to do that equal work is making a mockery of the whole notion of true equality.

The ways in which society prevents women from competing equally with men are perceived differently by different interest groups. At one end of the spectrum is the straightforward cheating, which sometimes goes on in the workplace, of classifying the jobs traditionally done by women as less skilled than those done by men. In this area the Equal Opportunities Commission ought perhaps to be able to be more effective than it is. As we become better at assessing the relative complexities of various jobs this area of inequality is, in theory at least, removable. At the other end of the spectrum is the very deep inequality which Kate Millett describes, when women are expected to fit into the existing male-created and male-dominated institutions and traditions.[2] Removing this inequality would involve scrapping the whole lot and starting again from scratch. However attractive a proposition this may sound in theory, it is certainly unattainable in practice if it is seen as a one-off sweeping reform. Somewhere between these two extremes is the inequality which results from the fact that women first of all bear children and then are landed with almost the whole responsibility for bringing them up.

The most widely proposed solution to this problem is that we need to recognize, seek out and destroy the deep-rooted causes of this inequality. Women, it is argued, cannot compete equally with men outside the home until men accept that they too have a role inside it. While women bear the whole burden of domestic responsibility, their ability to achieve true equality with men is impaired from the outset. The answer is clear; men must mend their idle ways and learn to take the family responsibilities which they have for so long managed to escape. The problem, of course, is how women are going to make them do this. The *status quo* suits most men very well; there is no obvious reason why they should volunteer for the dish-washing and the nappy-changing when they have always been able to rely on others to do these things for them.

One answer is some version of women's withdrawal from traditional duties. This can range from full separatism to selective strikes. We have already said that separatism is not a real choice for most of the human race. Selective strikes sound much more hopeful. Unfortunately, as Aristophanes so wickedly displayed in his play *Lysistrata*, withdrawal of labour in those fields which might actually affect men badly enough to make them notice affects women too. There is little point in refusing to wash up when you and the children are likely to be the first to succumb to the effects of botulism, or withdrawing sexual co-operation when this may be one of the few enjoyable things left to you in an otherwise pretty dreary life. Moreover, provoking men from a position of relative weakness does not really sound like the most sensible procedure for achieving important goals.

At this point we may be tempted to throw up our hands in despair. Changing men's attitudes, even if it is a realistic project will, it seems, take generations to effect. It will involve careful upbringing of young males to behave in ways which would have been unthinkable for their fathers. Deep-seated attitudes, expectations and beliefs are not changed overnight. How long will it all take? Will the sons of the first generation of feminists be all that different from their sires? However long it takes, it will certainly be longer than most women would prefer to wait.

When things look hopeless, those with courage do what they can. Those women who, in spite of the difficulties, decided that things *must* be improved had to find somewhere to start.

2. Equal rights

In the United States the natural place to start was with the law. From the beginning of the women's movement it had been observed and understood that occasional laws demanding things like equal pay or the right of women to enter bars made hardly any difference to the way things are. The British tend to be much less confident than the Americans in the efficacy of using the law to change attitudes. One of the most frequently heard objections to our racial anti-discrimination legislation was that it would not make the white population love the black minority any better. Martin Luther King agreed, but welcomed any law which made it illegal for a white man to kick him off the pavement just the same. It does seem reasonable to suggest, as Aristotle did, that the first requirement for goodness is the acquisition of good habits.[3] We tend to believe that what we are accustomed to is also right, and although this is sometimes dangerous, it is in fact sometimes true.

What the reformers saw was the inequality of the rights and treatment of women in law. It was therefore quite predictable that they should conceive the struggle as the struggle for equality, particularly the struggle for equal rights.

The fourteenth amendment to the United States Constitution (1868) had in theory given all citizens of the United States equal protection under the law. It states: 'All persons born or naturalized in the United States ... are citizens of the United States and of the State wherein they reside. No state shall ... deny to any person within its jurisdiction the equal protection of the laws ...'. This amendment, which applies equally to all persons, was not, however, interpreted as giving protection to women as a class against sex discrimination at work or in law. The challenge came in 1971 when, in the case of Reed v. Reed, the Supreme Court found that an Idaho law which provided that, all else being equal, a male was to be preferred over a female to administrate a deceased's estate, was in violation of the fourteenth amendment. Immediately the floodgates were open, and in 1973 Congress passed the Equal Rights Amendment (ERA), which stated this principle clearly and unequivocally. Section 1 reads: 'Equality of Rights under the law shall not be denied or abridged by the United States or by any State on account of sex'.[4]

Commenting upon this, Hazel Greenberg writes: 'In view of the multitudinous differences among people, sex is too broad a classification. Sex-based laws are unjust and irrational because they use gender rather than ability or need to determine an individual's rights, responsibilities and benefits.'[5] The task was thus interpreted as the identification and reform of any laws which use sex as a basis for discrimination. It looks like a good idea, and while it is used to make it illegal to treat women as mental or moral half-wits, it is. But it rather soon runs into trouble. As a piece of rhetoric it is admirable, but it does not stand up well to analysis. To begin with, if sex is an intrinsically unjust classification in law, it cannot be so merely because it is too wide. There are many other laws which depend on equally broad distinctions, for example those which distinguish between children and adults. Yet we presume that no one is going to demand that children of three should be sued for criminal negligence or invited to stand for parliament. The second part of the argument is no better. It is either question-begging – sex-based laws are unjust because they are sex-based – or it depends upon a probably false and certainly unproven assumption that there is never any connexion between gender and capacities and needs. It was this assumption which led to the move to reformulate all laws in 'sex-neutral' language. But this too created problems.

The advocates of the use of 'sex-neutral' language in the formulation of laws really do mean it to be universal. That is, it must be used not only when legislating about property rights, for example, but also when legislating about maternity rights. Hazel Greenberg sees that this poses certain problems.

> ... judges are human beings, not robots. The way in which the courts will apply principles of sex equality in difficult cases in part depends upon the judges' own socialization and expectations about men and women, especially where biology is concerned. For example, the Court may be psychologically predisposed, as it has been in the past, to approve sex classifications related to pregnancy. The equal rights amendment's legislative history makes congressional intent to prohibit such discrimination apparent. Nonetheless, obtaining judicial acceptance to this proposition is likely to require persuasive and expert litigation.[6]

Well, yes, it is. We would hesitate before trying to convince even a liberated American judge that the reason he thought that pregnancy was sex-related was because of his lousy upbringing. This is beginning to look frivolous.

Myra Harmon had similar problems at the Senate Hearings on the ERA in 1970. Harmon, then President of the National Federation of Business and Professional Women's Clubs, was asked whether she was concerned about laws 'aimed directly at the attributes of women as distinct from males, such as laws providing maternity benefits' (question 26, Senator Bayh). Harmon replied: 'It seems to me that these are special aspects of our life and would require special laws. For instance the maternity laws are provided to help the existence of the human race and not [just women]'. So far, so good. But then she added: 'If a man could bear children he would be under the same law'.

Elizabeth Wolgast comments: 'These are "special aspects of our life" ... but not special aspects of women's lives. To bring them into the form of equal rights she [Harmon] makes them applicable to pregnant men as well. It is comical reasoning.'[7] It also provided the opportunity for persuasive advocates to turn the tables on women.

In 1974, in the celebrated case of Geduldig v. Aiello, the Supreme Court decided that the Californian disability insurance plan which provided benefits for virtually all disabilities except those connected with pregnancy and childbirth was not in breach of the fourteenth amendment. Mr Justice Stewart gave the opinion of the court:

> We cannot agree that the exclusion of this disability from coverage amounts to invidious discrimination under the equal protection clause. California does not discriminate with respect to the persons or groups which are eligible for disability insurance protection under the program. The classification challenged in this case relates to the asserted underinclusiveness of the set of risks that the State has selected to insure. . . . There is no evidence in the record that the selection of the risks insured by the program worked to discriminate against any definable group or class in terms of the aggregate risk protection derived by that group or class from the program. There is no risk from which men are protected and women are not. Likewise there is no risk from which women are protected and men are not.

A note was added, presumably in case anyone had difficulty in following the reasoning. It read: 'The program divides potential recipients into two groups – pregnant women and non-pregnant persons. While the first group is exclusively female, the second includes members of both sexes. The fiscal and actuarial benefits of the program thus accrue to members of both sexes.'

Thus there was no sex discrimination. Pregnant women were excluded because they were pregnant, not because they were women. It was the disability and not the person or the group which was excluded. It was Myra Harmon's reasoning turned upside down. Pregnant men would not be entitled to maternity benefits either. This, in Elizabeth Wolgast's phrase, is 'sly logic' indeed.

3. 'Different and worse' or just 'different'?

Theorists devoted to equality tend at present to admit the need to take account of sexual difference very reluctantly, if at all, and try to find a fence which will encircle this area of difference and keep it as small as possible. It is sometimes described as the field of 'mere biology', but this usually turns out to mean just reproduction. In the conclusion of their fascinating book *Woman and the Law* Cary and Peratis write:

> Differences among people can be enormous – differences in skills, intelligence, hopes, aspirations, physical abilities, size, strength, social and cultural background. Law often should and often does take account of these differences. The question is whether gender alone is a difference that law should take account of. Except in a very narrowly prescribed area – reproduction – we think that the answer is clearly no.[8]

The longer one contemplates these statements, the stranger they seem. To begin with, Cary and Peratis present us with a list of differences such as skills and strength which they claim are differences that the law ought to take into account, and one, gender, that it should not. Now gender certainly is a different difference from skills or strength. It is more of a difference. It cannot be lost or acquired, it cannot be improved upon, it is not quantitative. No amount of redistribution or hard training will remove the difference of gender. It is unlike any other difference, including that of race. As Elizabeth Wolgast points out, different races are, in theory at least, assimilable in future generations. But different genders are not. We are, as she says, a two-sexed species. That is the way it is. It seems oddly perverse then to claim that the one irreducible difference should be the one to be singled out to be steadfastly ignored by law.

This difference does not go away because we close our eyes. The real problem is surely to identify those areas where the difference really is relevant, and we must try to do this from as open-minded a position as we can achieve. We have already seen how starting from a total commitment to an equality principle can lead us into silly situations like talking about pregnant men. Such situations are best avoided if possible, and we have the best chance of avoiding them if we start where we are rather than where we think we ought to be. Cary and Peratis themselves see the need for this, and they concede an exception to their general thesis, that 'very narrowly prescribed area – reproduction'. But what exactly do they mean this area to cover? They do not tell us here, but from the main body of the book it seems that they mean only that area connected with pregnancy and childbirth. But is this actually as narrow an area as they think? Pregnancy and childbirth have causes and effects. It is not obvious that these should not be taken into account at all. Babies have a disconcerting habit of staying around after birth. Women cannot ignore the fact that they are the ones who become pregnant. Has the law nothing to say about women in relation to these facts? Of course it does, but the current thinking on both sides of the Atlantic is that it should not. That is, it should not have anything to say on these matters which is aimed specifically and openly at women.

We understand, of course, why those who are concerned with women's rights tend to favour equality arguments over an appeal to difference. For centuries men have used women's 'difference' as an excuse for treating them abominably. And it is worth noticing that the claim that men and women are different is usually taken to be a simple assertion about women. It is not. 'Difference' is a relational concept. If men and women are different, then it is just as true that men are different from women as it is that women are different from men. But if you constantly mean only the latter, then it is an easy slide into using 'difference' to indicate 'deviance'. This is precisely what has happened in the past. When people held a hierarchical view of the world which gave pride of place to the human male, then it was inevitable that anything that was different in any way from the human male was to be regarded as 'worse'. However, this is a view which no one who wished to be taken seriously would dare advance today. The reasoning has changed, even if the old attitudes and prejudices are an unconscionable time a-dying. And once the world is no longer seen in neat hierarchical terms, then the simple equation of difference and inferiority is no longer tenable. There really is no necessary connexion between them. It is particularly irritating when well-intentioned feminist thinkers persist in talking as if there were. Hazel Greenberg again:

> In constructing social law on the basis of natural law, man has made much of the difference between male and female. He has given this factual differentiation a value and, by so doing, has imposed a patriarchal definition of reality on society. This definition assigns moral, practical and psychological meanings to neutral biological differences. This has resulted in sexuality being the first and foremost classification of persons and in females being defined as unequal to men within that classification system.[9]

This sounds as if *any* meaning assigned to a biological difference indicated inferiority, and as if that was the only possible reason for assigning it. But there are plenty of biological differences – such as that between old and young, child and adult – where there is no inferiority, but very important 'moral, practical and psychological' consequences still follow from the distinction. And feminists, of all people, seem committed to treating the sex distinction as one of these real differences, since they lay stress on the special bond of sisterhood uniting women and excluding men. This difference is not 'neutral', in the sense of insignificant, to anybody. The idea that it ought to be is one of the endless confusions introduced by the parallel of race. Race is indeed a trivial classification, so distinctions are not usually based on it except for oppressive reasons. The word 'racism' therefore combines the two ideas of making a trivial distinction and using it tyrannically. (Even on its own ground this makes for confusion about 'reverse discrimination', which is supposed to be a non-tyrannical use.) But when we turn to other differences, which are not in themselves trivial, the first idea no longer applies at all, and the second accordingly loses its foothold. Significant distinctions have real consequences. It is not 'ageism' which dictates that we do not all go to school, or receive old age pensions. Neither is it 'sexism' which brings it about that women do not have prostate operations, or men maternity leave. Some differences are real.

4. Rape without difference

One area where this becomes apparent is in the proposed reforms
of the laws relating to rape. On both sides of the Atlantic women
are advocating the abolition of the existing laws and subsuming
the crime of rape under some general title such as 'criminal
sexual conduct' or 'sexual offences'. In Britain there have even
been suggestions to abolish it altogether and prosecute rapists
under the assault laws.

In America the proposed reforms are part of the attempt to
use sex-neutral language in legislation. We may be forgiven for
finding the suggestion that sex crimes such as rape should be
described in sex-neutral language somewhat amazing. The result
makes the model rape statute in Brown, Freedman, Katz and
Price read somewhat oddly. First Degree Criminal Sexual Conduct begins: 'A person is guilty of criminal sexual conduct in the
first degree if he or she engages in sexual penetration with
another person and if any of the following circumstances exists
...' followed by a list starting '(1) That person is under 13 years
of age'. Sexual penetration is defined as 'sexual intercourse,
cunnilingus, fellatio, anal intercourse, or any other intrusion
however slight, of any part of a person's body or of any object
into the genital or anal openings of another person's body, but
emission of semen is not required'[10]. Apart from creating problems for doctors who may wish to take a child's temperature per
rectum, the reference to semen ought to be quite unnecessary.
But, of course, it is not. And in the introduction Hazel Greenberg
writes: 'The sex neutralization of rape laws will not in and of
itself prevent a rape victim from being treated as if she herself
were the criminal.'[11] Sexist stuff this! Why does she assume that
rape victims are women? We know why. Because they are. And
no amount of sex-neutral language is going to disguise that fact.
Women can be abused sometimes in ways that men can be
abused (e.g. anal rape), sometimes in ways comparable with men
(e.g. enforced sterilization, infection) and also in this other separate and different way (vaginal rape).

In Britain, the move to reform the rape laws springs from a
different source. Here, as in America, women have become

increasingly angry at the way in which alleged rape victims are treated by the police and the courts. Sometimes this is clearly shocking. But it is this which needs changing. If subsuming rape under different laws would help to bring the change about, we would have no objection to such a proposal. Or, rather, our objections would be concerned with practical matters, such as having to decide whereabouts in a wide range of potential assaults rape would figure for sentencing purposes. But as things are, our objection to these suggestions rests on our refusal to concede that laws which prohibit vaginal rape are discriminatory because they rely on a totally irrelevant difference between men and women.

As long as men and women are biologically distinct, it is vitally important to women that they keep pointing out the areas where this matters rather than accepting the old equation of difference and inferiority and trying to minimize the differences.

Women need laws to protect them during pregnancy and childbirth, and they need laws to protect them against certain forms of violence too. The fact that, for both biological and social reasons, men are capable of inflicting quite specific forms of abuse on women and sometimes do so, needs to be recognized and confronted as an evil, not hidden and protected by 'sex-neutral' language. Calling wife-beating 'spouse assault' does indeed 'mask centuries of oppression of women and contribute to their further oppression by neutralizing the very word that describes the continued practice of wife-beating'.[12] Similarly, talking about the sexual abuse of children can divert our attention from the fact that this is 'overwhelmingly a crime of adult men against female children',[13] and the 'rhetoric of mutual parenthood ... masks which parent retains control'.[14]

It is the use of sex-neutral language in the formulation of certain laws which causes us concern. Has such language any role to play when we are contemplating the fairness or otherwise of existing or proposed legislation? As a psychological device for reminding ourselves about the deep-rooted prejudices which obscure our judgements so often, a mental reformulation of the law in terms of 'people' rather than 'women' may act as a salutary indicator of its fairness. Such an exercise would fulfil a role akin to that of John Rawls's concept of the 'original position' which is 'a purely hypothetical situation characterised so as to lead to a certain conception of justice'.[15] In this 'original position' 'no one knows his place in society, his class position or social status, nor does any one know his fortune in the distribution of assets and abilities, his intelligence, strength and the like. ... The principles of justice are chosen behind a veil of ignorance.'[16] Perhaps we could pose the question – suppose you were about to be born into this society not knowing whether you were to be male or female, how would society look to you then? Or – suppose you or your wife is going to give birth to your next child, but you do not know which, how does the law look now?

As a psychological device this may have some use, but it is an extremely limited one. We do not propose to enter the philosophical mire surrounding this hypothetical position. Suffice it to say that we have got a very strange notion of a person here. If such a reformulation can work coherently at all, it is an *aide mémoire*, not a description of how the world is, ever has been or ever will be. And it is certainly not a prescription for how it ought to be. In formulating those laws which relate to areas of our lives in which sex differences are relevant, it is unusable. In the end 'sex-neutral' language is a myth. 'People' refers to the members of our species, and the members of our species are sexed.

5. Equal treatment

What about those laws which already refer to 'people' rather than to 'men' or 'women'? Do they offer any guarantee of fair treatment for women?

In Britain, until very recently, a person who wished to claim unemployment benefit had first to register at the Job Centre, i.e. he or she had to be seen to be looking for work. In October 1982 this requirement was waived. Nevertheless, it remains a principle of claiming benefit that a person should be 'available for work'. Recently attention was drawn to the invidious position of women with small children who try to register as unemployed. They too must declare their availability for work. Unfortunately, if their pre-school children are not receiving full-time nursery education then they are often not able to make this declaration. But the provision of nursery places is so slight that many nurseries operate their admission systems on a priority need basis. And a woman who is not in employment is not a priority need. Here we have Catch 22 – no unemployment benefit unless she has got a nursery place for her child, no nursery place unless she has got, or is likely to get, a job. It looks unfair. But in what way is it unfair?

It does seem reasonable that a person of either sex should not be able to register as unemployed if as a matter of fact they are unwilling or unable to take up suitable employment if it is found. This rule is not group-based. It applies to everyone, regardless of sex, race, colour and creed. It is non-discriminatory in the sense that it treats everyone in the same way. Yet it clearly operates to the disadvantage of mothers of young children. Well, tough. That is equal treatment under the law. And that is what women want, or say they want.

Another area in which the same kind of problem arises concerns the use of official council transport by local councillors. There is a widespread rule that local councillors should use official transport for official business only. Recently, women councillors in London have unashamedly admitted to using official cars for collecting their children from school. They claim that if they are not allowed to do this then those who could not afford to pay someone to collect the children would, in effect, be barred from council work. Again, this looks right. But again, the rule is non-discriminatory. It applies to all councillors. And, certainly, it seems reasonable that councillors should not be allowed to entertain their friends at the races or take the family on weekend jaunts at the ratepayers' expense. So what is the problem? Equal treatment is what the women are receiving. They really cannot have it both ways.

Something is obviously going wrong with the arguments here. If the application of an equal treatment rule actually prevents an identifiable section of the community from finding work or playing a part in the life of the community, it is time to think again. The first thing that might occur to anyone is that although this might seem unfair, it actually is not. There is a rule which states that in order to hold a driving licence one must pass a minimal eyesight test. This discriminates against an identifiable group in the community, but it could hardly be argued that this was unfair. Not being able to see is a rather serious handicap if you are driving, and is a positive danger to other road users. So, by analogy, perhaps having small children really is a disqualification from earning your living or helping to run the community? Put like this, the 'Well, tough' response now looks silly. Whatever the most traditional of us may believe about a 'women's place', the connexion between having children and an inability to work is just not like the connexion between driving and the inability to see. And even if it were, the unfairness lies in the way in which it discriminates against those women who are not well-off enough to hire a nanny, which would enable them to prove their availability for work or allow them not to have to rush off from council meetings to collect the children. These women, it may be argued, are precisely the kind of women who are most needed in local government.

Trying to identify the nature of the injustice, some women have complained that the availability-for-work condition is not being fairly applied. It is pointed out that men are not asked about the provision for their children when signing on. This is a red herring. Suppose they were asked. Most men would simply say that that was the wife's business. The most that could be achieved by asking men the same question is that you would land one or two men in the same mess as the unfortunate women. It might produce a temporary warm glow of revenge, but in the end it would achieve nothing. Making things difficult for a tiny number of our brothers without in any way improving the situation of a significant number of our sisters is a perverse notion of equality.

Perhaps the real complaint is about the miserable lack of pre-school education. The signing-on problem would not arise were all children in full-time nursery education. That is true. But it begins to look dangerous when we remember the discontent of the Russian and Swedish women who have been in this supposedly happy situation. Many women who need to work might nevertheless feel that if they cannot find employment, then their time is best spent with their children. A woman who put her child into a full-time nursery and then spent the next five years unsuccessfully trying to find work might reasonably feel that she had the worst of all possible worlds. In any case, a complaint about pre-school education or the lack of it is a separate issue from the immediate concern for the present injustice.

What the women concerned with these cases are really saying is that in the circumstances as they now are – however unjust those circumstances may be or appear to be – equal treatment under these rules acts to their disadvantage, even though the rules themselves are not unjust, and that what they need here is special treatment because they have special difficulties. It is perfectly true that you cannot work an eight-hour factory shift unless there is someone to take care of the baby, and that you cannot accept such a job until you have found someone who will. It is therefore technically true that if you have young children to look after and no help, then you are not available for work. But, nevertheless, it seems right to suggest that not being available for work because of the children is quite unlike not being available for work because it would interfere with pub opening hours. Similarly, using an official car to enable you to do your job is not like using it to take your chums to Epsom.

It is worth digressing for a moment to remark that a society which does think that these things are significantly alike has got its priorities sadly wrong. For too long we have accepted arguments about the unfitness of women to do certain things because of their inconvenient propensity to mess up the work situation by producing children. We regard pregnancy as a disability, children as a problem to be solved, mothers as tiresome non-beings who should not need to eat, let alone think or aspire. This is not simply a male nor an old-fashioned feminist point of view. It is still rampant in current equal rights talk, where, in order to avoid having to make special provision for women, maternity benefits are subsumed under disability allowances and exemption from jury service because of child-care responsibilities is incorporated into a general hardship category. This really is to stand life on its head. It is work that should be accommodated to fit these inescapable facts of our lives, not the other way round. Women cannot wait, however, until we acquire a new set of attitudes. They are engaged in living now. And right now, asking for equal treatment in all situations is beginning to look like a bad bet.

6. Rights and needs

So far we have argued that men and women are biologically different and that the difference is and ought to be important – even in legislation – if women are to be treated fairly. We have also said that equal treatment under the law sometimes acts to the disadvantage of some women. What are we saying? That we do not always want equal treatment. This is beginning to sound subversive. Are we then saying that what we want is unequal treatment and unequal rights?

In her powerful book *Equality and the Rights of Women*, Elizabeth Wolgast confronts this question. She points out that equality is essentially a quantitative notion which implies a measure. If two things are unequal in some respect, then one has significantly more of whatever it is we are measuring than the other. Two people are equal in regard to some property if they have roughly the same amount of it. The old doctrines used 'humanness' as such a property. Men were the most human of beings, women and children less so and slaves hardly at all.

Women, on this formulation, were unequal with men because they had less of this desirable quality. Today we do not subscribe to this view. This is why it now makes less sense to talk about equality over basic rights.

Similarly, when we have a society in which the distribution of wealth is grossly distorted in favour of a small, privileged minority it is perfectly proper to talk in terms of the desire for greater equality. Yet even here, in what may seem to be a paradigmatic situation for talk of equality, we can run into difficulties. On a recent television programme[17] Peter Shore began his speech with a rousing appeal for equality and ended twenty minutes later with the claim that what he really wanted to see was 'rational, controlled inequality'. What he was displaying is that equality works very well in those situations where things are very disparate, but begins to collapse as a simple principle when the grave inequality has been remedied. Then, even when we are talking about something as manifestly quantitative as money, we need to introduce new notions such as need and desert to take over where equality runs out.

There are other situations, however, where equality cannot get off the ground at all. When there is no common object between two groups for the application to be possible, then equality is a non-starter. Can a cat and a rose bush be equal? It would take an enormous amount of ingenuity to construct a situation in which such a question could have any real application. We would have to search for some common attribute which would enable equality talk to begin. It is no good saying that as far as being a good mouser is concerned, the cat wins paws down, and that therefore the rose bush is an unequal mouser. The rose bush is not a mouser at all, equal or unequal.

Talking about equality in relation to men and women poses special difficulties. In so far as they really are alike, then equality talk is possible and sometimes very helpful. In so far as they really are different, then it is neither.

In matters relating to pregnancy and childbirth equality talk cannot begin at all. Commenting on the case of Geduldig v. Aiello cited previously, Elizabeth Wolgast writes:

A medical insurance program needs to cover some disabilities which pertain to both sexes and some which pertain to only one sex. For example the California program covers prostatectomies and other difficulties pertaining only to men. To say as the Court did that women have the same right to this benefit as men puts 'equal rights' in a useless role. How does a woman have this right? Is it potentially hers in the event she should become a man? ... Better to say that men have some rights not applicable to women. This lays the ground for arguing that women should have some rights not applicable to men.[18]

Apart from a preference not to refer to pregnancy as a disability, we agree entirely. Apart from anything else, this looks like good psychology. Talking about pregnant persons is not as a matter of fact going to convince the man on the Clapham omnibus that he has equal rights to maternity benefits. It is more likely to make him wonder if women who talk like this have taken leave of their senses. Elizabeth Wolgast sees that the trouble lies at least in part in our curious desire to treat our two-sexed species as if it were only one-sexed. Both those who would have women competing with men in a male-dominated world and those who would have us tear down all our institutions and begin again would also have it that, with a little effort and goodwill all round, we could end up not noticing the difference between men and women. This is a view which is both false and unattractive. Much more, we all need to learn when the differences are relevant and when they are not. When they are, we should forget talk of equality and concentrate instead on appealing for fair treatment. We can base such arguments on the fact that the species is two-sexed and that there is no reason to ignore the pressing needs of either sex. That looks fair.

7. Theory and practice

So far we have concentrated on the need for appropriate treatment for women in matters relating to pregnancy and childbirth, and we have argued that the fairness or unfairness of such treatment cannot be decided under the banner of equal rights where this is interpreted as the right to equal treatment. The equal right which women need to claim is the right to have their particular needs attended to, and among these are needs connected with their reproductive role.

But biological truths are not the only truths. As the examples of the jobless mothers and local councillors show, the demand for equal treatment can adversely affect women beyond the child-bearing stage. It is a fact that, in our society, it is women who undertake the lion's share of child-rearing and care and the major part of general domestic management. Regardless of whether this stems from biological or social causes, or from a mixture of the two, it now happens, and while it does fair treatment for women must take account of the fact. This has two aspects. First, it means that women and men have different needs in more areas of their lives than the purely reproductive, and second, given the nature of these other tasks which women commonly perform, it means that we cannot readily compartmentalize women's lives into areas where equal treatment is appropriate and where it is not. Being 'responsible' for a child is not an action which is performed outside office hours only.

The traditional response to the recognition of the 'differentness' of most women's lives for at least part of the time has been to tell them that if they cannot stand the heat they should go back to the kitchen. The counter-response has been for women to sweat it out. And while equality is the main goal, then sweating it out is the only alternative. But once we escape from this ideal it becomes possible to demand treatment which looks positively advantageous in the world of work (like using the council's car to collect the children) to counterbalance the disadvantage of being the one who has to collect them in the first place. It enables us to make *more* radical demands than any that could be justified under an equal rights heading, without involving us in silly claims about the 'superiority' of either sex.

The Russians are beginning to learn this lesson. The Constitution of the Union of Soviet Socialist Republics (1936) included the following:

Article 122
Women in the USSR are accorded equal rights with men in all spheres of economic, government, cultural, political and other public activity. The possibility of exercising these rights is ensured by women being accorded an equal right with men to work, payment for work, rest and leisure, social insurance and education, and by state protection of the interests of mother and child, state aid to mothers of large families and unmarried mothers, maternity leave with full pay, and the provision of a wide network of maternity homes, nurseries and kindergartens.

The relevant article in the 1977 Constitution makes significant alterations:

Article 35
Women and men have equal rights in the USSR. Exercise of these rights is ensured by according women and men equal access to education and vocational and professional training, equal opportunities in employment, remuneration, and promotion, and in social and political, and cultural activity, and by special labour and health protection measures for women; by providing conditions enabling mothers to work; by legal protection, and material and moral support for mothers and children, including paid leaves and other benefits for expectant mothers and mothers, and gradual reduction of working time for mothers with small children.

This interpretation of equality, with its explicit reference to 'special' measures for women, is a response to the disastrous effects of the simple 'equal treatment' interpretation; disastrous for the state, the family and not least for women themselves. It is a far cry from Engels's conception of real social equality between men and women, which simply required the introduction of 'the entire female sex into public industry',[19] or, as Alexandra Kollontay saw it, 'a union of two equal members of the communist society, both of them free, both of them independent, both of them workers'.[20]

The matter then seemed a simple one. The main need was to get rid of domesticity and treat women like men. The only real difficulty was child-care, and this would be handed over to the community. When, however, the time came to put revolutionary principles into action, other problems and disagreements emerged. 'In the days of the civil war, such views were cited to justify promiscuity, free love and the *"nationalization of women"; for example, in Vladimir a decree was passed making every virgin over 18 years State property.'*[21] (Italics ours.) These measures, it should be noted, were not conceived as a product of the old casual, unthinking, patriarchal tradition which we have noticed as predominant in European thought, but as a piece of red-hot, brand-new enlightened egalitarianism. The extraordinary difficulty which people find in *thinking* about the position of women emerges once again. Naturally, such aberrations did not last. But official Soviet thought and practice has taken a long time to register that Engels's simple insight was not enough, and to revise its principles.

Whether or not this new interpretation can be made to work in the Soviet Union remains to be seen. What is clear is that the old one did not. But the old one was based on bad theory as well as subjected to bad practice – Russian men continued to leave all domestic duties to their wives – while the new version has the merit of recognizing the different needs of women at some stages and trying to accommodate them rather than denying that they exist. Similarly, in Western societies we need to escape from the outworn ideas of the Industrial Revolution.

We have already pointed out (in Chapter 2) how existing models of work suit women's needs very badly. The difference in pay and privileges between full- and part-time work is of crucial importance to many women, and it is one which need not exist. In 1979 the British voted against a European Commission recommendation that the distinction should simply be abolished, though many other countries saw no difficulty in the proposal. Its abolition could have some very beneficial results. For example, it is part-time work which is largely paid on a production-related basis. The discrepancy between full- and part-time rates of pay is often much greater than is realized. Abolishing the distinction would lead to paying for hours worked pro rata, which in many cases would improve considerably the pay which women obliged to work for fewer hours could command. It would also mean that those hours could be increased gradually as other commitments lessened. Such a measure would reflect much more accurately the actual situations in which women are placed, instead of facing them with the fearful all-or-nothing choice of the present system.

Maternity grants and benefits are in dire need of restructuring. To be of any real use to most people, the level of the maternity grant should be related directly to the cost of basic necessities such as cot and pram, and should be adjusted as often as price changes dictate. This could be done quite simply by fixing the grant as a percentage of the cost of standard items. But it is in the area of maternity benefits that radical new thinking needs to take place. Our present social system ties all but the most basic allowances and benefits to the amount of contributions paid by the potential recipient. In some instances this is not unjust or unrealistic, but in the case of many women who are starting a family it is. For many, those who are young, or who have been obliged to leave their employment to follow their husbands' careers, or who are having second or subsequent children, the contributory conditions for benefit are not possible to meet. Those who benefit most are often those who need help least. We do not have to be paid-up members of the Communist Party to feel uneasy about this.

Perhaps the single most significant piece of legislation which could be enacted to reflect the needs of many women is the introduction of the Infant Child Benefit proposed by Elizabeth Young in her SDP booklet *Men and Women: Equal but not Interchangeable*. Elizabeth Young proposes a massive increase in child benefit for infants up to the age of five. This would be paid to women in the same way as the present child allowance. Its main purpose is to make life easier for women who wish to remain at home and look after their small children. But, just as important, 'It would also signify that the community has at last become aware that mothers (and sometimes fathers) looking after small children are working . . .'.[22]

Another extremely effective move would be to give official recognition to the years spent looking after children as work experience. This may sound eccentric until we remember that it has been done before – for men, of course. Post-war Britain recognized the service years as relevant to the work experience of ex-servicemen for very good reasons. If it had not, many of those performing an essential service to the community would have had their long-term interest severely damaged by having those years simply written off. It enabled men to enter jobs at levels which their actual experience would not have justified. In many of the jobs in which women are concentrated the child-rearing years actually *are* relevant experience; in teaching, social work, nursing, jobs requiring domestic skills and, more directly than is sometimes realized, in middle management too. But even where it is not directly relevant, it is not obviously less work experience than being the company cook or a prisoner of war. In both cases, the work which causes the interruption is of real national importance.

No doubt in both there are problems about how best to recognize and reward this. People who have remained in a profession – including of course childless people – have their rights too. It would be unrealistic to suggest returners should have automatic seniority suitable to their age; this would often just make it impossible to employ them. But in any case such automatic age-based seniority is a bad principle for employment. It might be best if returners of both sexes, and also people moving into one kind of job from another, normally served a few years' probation in a grade lower than their age would suggest, sometimes in part-time work. But after that they should be allowed to catch up. And their first application for any post should not be viewed with suspicion simply because of their age. (It sometimes seems as if to be thirty-seven – or even twenty-nine – when one is expected to be twenty-seven is the most disastrous kind of disqualification possible, which cannot really be very sensible.) In any profession, continuous service can have bad

effects as well as good ones; the untypical experience can sometimes have surprising value. The more the world changes, and
jobs change, the more noticeable this effect is likely to be. People
of both sexes need to be able to move from one kind of work to
another with reasonable ease, instead of holding onto jobs which
have become useless, like feudal landlords, because they cannot
imagine making a living any other way. The rethinking which
would obviously be a lifeline for women here may really be the
only salvation for men as well.

Before men start to protest that they have worked longer
hours on the shop-floor to secure the same rights, let us remind
them that the solution in terms of equality really is up to them.
When they honestly do start taking on an equal share of domestic
responsibilities, women will be much more ready to discuss real
equality at work – perhaps a shorter working week for all.
Meanwhile, they look for the same rights, not for less work, but
for less of what men call work. The aim is not equality at every
level, but overall justice.

Tackling the problem in this way is probably the best way of
beginning to change men's attitudes to their homes and families.
If they see that women are able to combine paid work and
domestic life in ways that do not seriously impair their health or
long-term prosperity, perhaps they too will be prepared to try it.
If they do, so much the better for all of us.

8. Towards a broad principle of equity

The one thing that no one seriously disputes is that men and
women are both human. Most people believe that all human
beings, whatever their life-styles, are entitled to strive for the
happy life on earth. Those who live and die wretchedly ought to
concern us all; it should not be so. In our society we are becoming
increasingly aware of and indignant at the gross inequality between the affluent, industrial West and the grinding poverty of
the Third World. Our indignation is not just at the lack of

material wealth of those countries; were we all as poor we should not even notice it. Further, we often admire those who can live fulfilling lives without it. Mainly what offends us is the lack of what we call 'the quality of life' of their inhabitants in comparison with ours. It is not that we want to set up a foundation to supply Kalahari bushmen with televisions and deodorants, but that we do feel, however ineffectually, that we all ought to be able in the end to look back on a life that was in some sense worth living.

Where people are separated by distance, culture, tradition and preferences, straight comparisons about the quality of their lives are often very difficult to make. But where they live in close proximity, with shared life-styles, one of the things which invariably diminishes their happiness is the realization that they are eternally and radically worse-off in the things they value than their neighbours. This is not petty envy which resents any stroke of good fortune which befalls another. It is the perfectly understandable feeling that we all have a right to pursue happiness, albeit within limits, and a system which makes this a non-starter for any group of individuals is basically unjust.

The idea that we can, for some purposes, consider people's lives over a long stretch of time in order to decide upon the fairness of their treatment is not a new one. Men use it in quite specific contexts. For example, one of the arguments frequently used to justify the relatively large salaries paid to doctors is that their long training results in ten years' loss of earnings compared with their contemporaries who leave school at sixteen. For good measure, they point out facts like that the residential hospital requirements keep them out of the house-buying market for even longer than this, and that, therefore, their much higher salaries are required to give them parity over a long stretch of time. We make no comment on this except to note that the argument depends upon our looking at things in the long run rather than at a particular, isolated moment in time. This seems like a perfectly reasonable thing to do. And it is what we suggest as a broad principle of equity – fairness – rather than precise equality. Here too we can consider people's lives as a whole. We can begin to think in terms of a loose general principle that at the end of the day, whenever that is, we should be able to look back on our lives and say that no one group in our society was systematically and radically worse-off in those things which it values than any other. Of course, this hardly amounts to a neat philosophical theory of equality, which is probably not available. But it enables us to look at important issues from outside the sectarian position from which they are so often viewed, so that they can be assessed, as they actually occur, in relation to other parts of our lives.

This principle and its consequences are reminiscent of the definition of happiness supplied by that most gentle and honest liberal, John Stuart Mill:

> The happiness which they [certain philosophers] meant was not a life of rapture; but moments of such, in an existence made up of a few and transitory pains, many and varied pleasures, with a decided preponderance of the active over the passive, and having as the foundation of the whole, not to expect more from life than it is capable of bestowing. A life thus composed, to those who have been fortunate enough to obtain it, has always appeared worthy of the name of happiness.[23]

This broad definition leaves an enormous amount of scope for individual preferences and priorities. It does not permit a judgement about the happiness of one's life to be made by considering a single isolated incident.

Similarly our broad principle of equity does not demand that at every moment in our lives we should be receiving the same treatment or be in the same position as everybody else. It allows for the inescapable reality that there will be times in all our lives when, for various reasons, we will be worse-off than others. But it also requires that this inequality should not be systematic or permanent.

The search for blow-for-blow equality is almost always self-defeating. It is also no way to conduct our lives. It demands that groups compete with each other and rests on a self-interest ethic which is actually adapted to promote inequalities. The gruesome annual spectator sport of the pay-round is an example. Equality becomes an end in itself rather than a means to happiness.

9. Swings and roundabouts

This general principle of equity provides us with a very rough framework in which we can, for example, talk about things like relative job satisfaction and security and status as well as about money. It can help us to offset a deficit of one against a surfeit of the other. Again, this is very general, and it must operate within limits. Everyone needs a certain amount of all these things to provide the conditions under which a satisfying life is obtainable. What people want as well as what they get is important.

Yet again we must use this argument carefully and fairly. It is certainly open to abuse. It has been used in the most damaging way to justify denying women justice in the market-place. After all, they chose to have children, they are happy looking after them, why then should they want financial independence as well? We do not want to claim that no women enjoy looking after the children, or that they never derive any satisfaction from being competent home-makers. And it may be inevitable that while they are engaged in these occupations their financial position will be less good than it might otherwise have been. What we do want to insist on is that once these functions, which are finite, are complete, a woman should not find herself in a situation where her financial position can never improve and where she no longer has any compensation for its relative poorness.

Bringing up children can be immensely entertaining and rewarding, and a good reason for doing without certain other things at the time. But it is hardly adequate compensation for being condemned to a subsequent forty years of impoverished boredom. The broad principle of equity would accept the child-rearing years as ones of relative inequality, but then demand that action was taken to enable women to return to the non-domestic world of work on more equitable terms than they can at present. A suggestion has recently been made that the relative financial inequalities during the child-caring period could be eliminated at the outset by demanding pay for housework. It sounds like a good idea until we realize that employees can be fired and inspected and tested and graded. Most women would probably not appreciate being put in that situation.

Working within this principle would widen their options in a genuine way. A woman who knows that her move back from home to office or factory or whatever is going to be made easier when she is ready to make it, and that the years she spends at home are not going to affect her pension rights at retirement, has a much better chance of making a real choice about her preferences than she can in the all-or-nothing situation in which she is so often placed today. In many other areas of our lives we operate very happily with this swings-and-roundabouts mentality. We teach it to our children. They have to learn quite early on in life that they cannot always have the same as everybody else. But within a non-competing, trusting family structure they also learn that their turn will come. In politics this is where things get difficult. The attitude we are advocating does depend on a certain amount of trust in government, which is justifiably lacking at the moment. Jam tomorrow is not much help unless you have bread today and know that the jam will actually materialize. The issues here are frighteningly large and beyond the scope of this book. They involve changing the image of government and opposition from the protagonists in a day-to-day battle to the acceptable champions of the common good. How that can be achieved while preserving the democratic rights of argument and disagreement is a problem for the practical politician.

Extending genuine options within the principle of equity in the long run would benefit women particularly. Their needs and preferences change more frequently and more identifiably than men's do. But it could work well for men too. For example, the financial, social and personal problems encountered by many men at retirement are only just beginning to be recognized and met in any way by educational institutions and social services. They include a host of minor aids, from retirement courses to the provision of school dinners for pensioners. It must indeed be a strange feeling to wake up one morning and find you are not Joe Bloggs, factory foreman or family doctor, but Joe Bloggs, OAP. It is the kind of shock felt by women not only upon retirement, but at marriage and childbirth as well.

Suppose that instead of this 'today you work, tomorrow you don't' mentality we started to think more seriously about phasing people in and out of work wherever this was a sensible possibility. Many men, at sixty, might be quite glad to reduce their income gradually and trade the difference for increased leisure time, provided that their long-term interests such as pension rights were not damaged. The young, too, would frequently welcome a more gradual introduction into the workforce. They could also benefit from having more time for study and leisure between the ages of sixteen and twenty-one. It might even be possible to dovetail these to the benefit of all. In many jobs a man approaching retirement could phase himself out of work while phasing in a youngster. Not only would this suit their relative needs better than the present model, but it would also be a nice way to live. The older man could see himself not as a worn-out relic of his former self just waiting for it all to be over, but as a teacher, mentor and friend with a new positive value in society. The youngster would acquire new knowledge in a natural and personal way and have the opportunity to become acclimatized to the realities of adult life. None of these suggestions should be made mandatory, but there really is no good reason why we should not make such options available to those who want them.[24]

We believe that it is by thinking along these sorts of lines, asking for flexibility and overall fairness rather than for blow-for-blow equality, that women will make the most progress in rooting out the deep injustices which today still prevent so many of them from living satisfying and fulfilling lives. They have as much right as anybody else to pursue happiness and to expect that those in power will be even-handed in providing them with the opportunities to do so.

7 Biology, mere and otherwise

> 'She's a rum 'un, is Natur ... Natur', said Mr Squeers solemnly, 'is more easier conceived than described.'
>
> (Dickens, *Nicholas Nickleby*)

1. What sort of difference?

Is the difference between men and women natural, or is it produced by culture? Here is another false antithesis. In other fields today this one is usually nailed as false quite quickly, being unkindly referred to as 'the old nature-nurture controversy'. In most contexts, people now see that any aspect of human affairs can in principle have some biological sources in the genetic constitution of the species, and also some in recent culture and history. The two sets do not compete. The job of working out their details and relative importance is done by empirical enquiry, not by dying on the barricades.

Many feminists, however, still tend to resist this open-minded approach strongly. In the early stages of the movement they often dismissed any suggestion of natural sex differences as not only mistaken but wicked. Thus Kate Millett, complaining of 'the threadbare tactic of justifying social and temperamental differences by biological ones', writes: 'The sexes are inherently in everything alike, save reproductive systems, secondary sexual characteristics, orgasmic capacity, and genetic and morphological structure. Perhaps the only things they can uniquely exchange are semen and transudate.'[1] The extraordinary assumption that everything physical (the whole 'genetic and morphological structure') could be different and yet everything mental could remain the same was rather widespread at that time among social scientists. Although every cell in our bodies is sexed, and although there are marked sex differences in the structure of the brain and working of the nervous system, the human spirit was treated as a separate entity, somehow immune to such gross influences. This attitude, which is luckily less common now, will be our business shortly. We must notice first, however, that Kate Millett's position cannot stand in any case because it is inconsistent with some ideas central to feminism itself.

In itself, it is understandable as a reaction to confused male theorists, who have repeatedly justified local customs in this area which were just crude devices to protect masculine interests, or which were plain foolish, as laws fixed by unalterable dictates of nature. If what we want is merely to find food for satire and indignation, shooting them down can keep us occupied for a long time. But we do not only want that. Moreover, feminists need to be careful about shooting in this direction, since they may hit their own windows.

The assumption of natural causes is such a deep-rooted one that even those who officially disown it often find that they are using it. There are two prominent feminist concepts which seem to depend on that assumption. One is the idea of the natural superiority of women, either in general or in certain special respects. (It will be remembered that the strict, exclusive definition of feminism, to which Janet Radcliffe Richards referred, included belief in 'the inherent equality of the sexes *or the superiority of the female*'.[2] (Italics ours.) These two alternatives may look alike to the casual eye, but they call for opposite views on innateness.) The other is *sisterhood*, considered – as it usually seems to be – not just as an external community in misfortune, but as a natural bond of sympathy, resting on intrinsic likeness.

Neither of these ideas makes sense without the assumption of distinct, innate dispositions in the two sexes. We shall see that there is in fact nothing alarming in this suggestion. Innate difference does not have to be inferiority; it is just difference. And as we have already seen, people do not need to be standard, indistinguishable units like frozen peas, 'in everything alike', in order to be political equals. They need just enough minimal likeness to make them members of the community. We shall lose nothing by jettisoning the dogma that the two sexes have to be inherently indistinguishable. And if we want to retain the use of these two feminist concepts, we must jettison it. The use and standing of these concepts remains to be discussed. They are mentioned here just to point out that the question of natural difference is not a simple one, settled at once by reference to what is politically edifying. There are, too, some influential feminists, such as Elaine Morgan,[3] for whom biological considerations are central.

The issue is in any case a bit too serious for dogmatic bickering. We need the truth. In examining current attitudes to the sex difference and working to humanize them, we need the fullest understanding we can get of its real sources. To rule out the possibility of genetic ones in advance, simply because that area has been put to bad use in the past, is arbitrary. If there are such sources, even minor ones, we need to know about them. There is no substitute for this open-minded temper. Questions of fact cannot be settled in the lump on political grounds. If certain facts are dangerous, the remedy is, as usual, not suppression but more facts.

2. The fear of fatalism
All this may in general be admitted. But there is a special difficulty which apparently stops people from even considering propositions about human nature as candidates for belief. This is the suspicion of fatalism, usually described now as 'biological determinism' or 'genetic determinism'. People feel that, if our conduct had any genetically determined causes, we would be condemned to the status of automata, doomed to stick helplessly in our grooves. Must we not therefore believe instead only in social causes, so as to give ourselves the option of initiating change?

It is a very mysterious point about this way of thinking that it treats social causes as so much less compelling than genetic ones. As is often remarked, we are all 'conditioned by our culture'. This belief, however, is not thought to turn us into automata.

Yet the account of social conditioning can be built up, quite as easily as that of physical causes, in such a way as to make us seem like robots. And it has the extra disadvantage that it makes social change seem impossible. Since, however, we know that social change continually takes place, there must be something wrong with this notion of conditioning – which is, indeed, a very crude one. Human beings are not lumps of putty, passively accepting a mould, but active creatures with their own individual natures, able to select among the suggestions which they get, and to transform customs, gradually and cumulatively, by their distinctive responses. It is our individual natures, and the use we make of them, which save us from the tyranny of culture.[4]

There is no fatalism here. Fatalism is the belief that there are, not just causes, but overwhelming and unmanageable causes, opposing and dooming the enterprises that we value. In fact, originally fatalism is the belief in unbeatable hostile beings who are bound to get us whatever we do, as in the story of Oedipus. This is something quite different from determinism, which is just the modest assumption that events in the world may be expected to be regular. This assumption is needed for everyday science, though apparently not for the study of quantum mechanics. It need not rest on private information from heaven that events actually *are* regular. It is simply a convenient assumption, made for the sake of getting on with enquiry. Deterministic calculations can indeed sometimes be depressing, because they point out awkward facts about the world which we would have wished otherwise – such as that we are probably not going to be able to invent anti-gravity, so that weights will go on being heavy to lift. But we need to know these things. And just as often they point out welcome facts, such as the reliable good qualities of the plants and animals on which we depend. And in our observations of human conduct we depend on this calculation for our general expectations of good and evil alike. Human conduct is not random and unpredictable.[5]

No doubt there are problems about explaining the relation of these predictions to free will. But they are problems about description, not about the facts. Human choice is a matter of common experience, not a hazardous theoretical speculation. Both in ourselves and others, we are all familiar with the difference between normal, relatively free decision and decision driven by such things as threats and illicit influence from without, or by obsessions and diseases and neurotic compulsions from within. It is the latter which approximate us to automata. People do not, for instance, feel driven, automaton-like, by the talents and natural emotions which make up their inheritance. We do not think of a genius as a helpless automaton driven by a specially powerful motor. Yet genius certainly is thought of as a gift, as a piece of rather sublime luck for which the owner should be thankful, not as a pure achievement of the will. The same is true, on a more modest scale, of the gifts belonging to the rest of us. This idea of inherited gifts is not, and ought not to be, frightening. And it does not become so merely because scientists can discover a good deal about the working of our brains.

Biology is an enquiry, not a sinister force. All academic disciplines are tools, not empires. It is strangely common now for people to speak of being 'threatened by their biology' and the like. Thus Shulamith Firestone writes that 'women throughout history before birth control were at the continual mercy of their biology';[6] and that the substitution of *in vitro* pregnancy for current methods would 'free women from their biology'. [7] What this complaint really seems to express is a horror of the body – especially, of course, of childbirth – as a threat to the free mind and soul. We will discuss this idea shortly. But it clearly cannot be properly expressed in this way.

The impression that biology, and physical science in general, constitutes a threat seems to be a response to a certain kind of illicit scientific reductionism which brings out with an air of triumph, as if exposing a fraudulent medium, the claim that we are 'nothing but' certain scientific entities. About the physical basis of thought and feeling, this is usually done by claiming that the physical phenomena – secretions and the like – which accompany our experiences are their only real causes, and concluding that people are therefore really only the pawns or playthings of their secretions. The reducer's point is to exclude souls, vital force and other extras from the scientific scene, and this he is quite entitled to do. But to suggest that this shows ordinary experience to be unreal is sheer meaningless melodrama. Certainly we think and feel by means of our brains and nervous systems. If they fail us, our thought falters. But that is true of our hearts and livers as well, and is part of our general dependence on the physical world.

As whole beings, we think with our brains just as we jump with our legs. But to understand what we are doing requires much more than the physical sciences; it calls for a grasp of our purposes and the facts in the world to which they relate, all of which are perfectly real – indeed, their reality is far less problematical than that of, say, the basic entities of physics. The neurological explanation cannot therefore be the only one – or in some sense the only 'real' one – and the reduction fails. So, and more resoundingly, does the still odder and more recent sociobiological one, which says that all we are really doing is maximizing the spread of our genes ('the organism is only DNA's way of making more DNA').[8] This is not biology, it is rhetoric.

What is needed in order to prevent causes from looking like fates is a full recognition of their complexity. This will show the presence of genetic causes to be inoffensive in both the areas where it impinges on left-wing thought generally and feminism in particular. The first of these areas concerns capacity, the second, motivation.

3. Capacity and competition

Of these, capacity is the one which has been better ventilated and is now probably the easier to handle. That we do have inherited capacities – different from those of other species, and different again for each individual – is something which it makes little sense to deny, and which has no sinister consequences. What has made it seem dangerous is the insistence of theorists

on forcing these capacities into a ranking order by means of
concepts like IQ. The trouble with this is not really anything to
do with inheritance. Ranking people would be just as objectionable if their capacities really were, by some miracle, formed
during their childhood. It is still too late for them to do anything
about it. The trouble lies in our age's obsession with the race-
course model, the classic examiner's dream of a one-way scale
running from best to worst:

> The world and eke the world's content
>   And all therein that passes,
> With marks numerical (per cent)
>   He did dispose in classes;
>
> He did his estimate express
>   In terms precise and weighty,
> And vice got 25 (or less),
>   While virtue rose to 80.[9]

The crazy competitiveness of the modern world continually
distracts us with this way of thinking. In every area of life, down
to the most manifestly unsuitable, we fuss about ranking order
– about record-breaking, about exams and literary prizes, mu-
sical competitions, primacy in exploration, audience-ratings and
the accumulation of university degrees. The Greeks were obsessed enough with their Games, but we are far worse. The
worship of IQs is only one aspect of this strange obsession, and
the insistence that IQs are not hereditary does very little to make
it less sinister. It needs to be plainly said that people's general
capacities cannot be measured in this way. Measurement, by its
nature, always measures a special, limited capacity relative to
something already taken as a goal. But to consider people's
capacities in general is to wonder, much more widely, what
kinds of things each of them can or cannot do. This can call on
us to recognize things as achievements, as strengths, even as
aims, which we had not thought of as such before. It can alter
our whole idea of what an achievement is. It is in this sort of
spirit that we need to ask, with an open mind, whether there are

in fact, as has often been supposed, differences in capacity between men and women.

4. Yin, yang and others

Are there then any systematic differences, any specializations here? Let us look first at the tradition. It has been very widely believed that there are, and that they are profoundly, perhaps metaphysically, important. Many peoples believe that creation arises from a mystical marriage between male and female elements, often between heaven and earth, and still expresses a combination of these two natures. The Chinese notion of 'yin' and 'yang', and the Aristotelian one of form and matter,[10] are just two of many more sophisticated versions of this thinking. It has deep roots, and would not be easy to get rid of. These ideas have practical consequences, which are reflected back onto everyday life. They have also been drawn from that life in the first place. We need to look at their possible meanings.

They posit a sexual specialization which can look more or less alarming according to how you treat it. It can be formulated in a sweeping way which draws a firm line between the whole faculty of thought (male) and the faculty of feeling (female); or it can appear in a less drastic version which deals only with specialization within thought itself, and holds that men reason logically and articulately, while women use intuition – that is, they reach the same cognitive goals by different and more mysterious means. These are very different ideas, and need to be looked at separately.

We had better look first at the more sweeping yin/yang or reason/emotion kind of formula. Its symbolic and religious uses do not concern us now. At a very abstract level, it may have a real point. But we want to know what it says about actual men and women, and what consequences for them flow from accepting it. And here there is an obvious danger. Unless the interdependence of these elements is strongly stressed we will be landed with a sharp division of labour, in which women are not expected to think, nor men to feel. And though this sort of specialization cannot possibly be kept up in actual life, it does seem to have operated as a background ideal in our culture, and caused a mass of confusions.

Its clearest expression in modern times may have been that of Otto Weininger, the brilliant young Austrian follower of Schopenhauer, whose psychology influenced Freud. Weininger's MW theory posited two basic elements in every human being, never found in isolation but existing everywhere as polar extremes.[11] Of these, the M factor was responsible for everything positive, active and intellectual, while the W stood simply for emotion. Absolute W, if she existed, would be wholly unconscious. She has no cognitive element at all. (Weininger unfortunately shot himself when he found that his reasoning proved him to be homosexual, so he never explained his ideas further.)

The trouble about this kind of thing is that it rules out, *a priori*, any possibility of noticing the distinctive forms of female life and character. This is what made it so easy for Freud to give his account of women as a kind of shadowy, defective non-man, forever haunted by penis envy. Emotion on its own figures here as a kind of elemental force, a head of steam or water-power, which needs specifically male thinking before it can be translated into any kind of action. The formulation differs from the old Aristotelian one where emotion, equally with women, is treated as passive. Weininger seems to see both rather as the energy-source of all activity. He thus expresses, more directly than the older formulas, the terror of woman as a strange, uncontrollable force. But he calms this anxiety by keeping the idea that she is essentially formless and indeterminate. Until programmed by some male instructions, the whirlwind will not, it seems, know what to do.

5. Phantoms, angels, vampires and millstones

This is evidently a consoling thought, and no doubt it had a lot to do with the power and success of this idea of non-cognitive woman, which of course dates back in a less explicit form long before Weininger, and is quite an important element in the Romantic Revival.

> She was a Phantom of delight
> When first she gleamed upon my sight;
> A lovely Apparition, sent
> To be a moment's ornament ...
> I saw her, on a nearer view,
> A Spirit, yet a woman too,
> Her household motions light and free,
> And steps of virgin liberty; ...
> A creature not too bright and good
> For human nature's daily food;
> For transient sorrows, simple wiles,
> Praise, blame, love, kisses, tears and smiles ...
> A perfect woman, nobly planned,
> To warn, to comfort and command –
> And yet a Spirit still, and bright
> With something of angelic light. ...

Wordsworth's lady does (rather unexpectedly) *command*, and there is also a passing reference to her reason. But these are background elements. In the angelic tradition they play little part, and the guiding idea is that, as Charles Kingsley put it, 'men must work and women must weep' – though the women could of course do this selectively, like Ben Bolt's Sweet Alice,

> Who wept with delight when you gave her a smile,
> And trembled with fear at your frown.

The heroines of Dickens's early novels are entirely on this plan, and show some of its difficulties. Phantoms of delight, like Dora Copperfield and Ada Clare, have to give way, as soon as any practical demand appears, to angels in the house like Agnes Wickfield and Esther Summerson.[12] (Would you buy a used car from Dora Copperfield?) The total impracticality of the phantoms is interesting, because it marks a special element of unreality in their pedigree. The rising middle class wanted its women to be ladies, and believed that ladies did not work, even at home.

Uselessness was therefore a status symbol. The genuine upper class, having nothing to prove, attached much less importance to this. Florence Nightingale, herself an aristocrat, reported in exasperation that 'it is far more difficult to induce a "middle-class" woman than an "upper-class" one to go through as Head Nurse the incidental drudgery which must fall to her province or be neglected'.[13] The romantic and delightful elements of ladyhood were attached for the middle class to idleness. Accordingly, the practical angels in fiction, however badly they may be needed, leave the authors' imagination cold and turn out to be a dead bore. And this has proved a continuing difficulty. Betty Friedan's sad American ladies, conscientiously polishing their already perfect homes under the impression that this must be what people want of them, and then finding that their husbands have left them just the same, are victims of just this imaginative confusion. The role of advertisements in deepening and prolonging it can scarcely be exaggerated. But it became possible because of the nineteenth-century middle class's ambition to become something which it did not understand – an ambition which fed voraciously on the dreams offered in novels.

The aroma of falsity surrounding this kind of writing is no accident, but a sign of something radically wrong in the feeling. Ambivalence presses; the idealization is pregnant with hatred. Those who encourage phantoms always end up with some which are far from delightful. The angel is really a vampire. She cannot help being one, for she has no interests, no tasks, no wishes of her own. As they say, 'she lives for others; you can tell the others by their hunted look'. So she cannot let them go. And, as in the stories, those bitten by vampires may become vampires themselves. Hence, even among the rich and comfortable, there arose self-perpetuating domestic prisons, such as that in which Florence Nightingale groaned and struggled for so many years before she escaped. That men often regard domestic women as vampires and jailors in this way is well known. (It is very remarkable how Dickens's household angels are always rattling their baskets of keys.) This accusation is the burden of modern, post-Christian misogyny. From Schopenhauer on, woman is no longer dreaded especially as sinful and as the cause of sin, but as a dead weight, a parasite, a commonplace devourer, the domestic snare which holds back the aspiring male genius. Thus Freud:

> Women soon come into opposition to civilization and display their retarding and restraining influence. . . . The work of civilization has become increasingly the business of men, it confronts them with ever more difficult tasks and compels them to carry out instinctual sublimations of which women are little capable. . . . Thus the woman finds herself forced into the background by the claims of civilization and she adopts a hostile attitude towards it.[14]

You might think that running households and bringing up children had something to do with civilization, or that women helped their husbands, but no. By defining everything positive as male, and keeping women at home, it is easy to leave the women with no function but that of jailors. But this simple sex-drama collapses at once when we remember that those jailed are female as well as male, and that the jailors are male as well as female. Florence Nightingale's father was for long her most determined jailor, and he was not exceptional. Men have found it quite natural to demand that their womenfolk should stay at home and not go 'gadding about', a word which seems to be entirely sex-linked. Moreover, among the horrors which afflict jailed women, the fear of becoming in the end a jailor oneself has been one of the most dreadful. What Mary Kingsley and Charlotte Brontë and Mary Wollstonecraft and many others had said clearly enough has at last been said so loud by Germaine Greer, Shulamith Firestone and others that perhaps we can take it as read – women do not like being jailed any better than men do. And if the jailing is done in the name of affection, then it is time to remember that this emotion, like all others, needs to be informed by thought. The thought-free woman is a parasite on the thoughts and lives of others, and is moreover an encouragement to the development of that very dangerous monstrosity, the feeling-free man.

It is interesting, therefore, that this thought-free female angel has received something of a revival in the works of some feminist writers, such as Germaine Greer and Sheila Rowbotham. These quite often contain remarks like 'in most situations logic is simply rationalization of an infra-logical aim. . . . Male logic can only deal with simple issues; women, because they are passive and condemned to observe and react rather than initiate, are more aware of complexity.'[15] Germaine Greer is in fact talking here about the *misuse* of logic, about unfair and narrow-minded argument. But phrases like 'male logic' and 'logic is simply rationalization' certainly suggest more than this. They seem to mean that logic is itself something alien, something tainted and misleading, which women get on better without, or, alternatively, that male logic is like this; is there then a female kind? We will consider in a moment what this might mean if it is really just a remark about modes of knowledge – if we are dealing with the more limited antithesis between reason and intuition. That probably is, in fact, how Germaine Greer intends it here. But remarks of this sort also appear in relation to the much wider antithesis between thought and feeling as such. And here they really do seem wild. Logical thought is not something one can do without, any more than our bodies can do without a skeleton. Thought and feeling are not rivals or alternatives, any more than bone and flesh are. They are inseparable elements in all our experience. To be asked to choose between them really would be a monstrous false choice.[16]

6. The fear of feeling

It seems, then, that the dangers of seeing the sex difference as a sharp division between thought and feeling are rather grave. If not watched, the division easily grows into an exclusive one, and passes from a mere observation into a standard, banning intrusions by either sex on the province of the other. Forbidding women to think is damaging in an obvious way. The dangers of forbidding men to feel are slightly more subtle; they deserve attention.

We are all frightened of strong emotion. Where emotion is viewed as essentially female, that fear merges with another – the fear of femaleness, symbolizing the vast creative force which generated us all, or (to be more Kleinian) the fear of the all-powerful giantess who ruled our early lives. Now this can be a problem even for a woman, but at least she feels both forces also within herself. They can be frightening, but they are not really alien. For a man they easily do seem alien, and the fear can be serious. The less critical he is – the less he can distinguish between the forces of his own nature and the actual women around him – the more alarming his situation gets. But fear is itself an emotion, and one forbidden to men. Resentment and shame are added. His simplest remedy is to express his fear in the form of hostility and contempt for females. And unless he is helped to understand his situation and his reactions, this, evidently, is what he often does. Dale Spender, after giving many examples from her surveys of schoolchildren's attitudes, comments:

> That boys do not like girls – that they find them inferior and unworthy – and even despicable – is a conclusion hard to avoid when observing and documenting the behaviour of boys towards girls in schools. In the tapes that I have made in the classroom, there is the evidence that boys frequently make insulting and abusive – often sexually abusive – comments to girls. ... When I have asked why it is that such abuse is allowed to persist, even to go unchecked, the [teacher's] response has usually been in the form of an excuse; 'All boys behave like that at their age; it's a stage they go through' and 'It's best not to draw attention to it, they grow out of it, you know'. ... What is the effect on the girls of this vilification?[17]

It is a fair question. Even parents who themselves see through this attitude often do let it go on. Would they not do better to point out its falsity, to show that they do not accept it? The hope that 'they grow out of it' is manifestly mistaken. All comedians know that when they run out of actual jokes, they have only to reach into their bucket of non-jokes and pull out three crass items beginning 'my wife' to have their audience in stitches. Does it matter? Well, ask the Jews and the Irish. Sometimes it is harmless, but by no means always. Certainly there is sometimes retaliation. Girls, who have their own fear of the alien to cope with, can, when given the chance, return the compliment.

> I was once asked to take tea at a girls' school where one of my sisters was boarding. I was then about twelve years old ... I was left alone with the girls. The moment the mistress's back was turned, the head girl, who was about my own age, came up, pointed her finger at me, made a face and said solemnly, 'A na-a-asty bo-o-y!' All the girls followed her in rotation making the same gesture and the same reproach. ... It gave me a great scare.[18]

There was certainly something wrong with Samuel Butler's attitude to women, and perhaps this experience explains it. In any case the retaliation, even when it is possible, does not set right the original trouble but intensifies it.

Need this division between boys and girls ever arise? The idea that all could continue playing together in harmony is attractive. But, in the great range of cultures which have now been studied, the tendency of children to divide themselves spontaneously into distinct sex groups seems to be very widely, if not universally, found. Those devoted to excluding innate causes treat this as a mere reflection of the adult division into sex roles. But children do not reflect everything which goes on around them, and anyway that division itself remains to be explained. If the sexes are psychologically indistinguishable, why is it universal, which it certainly is? It would be very strange if these groupings did not reflect a natural difference. The important thing is to avoid loading that real difference with irrelevant and dangerous symbolism. And the symbolism which allots thought and feeling separately to the two sexes seems a particularly dangerous one. Sex differences, whatever they are, are likely to affect thought and feeling equally.

7. Reason, intuition and madness

What, then, about the less pretentious traditional idea that the sexes differ in their capacities for thought? This notion too can be treated in a way extremely flattering to women, crediting them with an intuition, a mysterious insight, with which men cannot compete. At the other extreme, it can show them as quite simply insane. A distinguished doctor and amateur philosopher, Sir Almroth Wright, developed this last view in a singular book called *The Unexpurgated Case Against Woman Suffrage* published in 1913. Sir Almroth explained that 'the woman voter would be pernicious to the State .... because of her intellectual defects',[19] though she also had still graver moral ones which will occupy us presently. Women were, in fact, always unbalanced and usually demented. The interest of the book lies in Sir Almroth's firm conviction that what he is saying is already well known, an obvious truth which is only concealed because everybody else is too scared to admit it. 'Woman has stifled discussion by placing her taboo upon anything seriously unflattering being said about her in public'.[20] This conviction of a hidden agreement has some basis. C.S. Lewis, a far more humane and subtle person, was, as his biographer says, 'firmly convinced from an early age that the female psychology was entirely different from – and largely inimical to – that of the male. In 1923 he and Barfield discussed the subject and agreed that "either men or women are mad" – not that they themselves had any doubt which sex was sane'.[21] This, too, was a belief about ability as well as about motivation.

Lewis wrote very differently on this sort of subject later when, in his fifties, love and marriage unexpectedly claimed him. But the reticent, upper-class British type of masculinity, which he shared with Almroth Wright, was and remains a very strong and persistent subculture. The suspicion about female insanity is natural to it, and indeed that suspicion may be a necessary counterpart to the idea about mysterious female intuition. Intuition, equally with madness, gives no account of itself. How can we know when it is working? Sometimes the prophetess is inspired; at other times she just raves. But we need to know whether to accept her voices today. Was she speaking *ex cathedra*? In a culture like our own, which venerates scientific proof and expects it to be available everywhere, this sort of situation is very disturbing.

What do we mean by intuition? In everyday talk the word means a hunch – a kind of knowledge which is real knowledge, not illusion, but for which we cannot account. Philosophers have pointed out that this is a worrying idea, because if we really cannot account for it, it may yet prove mistaken. The secretary claims to have an intuition that the new treasurer is dishonest. But it can only count as a real intuition when other evidence arrives, such as indiscretions or a bank-book. Without that, what seems like an intuition may be just groundless prejudice. Hunches, then, can perhaps only be identified as such by hindsight. But when we do identify them in this way we think of them as something more than luck. Typically, we think that the hunch-owners are practised and experienced in the appropriate kind of question, that they formed their opinions on a sound basis, even though they cannot explain them.

Looked at like this, intuition loses some of its mystery. It is not a special faculty with a route of its own to truth, bypassing all normal faculties. It is simply thought which, for some reason, has not been fully articulated. But then it is a very common thing for thought not to be fully articulated. In fact, to articulate any thought quite fully might be impossible. We know a vast number of things which we cannot prove, as we see when we try to do mathematics. Axioms are principles taken for granted because they are obvious. But to state these obvious things clearly and fit them together rightly takes real genius. It is the kind of work over which great mathematicians go grey.

8 Attending to the premises

Different things are obvious to different people. What is obvious to a given person depends a great deal on things like background knowledge, familiarity with like situations, attention and interest. In those areas where women are often thought to act intuitively, such as interactions with children or the sick, they are actually drawing on a fund of relevant experience and interest which those who find their insight miraculous simply do not happen to share. But this same thing can happen with men too. Experienced and devoted doctors, gardeners, engineers, even scientists (male as much as female) may equally astonish colleagues, who are more theory-bound, by unexpected perceptions for which they cannot on the spot give reasons. This does not mean, however, that they have passed out of the province of reason altogether. These 'intuitions' must not break the laws of logic. They are not, for instance, licensed to contradict themselves, nor any other known truths. If they do contradict something which is now believed to be true, either it or they will have to give way. They have to be on a route which reasoning can in principle follow, even if it has not yet done so. Otherwise they are just guesses.

Intuition, then, seems to be a name for informal, unarticulated but correct reasoning. And this is certainly not something confined to women. Are they in fact specially prone to it? There are two factors which make them seem so. One is their special familiarity with the field of experience just mentioned, centring on children's lives and extending to personal relations generally. This can make their insights mysterious to those lacking in that background, but perhaps not more so than an engineer's or a gardener's insight seems to those who lack those backgrounds. There may be no real asymmetry here.

There does seem to be an asymmetry, however, about the other factor, namely training in argument. Until this century that training was given only to men. It was part of the education which prepared them for the professions – notably for the church, for politics, and for the law. In all these professions, the power of effective speaking and writing – of presenting an argument in public – was crucial. Now in theory this skill is always supposed to be linked with the deeper and more serious one of following an argument disinterestedly wherever it may lead, as a path to the truth. But in practice the aims of truth and persuasion diverge so sharply that an obsessive interest in winning arguments must eventually kill the passion for truth. They cannot survive together. And, even in less extreme cases, training in argument can obstruct the honest handling of disagreements by making it too easy to produce some kind of façade of reasoning to make one's own case plausible, and to write off the less well-trained opponent who cannot at once see what is wrong with it. Thus Bertrand Russell congratulated himself on having convinced his small son by argument that it was foolish to be afraid of the dark (since it contained no real dangers), and thus stopped him asking for company or a night-light. The boy gave in, because he could see no flaw in his father's reasoning. But his terror continued for years, and in his sister's opinion did him lasting harm.[22]

Russell's mistake here was one very common in people who pride themselves on their logic. He had far too narrow a set of premises. He simply had not noticed a whole range of crucial questions about the nature of children's feelings. What small children fear or like is not determined by prudent considerations about future danger or advantage, but by cues which sometimes seem to work as directly as innate releasing mechanisms in animals. The feeling will not go away just because prudence gives no grounds for it. It will gradually be integrated into experience and resolved into various elements which are made compatible with prudence, so that it does not just dominate life. But many of these primitive feelings remain as important elements in adult experience. The horror of darkness does not simply fade out of our consciousness, any more than the love of what is bright and sparkling. It remains as a necessary thread in our symbolism. This is not surprising, since in diurnal creatures fear and avoidance of darkness has a useful evolutionary function, and is shared by many animals. To expect to get rid of such fears instantly, just by talk, is quite unrealistic and Russell's attempt to do so was itself as irrational as the attempt to boil a kettle by putting it on a cold gas ring.

His mistake, however, was a very common one. His premises differed from his son's, and in fact were defective, but he did not attend to or criticize his premises at all. There seem to have been two faulty ones. The first was something like 'we should not fear anything unless we know exactly what harm it can do us'. This is false, because we do well to be cautious also about the unknown. Russell, however, assumed that everyone else must share this belief, and that the boy was therefore irrational in being all the more disturbed because he did not know what it was that he was afraid of. The second false premiss was the belief that people can always control their fears, which is not true of adults, let alone small children.

Russell fell into a trap which lies in wait particularly for people who are very confident in their powers of reasoning. Fascinated by his own consistency in a small area, he ignored the background, and was left saying 'you are inconsistent because you act and speak contrary to *my* premisses'. This, of course, is actually bad logic. To grasp 'the logic of a problem' is to map out its general shape, to see what kind of reasoning it involves and what considerations are relevant to it – which includes surveying both one's own premisses and those of one's opponent. But the more confident people are, the less likely it is to occur to them as possible that other people might have different premisses at all.

Their confidence often extends to the still stranger habit of calling other people illogical just for not having a particular piece of information. This accusation can be made even by people who ought to have provided that information themselves. We have no wish to pile on horror stories, but here is an example. A consultant turns round from examining a patient, whom he finds to be pregnant, and, addressing the rest of the ward, says 'You women are all the same. You're completely illogical about this. You think, just because you've been sterilized, that it's going to last for ever. But it can always fail, you know.'

Now this kind of put-down could certainly be used against uneducated men as well. It could even be used in principle by a professional woman, if she were exceptionally confident. But the first sentence is significant. The contrast between rational, clear-headed professional and goofy, disorganized amateur is very easily lined up with the sex difference. And those who are convinced all along that they are dealing with disorganized goofs do not tend to listen very carefully to what they say. To a much greater extent than we normally realize, irrationality is expected of women and even thought fitting for them. This is so customary a way of thinking that men often are not aware of how grave a barrier it can be to understanding. Even very considerate men, not at all like this consultant, may overlook the need to listen to what their wives actually say, as well as just getting a general idea of what they seem to be demanding. This theme stands out remarkably when women explain their difficulties to those trying to help them find employment or retraining courses. It has often been impossible for them to discuss their plans constructively with their husbands. It seems that, as so many jokes suggest, men have a specific difficulty in listening to women, one which perhaps arises out of the pre-verbal relation of mother to child, and which anyway needs to be taken seriously by both sides. (The fact that research now seems to show that women talk less than men, rather than ten times as much, as folklore suggests, is surely significant.) The effect of all this is of course to make eventual disagreement sudden and violent, because it has been impossible to prevent this by dealing with it gradually. This confirms the initial assumption that women are illogical. And the general remark that women are illogical – and therefore wrong – is often used to settle disputes in advance without further trouble. Altogether, it is not hard to see how 'logic' became something of a dirty word to feminists.

9. The question of motivation

It should, however, be clear by now that the fault does not lie in logic, any more than arithmetic is responsible for financial frauds. In cases like those just cited (which are common enough), the logic itself is bad and the use made of it fraudulent. And it is often brought in, as it seems to be in both these cases, to distract attention from the arrogant person's own deficiencies. In these areas, we are not dealing with a difference in cognitive capacity between those who win arguments and those who lose them, but with the motivation which insists on winning, and that which accepts losing. The entanglement of this question with questions about capacity makes it impossible to deal with the cognitive questions on their own.

The whole question of sex differences in capacity therefore opens up at this point into that of differences in motivation. Unless you have understood what people are trying to do, it is idle to talk of discovering how good they are at doing it.

A small but significant example of this emerges over games. Excellence at chess is highly sex-linked. Very few grand masters are women. This is usually seen as a difference of capacity, or at least an unfair lack of opportunity. But what is the point of playing chess anyway? This may seem a philistine question, but it is one which does look very different to people of differing emotional temperaments. It raises questions about motivation, not just in the rather thin sense of 'how much do you want to do it?' but in the fuller sense of '*what* do you want to do?'. Is your attitude that of Diomedes in the *Iliad*, dedicated 'to always being first and excelling all the others',[23] or is it rather that of Fanny over the card game in *Mansfield Park*, when Henry Crawford cries, ' "The game will be yours, it will certainly be yours" – "And Fanny would much rather it was William's", said Edmund, smiling at her. "Poor Fanny – not allowed to cheat herself as she wishes".'[24] Capacity is not in question here. If something of real moment arises, there is no reason to expect this kind of person to be either more or less able and 'motivated' – that is, keen – to deal with it than a Diomedes. Both temperaments (and many others too) have their advantages and their drawbacks. But the difference is one of priority system, of motivation, not of ability.

If, then, we turn from questions about capacity to questions about motivation, what objections do we really find to the very natural idea that women's motivation is in some ways characteristically different from men's?

First, there might arise the very sweeping and wholesale behaviourist objection that there is simply no such thing as natural motivation at all; that all human beings are standard blank paper at birth. There is not room to go over fully all the objections to this strange doctrine here,[25] but we have pointed out that it is not really needed as a defence against fatalism. Certainly the reductive misuse of biological argument can be fatalist, but then so can the reductive misuse of any other kind of argument, such as argument from economics. Human freedom does not require us to have no bodies.

Next – and this is more likely today – objectors might concede that people do have their own individual physical constitutions, and that the peculiarities of their brain and nervous system, and indeed of their whole physique, might make a great difference to their personality. (Were this not true, it would scarcely be possible to account for individuality at all.) But they would still reject the idea of a natural, characteristic difference in personality between the sexes. They view all character traits as in principle equally likely to be found in either sex. They see the distribution of them as entirely due to social forces.

Now this objection is traditionally put as a sceptical one. As Mill expressed it, 'I deny that anyone knows, or can know, the nature of the two sexes, as long as they have only been seen in their present relation to one another'. [26] But the purpose for which it is invoked is far from sceptical: it is dogmatic. As a genuine piece of scepticism, it would have to cut both ways. If we really do not know anything about these two natures, we certainly cannot know that they are the same, or that they cover the same range. There is no path from this sceptical position to the dogmatic certainty with which Kate Millett expresses that the two sexes 'are inherently in everything alike'.

Genuine scepticism, then, will not do the job which feminists want it for, and will indeed make that job impossible. Is it, however, still a respectable position in its own right, with a claim on our attention? It scarcely seems so, because it is far too sweeping. It is true that we do not know the entire nature of the two sexes – nor, indeed, of most other things. It is also true, and is what Mill chiefly meant, that we do not know that those natures are just as tradition paints them, for we have reason to suppose that they are not. But to say this is already to claim that we do know something about them.

10. Sisterhood and motherhood

And indeed we do. Determined scepticism about our understanding of sex differences merges into the slightly unreal general scepticism which people sometimes express about anthropology. It is true that we cannot study human affairs by control experiments, but that does not make either history or anthropology impossible. Indeed, we know more of human life than we do of the life of fruit flies, because we make use of the special advantages which go with an inside view. (Were a practised experimenter to be turned into a fruit fly, the knowledge of fly life which he had gathered in his scientific career would almost certainly not enable him to take his place in society with credit.) Mill wants controls. ('If men had ever been found in society without women, or women without men, or if there had been a society of men and women in which the women were not under control of the men, something might have been positively known about the mental and moral differences which may be inherent in the nature of each.')²⁷ But we do not need to wait for this to know something about them, any more than anthropologists have to give up hope of knowing anything about the many other things which go on, more or less, in every human society, and to wait till they find one which is an exception. What they do in such cases is to compare the different ways in which these things are done.

Now we have today an immense amount more knowledge of various cultures than was open to Mill. The degree to which male dominance is a general feature of them has been questioned. But there is no doubt about something else, which has to be happening before that question can even arise – namely the universal division of men and women into separate groups, with distinct social roles. Why would this happen if they did not differ in character? It is no use accounting for this as a case of the strong oppressing the weak, because that can be done without any division of roles at all. Some women, too, are stronger than some men, and in any case many of the differences do not seem to have anything to do with oppression. They are just differences, not tyrannies.

This notion of a natural, irremovable likeness binding women and distinguishing them from men is taken for granted as underlying the notion of sisterhood, which has been so important to the women's movement. It is scarcely possible to think of that bond as just a link connecting fellow-sufferers from a particular kind of deceptive or distorting treatment – a conditioning which has persuaded women that they were different. If that were the idea, women's groups would surely want to *cure* them of the illusion, and send them out into the world as individuals who would no longer specially need each other's company. Far from this, women cultivate their own distinctness, and find great relief in discovering not just that other women share their misfortunes, but that they respond to them similarly. This cannot possibly just mean that, as behaviourism requires, they have been stamped in the same mill.

The thinking of the women's movement, then, already agrees with the anthropological evidence which indicates that women and men are not a single standard item. This same conclusion is, of course, also supported today by a whole mass of physiological evidence which was not available to Mill. Characteristic sex differences in the average levels of hormones have long been known, and more recently considerable differences in the arrangements of the two brain hemispheres are also emerging. Of course misuse of this evidence must be resisted, but that is a different thing from dismissing it all wholesale as irrelevant to psychology. That dismissal shows not just a disregard for the unity of science, but also a more than Christian desire to detach the soul from the physical world, which we must presently consider.

Against all these considerations, what horrific objection still stands? Undoubtedly, the obstacle is still the peculiarly crude and unreal idea, still current, of what an innate disposition is. This is well seen in Elisabeth Badinter's book, *The Myth of Motherhood*.[28] This book is devoted to proving that women have 'no natural maternal instinct'. The word 'instinct' is freely used in it, but the author refuses to define that word, saying that everybody knows perfectly well what it means. But unluckily they do not, as she herself shows. She cites evidence from history to show many cases where women have neglected and ignored their children. This shows indeed that there is no automatic, simple, unfailing mechanism which secures that women will care for children. But then instincts never are mechanisms of this simple unfailing kind. Even weaver birds, whose nest-building is indeed instinctive, can fail to build nests at the proper time, or can build them badly: something can go wrong. In any case the parental instincts of animals are not, properly speaking, detailed, 'closed' instincts of this kind at all. They are what Tinbergen has called 'major instincts' – general tendencies to a *kind* of behaviour.[29]

Other examples, comparable to parental interest, are curiosity, hunting, cleanliness or fear. Each of these general groupings typically contains a number of more specific behaviour patterns which are appropriate to it. A bird with strong parental motivation is likely to brood its chicks, and also to bring them food if they are hungry. But this same motivation can also lead to a wide variety of other, miscellaneous, activity which is not in itself instinctive at all, such as protecting them from new dangers and helping them out of new difficulties. Thus a mother elephant, swept away with her calf by a flooded river, was seen to perform the unparalleled feat of lifting the calf with her trunk and placing it on a ledge in safety from the water.[30] The action resulted from general maternal instinct, but was not regular 'instinctive behaviour' in the simple sense of a fixed action pattern like nest-building. In a dangerous and changing world, this range of behaviour is highly variable and complex, especially with intelligent creatures.

Of course, neither the general motivation nor the specific behaviour is infallible and automatic. In any species it can fail, as a whole or partly, and it is particularly likely to do so with the first birth. All this can be studied in great detail in birds, which need to give their helpless young a great deal of care. Any given bird may fail in some aspect of it, whether from sheer lack of the appropriate motivation or from the presence of another, stronger one which conflicts with it. Birds constitutionally inclined to do this, however, usually leave few descendants. Accordingly, their characteristics can never be transmitted so as to spread through their species. All surviving birds must be descended from ancestors whose parental motivation was quite strong.

This evolutionary consideration, of course, applies equally to all other species where the young need prolonged care. And of this group *Homo sapiens* is the most outstanding example. Our young have the longest period of dependence in the animal kingdom. On any view, at least up to the stage where social conditioning may be supposed to take over, the survival of our ancestors depended, as much as or more than that of other mammals and birds, on strong, natural parental motivation.

Primate mothers are in general particularly devoted parents. Because of their high intelligence baby primates cannot mature quickly. They need a long period of dependence, during which they learn flexible behaviour, instead of relying on a few basic instinctive patterns and a little experience to make them independent. Mothers must therefore not just keep their babies alive, but take a real interest in them, play with them, show them what they need to know and generally draw them into the community. They are not left alone to do this. Males, other females and particularly other young play a very important part in the process. A liking for children thus becomes a strong general emotional tendency in primates, as in other very social creatures. In some species, too, fathers or other males play a special part in this bonding. And it seems clear that our own species owes its success to an important degree to becoming one of these. All the same, even in these species the mother remains the irreplaceable centre of her infant's life. Although bouts of exploration soon interrupt the period of total dependence and grow longer and longer as growth proceeds, they are still for a very long time alternated with returns to the mother for comfort and reassurance, particularly if anything goes wrong. This rhythm of adventure and return to base is fundamental to the development of the young. Primate mothers have to show, and commonly do show, just those qualities of devotion, patience and intelligent affection for which human mothers are justly celebrated.

11. The existentialist protest

Are we, however, forbidden by respect for human dignity to draw any conclusions from this about maternity in human beings? Was there a total change – a miraculous Rise of Man, in which our species levitated away from the physical world altogether – when this whole instinctive mechanism vanished and was replaced by the radically different workings of social conditioning? Or did advanced intellect and culture emerge rather as a further development, enriching and organizing these simpler motivations into a new and splendid whole, not needing to destroy them first?

The first idea, which treats nature and culture as sharply exclusive alternatives, is one of the false antitheses which are the main business of this book.

This awkward cleavage is still popular among some social scientists; but no adequate reason for it, or plausible story about how it could occur, has ever been given. And in any detailed application it produces endless difficulties, of which the batch concerning motherhood are typical. How is it really supposed to work? Are the hormonal arrangements (which in human beings are very similar to those in the higher apes) supposed to have lost their function, become idle and ceased to be connected with the emotions? Or do they stay connected but only one way round – are they now passive, accepting social conditioning from outside but contributing nothing of their own? Is there now one-way causation? If this strange state of affairs were really working, nobody surely ought to be able to have emotions which their society did not demand of them. But they do, and it happens notoriously in this very case of motherhood.

On the one hand, some mothers cannot feel the love for their children which their society unanimously demands of them. Their instinctive responses fail, as do those of some apes. On the other, mothers often persist tenaciously in loving and clinging to babies whom their societies require them to forget. This has often happened in the case of illegitimate babies. To retain them was often certain to wreck the mother's life. Some indeed were lightly abandoned:

> Sink ye or swim ye, my bonny babe,
> For ye'll get no more of me.[31]

But many were kept in the face of appalling difficulties and continued to supply the central motivation of their mothers' lives, compensating for the general rejection of society. There have been recent cases, too, of girls arranging to have their babies adopted, and finding to their intense surprise after the birth that they could not do so because of the unexpected bond which had developed. (It is a common experience of mothers to be surprised by the nature and strength of this bond, even when they expected, in a general way, that something of the sort would appear.) If we are tempted to say that what happens here is still some expression of local Christian ideas on what ought to happen, it is worth noticing how things go in societies where ideas are different. In classical Greece, a poor country where infanticide was socially accepted as a proper and necessary way of controlling population, mothers (it is said) still voiced their indignant protests in the teeth of respectable opinion.[32]

Those who are determined to admit only social causes usually deal with this kind of evidence by saying that the conditioning must have been more complex than it looked – that there has been counter-conditioning at a deeper level, producing the conflicting motives. At this point, however, the notion of conditioning stops being an empirical one at all. If unnoticed conditioning can always be invoked as a hidden cause, anything goes.

It is very interesting that feminists should treat motherhood so differently from sisterhood. Obviously, one reason for this is the way in which the idealization of motherhood has been mis-used to justify narrowing women's lives. (The real point of Elisabeth Badinter's book *The Myth of Motherhood* is to resist this misuse.) But there is also a deeper and more important philosophical distortion, for which Nietzsche and Sartre are responsible. Simone de Beauvoir, among many others, declares that there is something not just frightening, but metaphysically degrading, about pregnancy and childbirth. A pregnant woman is, she says, 'alienated'; in her, the species is taking over the individual; she is 'in the iron grip of the species'. Both the father and the child are violating her sacred individuality.

Moreover, she will not be recompensed for this outrage by achieving anything of value. She is merely being used as a passive, uninvolved vehicle:

> The [primitive] woman who gave birth, therefore, did not know the pride of creation; she felt herself the plaything of obscure forces, and the painful ordeal of childbirth seemed a useless and even troublesome accident. But in any case, giving birth and suckling are not *activities*, they are natural functions; no project is involved; and that is why woman found in them no reason for a lofty affirmation of her existence – she submitted passively to her biologic fate.[33]

The premiss needed to make sense of this amazing piece of nonsense is the existentialist one that no act has value unless it is an entirely solitary choice and achievement. Since most human enterprises are in fact communal, it is hard, by these rules, to find anything at all which is worth doing. Everybody (including, of course, the artist) relies deeply on tradition. Everybody wants their achievements to be received and valued by others. The romantic idea of a dignity which could be sustained in solitude is grotesque. The examples which Simone de Beauvoir gives of genuine, male, forms of creation are the invention of 'the stick and the club with which he armed himself'. These, it seems, are new, whereas going on having the same old babies and decorating the same old houses, century after century, 'imprisons her in repetition and immanence'. But if creativity means only doing a thing for the first time, it seems rather a minor value, and men are going to spend as much of their time without it as women. What matters, most of the time, is doing the expected thing in the right way, which will sometimes (but not always) be a new and better way. This plainly can just as well be done when practising the difficult arts of childbirth and suckling and house-decorating as when hunting. The idea that there is something specially passive about these demanding occupations is a piece of ignorant traditional foolishness. Occasionally Simone de Beauvoir does see this, at least over sexual intercourse:

> As a matter of fact, man, like woman, is flesh, therefore passive, the plaything of his hormones and of the species, the restless prey of his desires. And she, like him, in the midst of the carnal fever, is a consenting, a voluntary gift, an activity; they live out in their several fashions the strange ambiguity of existence made body.[34]

That goes for childbirth too. There is plenty of scope for initiative in both activities. Nietzsche and Sartre, moreover, were not just making a mistake. They were making a special kind of directed mistake. Their peculiar idea of human dignity and independence is specifically a male one and is designed as such. One point of it is to elevate the male condition and represent the female one as degraded. It is just as easy, if one is interested in this sort of game, to exalt the female as being the only one who can break through the bounds of solitude, who can have the mystical experience of being both one and two, and who therefore is not afraid of otherness and constitutes our species's link with the glories of the physical universe. Either sex can, if it likes, claim superiority. You can take your choice. But it is best to take it while remembering that both parties are here for keeps.

Part Four:
Conclusion

8 Epilogue: what next?

'Will you never be done talking?' shouted the Thin Woman
passionately.

'I will not', said the Philosopher. 'A woman should be seen
seldom but never heard. Quietness is the beginning of virtue. To
be silent is to be beautiful. Stars do not make a noise. Children
should always be in bed. These are serious truths, which cannot
be controverted; therefore, silence is fitting as regards them.'

(James Stephens, *The Crock of Gold*)

Have we found the answer? We have not. Our main hope has
been to sort out the questions, and even that will take a long
time yet. Readers who are still with us will by now have seen
reason to think it unlikely that the women's movement will just
melt away. Feminism was never only an eccentric fad, and it is
not so today. It is rooted in serious troubles affecting the lives of
large numbers of ordinary people. But on the other hand, neither
can it be expected just to 'conquer'. It is not the one key cause,
with automatic priority over all other good causes. Nor has it a
magic universal efficacy, so that if favoured it would bring those
other causes to success automatically, without further attention
to them. Certainly its successes can help other good causes
forward, but then that process is mutual, and makes it impossible
to isolate feminism and pursue it alone. (For instance, the idea
of promoting women to positions of power would, by itself, only
lead to promoting more women moulded in the existing traditions, which would scarcely transform politics.) It needs to be
put in the context of a full set of ideals and a fair programme of
other humane enterprises.

In that wider context, righting the injustices which affect
women – which we noticed in our Introduction as the central
business of feminism – takes its place as part of the more general
business of righting injustice. In this work many men are allies,
and men as such are not conceivably the enemy. The aim is not
that women – or even feminism – will 'conquer' anything or
anybody, but that both will make their special contribution to

the general good. It should (for Heaven's sake) surely be a key part of that contribution to get rid of the language of fighting and conquering, and of the whole competitive way of thought which they express, so far as possible from the whole field of practical endeavour. If we look round at the amount of needless confrontation which goes on in every field of public life, from foreign policy to trades union bargaining, and also in academic controversy, and consider dispassionately the part played in it by mere habitual feuding, some of us may well conclude that these habits are the main danger confronting our species today, and that our most dangerous enemies do not lie outside us, but within. Even those who find this view too extreme would probably agree that feuding is a bad and wasteful habit. But it is a habit supported by an essentially male way of thinking which in general exalts truculence and despises willingness to compromise, regardless of what they will produce on any given issue.

The idea that women are not serious, that they cannot be allowed to intrude on important business – an idea which played a main part in the eighteenth century's refusal to grant them political rights, and still to this day keeps most of them out of politics – seems to rest centrally on their having a low opinion of confrontation as a way of settling disputes. They get excluded from councils of war because they would tend to argue for peace. They are inclined to take truculence less seriously than men do, and on the whole less likely to go into politics in order to indulge it. With the dangerous level which disputes have reached in the world today, this general tendency (it is of course not universal) is surely an asset which women should cultivate, and which the rest of the community, looking round and seeing what has been achieved by other methods, should welcome and imitate. Of course this is not to suggest that men are all quarrellers, nor to play down the great achievements of peace-making, constructive work so far. Endless credit is due to all those who have seen to it that things are no worse than they are. But these efforts still have a terribly long way to go. The trouble is, as has repeatedly been pointed out, that polemical methods which did no serious harm when all human affairs were on a much smaller scale and people were more isolated, have with our present technology and degree of crowding become disastrous.

In this alarming situation, the fact that some feminists have in their turn dropped peace-making and begun to wave sabres is depressing but not surprising. It should make us notice the difficulties raised by contemporary controversial habits. Where sabre-waving is the rule, it is hard to get noticed at all unless you buy yourself a sabre and wave it in something like the accepted style. Possibly some minimal element of sabre-waving is even a psychological necessity for controversy. We have waved the odd sabre in these pages ourselves, though we have tried hard to do it about particular issues and not on purely tribal grounds. With so tribal an issue this is difficult, and the shocking record of earlier philosophers goes near sometimes to making it impossible. That impartial third sex, if it has been watching, will certainly have some follies to charge against us. But feuding ought never to be seen as anything better than a necessary evil. The amount of it which goes on today, and the extent to which practical matters like industrial disputes and the manufacture of armaments are controlled by it, is plainly excessive. That background has forced some truculence on even quite co-operative feminists.

There is also a troublesome kind of optical illusion by which any woman who gets seriously involved in controversy tends to look shrewish, even if her actual arguments, over a different signature, would look quite inoffensive and cool. Mary Wollstonecraft could hardly have said less than she did if she was to talk at all about the views of Rousseau and other contemporaries, nor is her style polemical. But she met with widespread fury, and Horace Walpole called her a hyena in petticoats – a singular picture which still awaits an illustrator. So she got a reputation for extremism, which prevented her from being read. It is hard to see quite how to beat this bug. It is not surprising, then, that some women have eventually tried the method of accepting the charge and taking on the misogynists at their own game. They have done it well, earning a high place in any future anthology of good invective, and expressing many overdue truths. And the outcome shows, somewhat depressingly, that up to a point they were right. Stink-bombs can indeed get you listened to when patient, honest argument cannot. But of course it by no means follows that stink-bombs are all you need. Once people start listening, it is important to have something to say.

There is plenty to say, including many things of great importance which we have not been able even to touch on in this book. But the central point is just this very simple one. We have come to the end of the road for sex-linked individualism. It has been rumbled. The idea that every man should properly look out only for himself, while every woman should stand staunchly and obediently behind him as he does so, is not sensible and will not wash once attention has been drawn to it. We have a choice. We can either extend the individualism which has been almost a religion in the West since the eighteenth century consistently to *both* sexes, or we can admit its limitations, treat it with much more caution, and put it in its place as only one element in a more realistic attitude to life for everybody.

Modern feminists of the early, Firestone vintage went all out for the first option, demanding total independence for all. They did us a service by pointing out what this involved. More lately there has been something of a swing the other way. But what really is no longer possible is to deceive oneself into thinking that extreme individualism is an easy, untroubled option. To appear so, it has always relied on an inconsistency – on assuming that, while men regard themselves as isolated, competitive individuals, each hell-bent on his own interest, women will continue to see themselves as social beings, organically linked with those around them. More generally, of course, it has assumed that the unthinking mob in general will do a good deal of this, since without a background of co-operation both practical and emotional life would grind to a halt and supermen would be unable to operate.

The depressing fact that extreme individualism is exploitative has been blurred for us by more than a century of romantic propaganda which pilloried the bourgeois vices, ignored the bourgeois virtues, and sentimentally indulged the individualistic vices – conceit, ingratitude, self-dramatization, infidelity, hard-heartedness, uselessness and the fear of intimacy. This is a morality tailored to fit only adolescents at the moment of leaving home, young Werthers who remain perpetually young. Women's life-cycle is such that, even if they enter this narcissistic realm, they can seldom stay in it. They have therefore done very badly out of this system, and it is no chance at all that Nietzsche excluded them from his thinking. Of course they are not the only people who have done badly; the blight is a general one. But among its victims they are (as perhaps we should repeat) not just an atypical, eccentric minority. They are half the human race.

It is small wonder that the original prophets of the Enlightenment wanted to avoid seeing this difficulty. By putting their heads in the sand with uncommon firmness and unanimity they managed to delay for a couple of centuries the need to face the question 'are their ideals really a sufficient set for the whole of humanity, or not? Is the apparent sufficiency of those ideals parasitic on the existence of a class to which they are *forbidden*, a class which rejects them and remains reliably devoted to their opposites?' The best way to avoid this question was no doubt the one Rousseau took – not only to deny women freedom, but to keep their lives as different as possible from those of men, so that the difference in ideals could pass unnoticed. If industrial development had not transformed our lives so deeply, and tossed so many things into the melting-pot, this might even have worked. Women, who are much less bothered about the outward signs of dominance than men, would not necessarily have made a determined fuss about political power had that stood alone – had men been willing to attend to the problems which women saw as important. But when the networks necessary for private life were deeply disrupted, and at the same time access to the controls of public life, from which help was needed, was largely barred to them, women were forced to act, whether they liked it or not.

In trying to act, they must at once confront this general question about direction – do we want more individualism or less? It is a choice not only for them but for everybody. There is no doubt that individualism, like salt, is a very good and necessary thing, and that the eighteenth-century thinkers did quite right to shout for it. They provided a real Enlightenment. But how about a diet of salt alone? In romantic fiction, the problems posed by clashes of individuality are resolved, and could only be resolved, by death. Goethe, who first introduced the full-scale individualist hero, understood this very well, and if he left any 'i's undotted or 't's uncrossed in the proposition, Thomas Mann has finished the work. It has also been fully illustrated in real life by numbers of enthusiastic martyrs for the cause, from Byron and Rimbaud to Howard Hughes. Unmitigated individualism is a death-wish. Of course that may be one's choice, and unquestionably death is always available. But it is a decision which one ought to notice that one is taking.

Notes

Chapter 1

1 A concept developed by Elizabeth Wolgast in *Equality and the Rights of Women* (Cornell Press 1980), chapter 6.

2 For this impression that women's work is not real work, see Elizabeth Young, *Men and Women; Equal but not Interchangeable* (SDP Open Forum Paper 8, 1982).

3 See M. McAndrew and J. Peers, *The New Soviet Women – Model or Myth?* (Change International Reports, 1981, p. 18). Russian women's difficulties in coping with their 'equal' status at work have produced a drastic fall in the national birthrate to an average of 1.6 per family, and have compelled the government to provide them with more flexible hours and a year's maternity leave. (BBC *Summary of World Broadcasts* 6949(i), 9 February 1982.) See also chapter 6, pp. 174–6.

4 *Thus Spake Zarathustra*, part 1, last chapter, 'Of Bestowing Virtue', section 3. Also in *Ecce Homo*, chapter on 'Why I am a Destiny', section 1.

5 *Thus Spake Zarathustra*, part 1, 'Of Old and Young Women'

6 Schopenhauer's views may be found in his essay 'On Women', published in his *Collected Essays*. Its main points are that 'women are ... childish, foolish and short-sighted – in a word, are big children all their lives. ... The fundamental fault in the character of women is that they have no sense of justice ... they are instinctively crafty, and have an ineradicable tendency to lie. ... From [this] spring falseness, faithlessness, treachery, ungrateful-ness and so on', so that, as he intriguingly adds, 'they see through dis-simulation in others easily; therefore it is not advisable to attempt it with them.' There are no redeeming features. Women are quite useless, and must so far as possible be excluded from society.

7 *A Room of One's Own* (Hogarth Press 1929), p. 132

8 Statement reprinted in *Sisterhood is Powerful*, ed. Robin Morgan (New York 1970), p. 18

9 Quoted in *Sweet Freedom; The Struggle for Women's Liberation*, by Anna Coote and Beatrix Campbell (Picador 1982), p. 25

10 *The Sceptical Feminist* (Routledge and Kegan Paul 1980), p. 2

11 ibid., p. 3

12 A term strongly defended by Kate Millett in *Sexual Politics* (Virago 1977), p. 55 as suitable to describe women, though they are about 51 per cent of the population.

13 *Modern Man in Search of a Soul* (Kegan Paul 1945), p. 38

14 *Social Origins of Depression; A Study of Psychiatric Disorder in Women*

by George W. Brown and Tyrril Harris (Tavistock Publications 1978). We have had to sketch this very careful and balanced survey lightly, in order to summarize its conclusions here. They should be read in full to appreciate the complexity of the problem.

15 ibid., p. 281
16 Margaret Britton, *The Single Woman in the Family of God* (Epworth Press 1982), p. vii
17 Anthony Sampson, *The Changing Anatomy of Britain* (Hodder and Stoughton 1982)

Chapter 2

1 See *Politics*, Book 1, chapters 3, 5, 12 and 13; Book 2, chapter 9, and a good discussion in *Women in Western Political Thought*, by Susan Möller Okin (Virago 1980), chapters 2 and 5. Okin, though not a reliable guide to Aristotle's general thought, gives a most useful and astute account of the political issues connected with the present topic, not only for Aristotle but for a great number of other theorists. The present discussion owes a great deal to her. For Plato's views see *Republic*, Book V, 451–7.
2 *Generation of Animals* (trans. A.L. Peck, Loeb 1943), Book 4, 775a and 776a
3 *Physics*, Book 1, 192b 23
4 *The Subjection of Women* (MIT Press 1970), chapter 1, p. 35
5 'If women be in general inferior, it is because in general they receive a still worse education.' Helvetius, *A Treatise on Man*, vol. 1, p. 156.
6 'His articles, appearing in a number of Pennsylvania journals, dealt with such topics as Negro emancipation, justice for women, and cruelty to animals.' Introduction by Henry Collins to Pelican edition of *The Rights of Man* (1969, p. 16) describing Paine's first years as a journalist in America.
7 *Emile* (trans. Barbara Foxley, Everyman edn), Book 5, pp. 424 (social contract), 322, 332. See also *Women in Western Political Thought*, part 3, and a fuller discussion of the chronic liability of officially egalitarian thought to such aberrations than can be given here, in *Animals and Why they Matter* by Mary Midgley (Penguin 1983), chapters 6 and 7.
8 See for instance Dale Spender's justification for this approach in the introduction to *Women of Ideas and What Men have Done to Them* (Routledge and Kegan Paul 1982).
9 *Kant's Political Writings* (trans. H.B. Nisbet, ed. Hans Reiss, Cambridge 1970), pp. 158–9. Summary given here is Okin's, *Women in Western Political Thought*, p. 6.
10 *Philosophy of Right*, paragraphs 158–81

11 'Let the woman learn in silence, with all subjection' (St Paul, first Epistle to Timothy, 2.11). 'Man is the beginning and end of woman, just as God is the beginning and end of all creation' (St Thomas Aquinas, *Summa Theologica* 1a.92.2. ad 1).

12 In a discussion of 'Prostitution in London', in Henry Mayhew's *London Labour and the London Poor*, vol. 4 (London 1851-62). Quoted by Peter Cominos in *Suffer and be Still*, ed. Martha Vicinus (Methuen 1980), pp. 166-7.

13 The name of a very popular Victorian poem by Coventry Patmore, well discussed in 'Victorian Masculinity and the Angel in the House' by Carol Christ in *A Widening Sphere; Changing Roles of Victorian Women*, ed. Martha Vicinus (Methuen 1980).

14 *The Screwtape Letters* (Geoffrey Bles 1942), Letter XX, p. 104

15 A point well discussed by Anthony Stevens in *Archetype, A Natural History of the Self* (Routledge and Kegan Paul 1982).

16 It is alarming to see what difficulty working women arrested under the mid-Victorian Contagious Diseases Acts as prostitutes had in proving that they had been wrongly suspected. See 'The Making of an Outcast Group' by Judith Walkowitz in *A Widening Sphere*.

17 In *Suffer and be Still*

18 This revolution in the modern world, and particularly the immense potential which it should leave to older women, is very well documented by Alva Myrdal and Viola Klein in *Women's Two Roles* (Routledge and Kegan Paul 1956).

19 Elizabeth Young, in *Men and Women; Equal but not Interchangeable* (SDP Open Forum Paper 8, 1982), pp. 11 and 21, quotes the following figures. Number of one-parent families in Britain: about 2½ million. Number of families kept above official poverty line by wife's earnings: about 825,000.

20 *Sweet Freedom; The Struggle for Women's Liberation* (Picador 1982), p. 243

21 In *Kitchen Sink or Swim?* (Penguin 1982), p. 251

22 Figures supplied by the Equal Opportunities Commission

23 For information on the original design see a paper called 'New Opportunities for Women' by Ruth Michaels, obtainable from her at Hatfield Polytechnic, and on fuller developments one by Jonathan Brown and Eileen Aird called 'New Opportunities Courses at Newcastle', obtainable from the Adult Education Department, University of Newcastle-on-Tyne.

Chapter 3

1 *Essay on Liberty* (Everyman edn), p. 159
2 ibid., p. 160
3 *Confessions*, Book 9

4 *Emile*, Book Five. For an excellent discussion of this strange thinking see Susan Möller Okin, *Women in Western Political Thought* (Virago 1980).

5 *Essay on Liberty*, Introduction, p. 73

6 *The Dialectic of Sex; The Case for Feminist Revolution* (The Women's Press 1979), p. 215

7 ibid., p. 222

8 ibid., p. 217

9 ibid., p. 193

10 ibid., p. 194

11 Its main source is Philippe Ariés's book *Centuries of Childhood; A Social History of Family Life* (Cape 1962).

12 Barbara Ehrenreich and Deirdre English, *For Her Own Good* (Pluto Press 1979), p. 203

13 *Thus Spake Zarathustra*, part 1, 'Of Womenkind, Old and Young'

14 See Susan Möller Okin, *Women in Western Political Thought* for the meaning and history of this powerful move.

15 For the story of this uphill campaign see 'Victorian Wives and Property; Reform of the Married Women's Property Law, 1857-1882' by Lee Holcombe in *A Widening Sphere; Changing Roles of Victorian Women*, ed. Martha Vicinus (Methuen 1980).

16 *Psychological Care of Infant and Child* (1929), pp. 81-2

17 *Infant Care*, by Mrs Max West. Cited in Robert E. Bremner (ed.), *Children and Youth in America, A Documentary History Vol. ii, 1866-1932* (Harvard Press 1971), p. 37. Well discussed by Ehrenreich and English, *For Her Own Good*, p. 182.

18 *Psychological Care of Infant and Child*, pp. 5-6

19 ibid., p. 82

20 *The Female Eunuch* (Paladin 1971), p. 235

21 ibid., pp. 234-6

22 *Emile* (trans. Barbara Foxley, Everyman edn,), p. 148

23 *The Dialectic of Sex*, p. 197

24 *Republic*, Book 5, 460-62. His reasons were of course very different, centring on producing harmony in the state.

25 *The Subjection of Women* (MIT Press 1970), chapter 4, p. 80

26 See Elizabeth Young, *Men and Women; Equal but not Interchangeable* (SDP Open Forum Paper 8, 1982), p. 20

Chapter 4

1 We have added Tertullian and Abbot Conrad merely for balance and to avoid the charge of sexism. Tertullian, though an extremist who was eventually excommunicated, differs only by the picturesqueness of his language from the most respected Church fathers. Simone de Beauvoir

gives an interesting collection of their views in *The Second Sex* (trans. and ed. by H.M. Parshley, Penguin 1972), p. 129. Abbot Conrad is cited by Brian Easlea in *Witch-Hunting, Magic and the New Philosophy* (Harvester 1980), p. 34 as 'scarcely atypical' of his age. The combination of an Aristotelian background with the accusation that Eve brought about the fall of man was ruinous.

2 The idea that it is *men* who particularly need liberating from bad habits, from a foolishly constricting role and an obsession with dominance and rank-order, is developed in a lively book called *The Liberated Man* by Warren Farrell (Bantam Books 1975).

3 *Women of Ideas and What Men have Done to Them; From Aphra Behn to Adrienne Rich* (Routledge and Kegan Paul 1982), pp. 13–14

4 Report of the World Conference of the United Nations Decade for Women, Equality, Development and Peace, Copenhagen, July 1980. *Women and Work* by Sheila Lewenhak (Fontana 1980) gives an impressive bird's-eye view both of the history and the current scope of this problem. See also *Women and Work; Overseas Practice* (Department of Employment Manpower Paper 12).

5 *The Second Sex*, p. 96

6 The Redstockings' Manifesto seems to take this line in saying 'we define our best interest as that of the poorest, most brutally exploited women'. But there may be a fatal ambiguity in the phrase '*our* best interest' when theirs should surely be the issue.

7 *The Second Sex*, p. 729

8 *The Subjection of Women* (MIT Press 1970), chapter 2, pp. 35–6

9 *Leviathan* (Everyman edn), part 1, chapter 13, p. 64

10 A point discussed at length in *Beast and Man* by Mary Midgley (Harvester 1979, Methuen University Paperback). See particularly index s.v. Hobbes.

11 See the *Communist Manifesto* (Martin Lawrence 1930), p. 39

12 'The failure of the Russian revolution to achieve the classless society is traceable to its half-hearted attempts to eliminate the family and sexual repression.' *The Dialectic of Sex; The Case for Feminist Revolution* (The Women's Press 1979), p. 198.

13 *Sweet Freedom; The Struggle for Women's Liberation* (Picador 1982), pp. 31–2. Their discussion is altogether very helpful.

14 See the admirable and balanced account given by R. Emerson Dobash and Russell Dobash in *Violence against Wives* (Open Books 1979). Also *Leaving Violent Men, A Study of Refuges* and *Housing for Battered Women* (Women's Aid Federation 1981).

15 *Violence against Wives*, p. 227

16 *The Subjection of Women* (MIT Press 1970), p. 35

17 ibid., p. 46

18 *Violence against Wives*, p. 221

19 This was the solution proposed by Germaine Greer in 1971 (*The Female*

Eunuch (Paladin), p. 329). It is still the central proposal of Dale Spender in 1982 (*Women of Ideas and What Men have Done to Them*, p. 530). It does not seem to have gained any clearer meaning in the interval.

20 The name *radical* seems to have been chosen chiefly because of the need of each group to appear more extreme than its rivals, without asking too carefully whether they were going in the same direction. 'It [radical feminism] refuses to accept the existing leftist analysis not because it is too radical, but because *it is not radical enough*.' *The Dialectic of Sex*, p. 43.

21 *The Wanderground: Stories of the Hill Women*, by Sally Miller Gearhart (Persephone Press, Massachusetts 1979)

22 In *On the Problem of Men; Two Feminist Conferences*, ed. by Scarlett Friedman and Elizabeth Sarah (The Women's Press 1982)

23 An issue well discussed by Dale Spender, *Invisible Women; The Schooling Scandal* (Writers and Readers Press 1982), parts 2 and 3.

24 *Sexual Politics* (Virago 1977), p. 23

25 These conflicts, and others concerned with relating feminism to Christianity, are very well discussed by Margaret Britton in *The Single Woman in the Family of God* (Epworth Press 1982).

26 *Invisible Women; The Schooling Scandal*, pp. 11-12

27 *A Room of One's Own* (Hogarth Press 1929), pp. 40 and 149

28 *Invisible Women; The Schooling Scandal*, p. 143

29 *SCUM Manifesto* (Olympia Press 1971), pp. 41-2

Chapter 5

1 See *The Sceptical Feminist* (Routledge and Kegan Paul 1980), pp. 182-206

2 N. Tinbergen, *Social Behaviour in Animals* (Methuen 1953), p. 66

3 In T.S. Eliot's poem 'Sweeney Erect'

4 *Three Complete Novels and Other Writings* (Grove Press Inc., New York 1966), p. 733

5 *Sexual Politics*, chapter 1

6 Henry Miller, *Sexus* (Grove Press, New York 1965), p. 179. Quoted by Kate Millett.

7 *Growing up in New Guinea* (Penguin 1967), p. 67

8 Dale Spender, *Man Made Language* (Routledge and Kegan Paul 1980), p. 17

9 ibid., p. 15

10 ibid., p. 18

11 In *Fighting for Life; Contest, Sexuality and Consciousness* (Cornell Press 1981), pp. 71-2

12 *A Room of One's Own* (Hogarth Press 1929), p. 147

Chapter 6

1 *Sweet Freedom, The Struggle for Women's Liberation* (Picador 1982), p. 48
2 *Sexual Politics* (Virago 1977), chapter 2
3 *Nicomachean Ethics*, Book 2, chapter 1
4 In 1982, ten years after it was passed by Congress, the ERA failed to be accepted by sufficient states to enable it to become a constitutional amendment.
5 *Women's Rights and the Law* by B. Brown, A. E. Freedman, H. N. Katz and A. M. Price (Praeger, New York 1977), introduction (by Hazel Greenberg), p. 3
6 ibid., p. 5
7 *Equality and the Rights of Women* (Cornell Press 1980), p. 92
8 *Woman and the Law* by E. Cary and K. W. Peratis (National Text-book Co., Illinois 1977), p. 197
9 *Women's Rights and the Law*, p. 9
10 ibid., p. 61
11 ibid., p. 6
12 *Violence Against Wives* by R. Emerson Dobash and Russell Dobash, pp. 11-12
13 'The Sexual Abuse of Children in the Home' by Sheila Jeffreys, p. 56, in *On the Problem of Men*, ed. Friedman and Sarah (Women's Press 1982)
14 ibid., 'Fatherhood - Bringing it all Back Home' by Jo Sutton and Scarlet Friedman, p. 119
15 *A Theory of Justice* (Harvard 1971), p. 12
16 ibid.
17 *Futures*, BBC 15 September 1982. For the considerations which force any realistic analysis in this direction see J. S. Mill, *Utilitarianism* (Everyman edn), chapter 5, pp. 40-41.
18 *Equality and the Rights of Women*, p. 88
19 *The Origin of the Family, Private Property and the State* by F. Engels (1884). This and the quotation from Kollontay which follows are from passages quoted in *Politics and Society* by David Lane (Martin Robertson, revised edn 1978), p. 322. In chapter 11, 'The Family', Lane traces the changing attitudes to the family in Russia during the nineteenth and twentieth centuries.
20 *The New Morality and the Working Classes* by A. M. Kollontay (1918). Quoted in Lane (see above), p. 375.
21 *Politics and Society*, p. 345
22 *Men and Women: Equal but not Interchangeable* by Elizabeth Young (SDP Open Forum Paper 8, 1982), p. 23
23 *Utilitarianism*, chapter 2, p. 12
24 The 1983 Budget proposals included measures relating to part-time work which move in this direction.

Chapter 7

1 From 'The Debate over Women; Ruskin versus Mill', in *Suffer and be Still; Women in the Victorian Age*, ed. Martha Vicinus (Methuen University Paperback 1980), p. 126

2 See chapter 1, p. 21

3 See her interesting book *The Descent of Woman* (Souvenir Press 1972), which was the first serious feminist challenge to the crude myth of 'man the hunter'.

4 This point can only be briefly dealt with here; it is more fully argued in *Beast and Man* by Mary Midgley (Harvester 1979).

5 That it does not need to be so for freedom is an important truth pointed out by many philosophers, notably David Hume (*Enquiry Concerning Human Understanding*, section 8, 'Of Liberty and Necessity').

6 *The Dialectic of Sex; The Case for Feminist Revolution* (The Women's Press 1979), p. 17

7 ibid., p. 193

8 Edward O. Wilson, *Sociobiology* (Harvard Press 1975), p. 3. The meaning and function of this kind of claim is discussed in *Heart and Mind; The Varieties of Moral Experience* by Mary Midgley (Harvester 1981, Methuen University Paperback), chapter 1, pp. 15–24.

9 From 'In Memoriam Examinatoris Cuiusdam' by A.D. Godley, in *Fifty Poems* (Oxford University Press 1927)

10 The unfortunate way in which this has affected ideas about women is admirably traced in *Women in Western Political Thought* by Susan Möller Okin (Virago 1980). In other areas it has of course been a metaphysical framework of great power and value.

11 Developed in his book *Sex and Character* (*Geschlecht und Charakter*) published in 1903

12 See chapter 2, note 13, and also Kate Millett's admirable paper, referred to in note 1 of this chapter. The difference between Millett the critic and Millett the political orator is that between day and night.

13 Cecil Woodham Smith, *Florence Nightingale* (Constable 1950), p. 482

14 *Civilization and its Discontents* (Hogarth Press 1930), pp. 103–4

15 Germaine Greer, *The Female Eunuch* (Paladin 1971), pp. 108–9. Compare Sheila Rowbotham, *Women, Resistance and Revolution* (Penguin 1974), p. 12, and *Woman's Consciousness, Man's World* (Penguin 1973), p. 16. The issue is well discussed by Janet Radcliffe Richards in *The Sceptical Feminist* (Routledge and Kegan Paul 1980), p. 17.

16 This is the central theme of *Heart and Mind* by Mary Midgley, particularly of its opening chapter 'The Human Heart and Other Organs'. Again, it cannot be fully developed in this book, though it has a great deal to do with the disastrous division of the sexes.

17 *Invisible Women; The Schooling Scandal* (Writers and Readers Press 1982), p. 63

18 Samuel Butler, *The Way of All Flesh*, chapter 10
19 p. 35
20 p. 1
21 Humphrey Carpenter, *The Inklings* (Allen and Unwin 1978), p. 164
22 Kate Tait (*née* Russell), *My Father, Bertrand Russell* (Gollancz 1976)
23 *Iliad*, Book 6, line 208
24 Oxford edn, chapter 7, p. 244
25 It is discussed in *Beast and Man* by Mary Midgley, part 2.
26 *The Subjection of Women* (MIT Press 1970), p. 22. It is interesting that Kate
   Millett reproduces this reasoning exactly in *Sexual Politics*, p. 29. It is not
   really a defensible view today. For a good, recent summary of the now
   overwhelming physiological material see *The Tangled Wing; Biological
   Constraints on the Human Spirit* by Melvin Konner (Heinemann 1982),
   chapter 6. He is especially good on the effects of sex hormones on the brain.
   For the anthropological evidence, Margaret Mead's *Male and Female*
   (1949, Penguin edn 1962) is still a classic statement. Though she wrote it
   before becoming fully converted to a strong emphasis on innate causes of
   human behaviour, she had no doubt that there must be marked, innate
   temperamental differences between the sexes.
27 *The Subjection of Women*, p. 22
28 Trans. by Roger de Garis (Souvenir Press 1981)
29 See N. Tinbergen, *The Study of Instinct* (Oxford University Press 1969),
   chapter 5. The word 'instinct' is currently less favoured among ethologists,
   but the general way of thinking remains unchanged. For more recent
   developments see *Ethology* by Robert A. Hinde (Fontana Masterguides
   1982).
30 See Richard Carrington, *Elephants* (London 1958), p. 60
31 *The Ballad of the Queen's Maries*
32 Plato, *Theaetetus*, 151
33 *The Second Sex* (trans. and ed. by H.M. Parshley, Penguin 1972), p. 94
34 ibid., p. 737

Index